Contents

Why You're Going to Love This Book iii

Introduction: How to Use This Book 1

Part I: Which Majors and Careers Might Suit You? 9

Your Interests 11

Your Skills 22

Your Favorite High School Courses 37

Your Work-Related Values 65

Your Hot List of College Majors and Careers 75

Part II: Facts About College Majors and Careers 79

Accounting 80

Actuarial Science 82

Advertising 84

Aeronautical/Aerospace Engineering 86

African-American Studies 88

Agricultural Business and Economics 90

Agricultural Engineering 92

Agronomy and Crop Science 94

American Studies 96

Animal Science 98

Anthropology 100

Archeology 102

Architecture 104

Area Studies 106

Art 108

Astronomy 110

Biochemistry 112

Bioengineering 114

Biology 116

Botany 118

Business Education 120

Business Management 122

Chemical Engineering 124

Chemistry 126

Chinese 128

Chiropractic 130

Civil Engineering 132

Classics 134

Computer Engineering 136

Computer Science 138

Criminology 140

Dance 142

Dentistry 144

Dietetics 146

Drama/Theater Arts 148

Early Childhood Education 150

Earth Sciences 152

Economics 154

Electrical Engineering 156

Elementary Education 158

English 160

Environmental Science 162

Film/Cinema Studies 164

Finance 166

Food Science 168

Forestry 170

French 172

Geography 174

Geology 176

Geophysics 178

German 180

Graphic Design, Commercial Art, and Illustration 182

Health Information Systems
Administration 184

History 186

Home Economics Education 188

Hospital/Health Facilities
Administration 190

Hotel/Motel and Restaurant
Management 192

Human Resources Management 194

Humanities 196

Industrial Design 198

Industrial and Labor Relations 200

Industrial Engineering 202

Industrial/Technology Education 204

Insurance 206

Interior Design 208

International Relations.............................. 210

Japanese 212

Journalism and Mass
Communications 214

Landscape Architecture 216

Law.. 218

Law Enforcement....................................... 220

Library Science.. 222

Management Information Systems 224

Marketing 226

Materials Science....................................... 228

Mathematics.. 230

Mechanical Engineering 232

Medical Technology................................... 234

Medicine 236

Metallurgical Engineering 238

Microbiology/Bacteriology 240

Modern Foreign Language 242

Music.. 244

Nursing (R.N. Training) 246

Occupational Health and Industrial
Hygiene 248

Occupational Therapy 250

Oceanography 252

Optometry.. 254

Orthotics/Prosthetics 256

Parks and Recreation Management 258

Petroleum Engineering 260

Pharmacy.. 262

Philosophy 264

Physical Education 266

Physical Therapy 268

Physician Assisting 270

Physics 272

Podiatry 274

Political Science 276

Psychology 278

Public Administration 280

Public Relations 282

Religion/Religious Studies 284

Russian 286

Secondary Education 288

Social Work 290

Sociology 292

Soil Science 294

Spanish 296

Special Education 298

Speech Pathology and Audiology 300

Statistics 302

Transportation and Logistics
Management 304

Urban Studies 306

Veterinary Medicine 308

Wildlife Management 310

Women's Studies 312

Zoology 314

Indexes **317**

Careers Index 317

College Majors Index 322

High School Courses Index 325

Interest Areas Index 326

Work Groups Index 326

Quick Guide to
COLLEGE MAJORS AND CAREERS

Laurence Shatkin, Ph.D.

Quick Guide to College Majors and Careers

© 2002 by JIST Publishing, Inc.

Published by JIST Works, an imprint of JIST Publishing, Inc.
8902 Otis Avenue
Indianapolis, IN 46216-1033
Phone: 1-800-648-JIST   Fax: 1-800-JIST-FAX   E-mail: info@jist.com

Visit our Web site at **www.jist.com** for information on JIST, free job search information, book chapters, and ordering information on our many products! See the back of this book for additional JIST titles and ordering information. Quantity discounts are available for JIST books. Please call our Sales Department at 1-800-648-5478 for a free catalog and more information.

Development Editor: Beverly Murray Scherf
Production Editor: Lori Cates Hand
Interior and Cover Designer: Aleata Howard
Proofreader: Mary Ellen Stephenson
Indexer: Tina Trettin

Printed in the United States of America
06 05 04 03 02   9 8 7 6 5 4 3 2

Library of Congress Cataloging-in-Publication Data
Shatkin, Laurence.
    Quick guide to college majors and careers / Laurence Shatkin.
        p. cm.
    Includes index.
    ISBN 1-56370-834-5
     1. College majors--United States--Handbooks, manuals, etc. 2. Vocational
guidance--United States--Handbooks, manuals, etc. I. Title.

LB2361.5 .S53 2002
378.1'9425--dc21

                                                                2001038349

ISBN 1-56370-834-5

Why You're Going to Love This Book

Decisions, decisions. Which comes first: choosing a college major or choosing a career? The truth is that this is a chicken-and-egg problem, which people disagree about.

Some people say that first you should decide what career you want to pursue, then choose a major that helps you prepare for it. They tell you success stories about students who graduated with degrees in accounting, computer science, or some other career-oriented major, then got high-paying, fast-track career offers from businesses.

Other people take the opposite approach. They say that first you should decide on a major you really love, then choose a career that can take advantage of what you've learned. They tell you horror stories about students who declared a major in a career-oriented field such as engineering or business, only to discover that the coursework was so boring that they dropped out of college, or changed majors and delayed graduation by one or more years.

Both approaches have elements of truth. And *the reason this book is so special* is that it lets you choose a four-year college major and a career *simultaneously,* instead of considering just one or the other. It links 118 majors to 286 careers. It informs you about what the career is like, and also about what you would study in the major. It tells you which careers are commonly associated with the major, and in some cases how graduates may go into careers in unexpected fields.

So the choice is yours: You can sign up for an expensive battery of personality tests and counseling sessions; you can dig through piles of college catalogs, examining and comparing the requirements for the majors; you can search through massive databases of career information, taking pains to determine the skill requirements and the income you can expect—or you can use this book to obtain self-understanding and get concise and authoritative facts about majors and careers that might suit you.

If the choice is not obvious already, turn to part I and start the exercises. You'll be surprised by how quickly you'll start seeing the connections between who you are and where you want to go.

Dedication

*Dedicated to the memory of Sidney Shatkin, who
completed his college major (history) at age 58.*

Acknowledgments

This book would not have been possible without the help and encouragement of some remarkable people:

LaVerne L. Ludden introduced me to the fine folks at JIST Publishing

J. Michael Farr saw the potential in this book and believed that the show must go on.

Beverly Murray Scherf provided invaluable editorial guidance.

Nancy Decker Shatkin supported my labors and did not complain when I monopolized the computer every evening.

Introduction: How to Use This Book

This section shows you how to use this book for your specific needs. First it explains who will benefit most from reading the book, as well as how it can help you. Then it details the different elements of parts I and II. Finally, it describes how you can get the most out of the book depending on your needs.

Who Really Needs This Book?

Lots of people need to make decisions about college majors and careers. Read over the following list to see where you fit in:

- **Young people choosing a major or career who don't have a clear idea which major or career might be best for them.** This book can help you look at yourself and see what majors or careers might be good choices for you. For example, you may be a high school student trying to decide which college to go to. Your choice may depend partly on your intended career and major. This book can help you narrow your choices by getting you interested in some specific careers and majors. It can also *broaden* your choices by informing you about certain majors and careers that are new to you.

- **Or perhaps you're not even sure you want to go to college at all,** but you are exploring your options. This book may get you excited about certain college-related career paths and help make the decision easier.

- **Young people who have a major in mind but are not yet certain about it.** With this book, you can get facts that will help you make up your mind and start planning. For example, you may be a college student who will soon have to declare a major. Maybe you're at a two-year college and you're thinking about going on for a four-year degree, but in what major? This book may suggest majors and careers that you haven't considered before, or it may give you concrete facts to help you evaluate majors that you already have in mind.

- **Midlife career changers.** You can find ways to use your accumulated skills and experience in a new career. For example, perhaps you're considering taking college classes and want to find a major that can help advance your career. This book gives you dollar figures about careers and useful information about coursework in college majors.

- **Or perhaps you already have a degree** and want to (or need to) change careers while still taking advantage of your educational credentials. You don't have to let yourself be boxed in by traditional connections between majors and careers. With the information about skills and work groups in this book, you may explore non-traditional career pathways that you have not previously considered.

- **People who are making the transition from college to a career.** You can see which careers might make good use of what you've learned. For example, perhaps you're a college student who will graduate soon, and you're wondering how you might "use" the degree you're about to get. Be sure to look at the career suggestions in this book and think about using the information about skills when you start preparing your resume.

- **People who are applying for jobs.** You can get ideas for your resume, cover letter, or job interviews. For example, you can review the Career Snapshots in the book so that you will use appropriate job-related terms when you write your letter and resume.

- **Professionals who are helping others make decisions about majors and careers.** For example, maybe you're a guidance counselor, academic advisor, or librarian and need to help other people make these decisions. You can help them clarify their priorities, explore options, and plan their next steps. You can see from the bulleted items above that this book can help a broad variety of people.

What's in This Book?

This book is set up so that you can find information quickly, in a variety of ways. Looking at the table of contents, you'll see that the book is divided into two main parts. Part I asks "Which Majors and Careers Might Suit You?" Each section in it offers an exercise to help you assemble a Hot List of majors to explore in part II. Part II offers "Facts About College Majors and Careers," and it lists the 118 college majors alphabetically.

Here's what you'll find for each college major in part II:

- **Career Snapshot:** A one-paragraph definition of the subject and an explanation of what sorts of careers (and additional education) graduates typically go into.

- **Related Specialties and Careers:** This is a list of areas of concentration that people in this field pursue, both in college and later in jobs. Depending on your interests, you could go in many different directions.

- **Related Job Titles, Projected Growth, and Earnings:** Here's where you'll get very specific facts about the jobs that the major most frequently leads to. You'll see whether the job openings are growing, shrinking, or holding steady, and what the average income for everyone in the job is. You'll also see a code number for each job (for an explanation of this code, see the paragraph below about "Other Information Sources").

- **Typical College Courses:** This is a list of the college courses that are often required for this major. Naturally, each college has its own set of requirements, but this is a general look at what to expect.

- **Some Suggested High School Courses:** If you're still in high school, this list can recommend coursework that would be good preparation. If you're beyond high school, you'll see whether you have an appropriate background.

- **Essential Knowledge and Skills:** These are the skills that are most important for the careers related to this major. Keep in mind that different majors may require somewhat different sets of skills—for doing research, writing papers, and so on.

- **Values/Work Environment:** Here you'll see some of the rewards of being in the related jobs—such as creativity, achievement, or recognition. You'll also see whether the work will have you mainly sitting, standing, working outdoors, and so on.

- **Other Information Sources:** Here each major is linked to a program in the Classification of Instructional Programs (CIP), a naming scheme used by the U.S. Department of Education. You can get additional information about any CIP program on the Web at ftp://ftp.xwalkcenter.org/download/cip2000/. For each major, you'll also see one or more GOE Work Group codes, showing a related family of jobs. You can learn more about these work groups in JIST's *Guide for Occupational Exploration*, Third Edition.

O*NET codes listed under "Related Job Titles, Projected Growth, and Earnings" can lead you to resources with detailed information about each job—for example, JIST's *O*NET Dictionary of Occupational Titles, Second Edition.*

Finally, an appendix cross-references all the college majors to the code numbers referred to in the previous paragraph.

Note that you can also use the index to look up occupations and find the related majors in part II.

How You Can Benefit from This Book

This isn't the only book about careers or college majors, but it is specially designed to knit the two tightly together so that you can decide about both at the same time. You can benefit from using the book in the following ways:

- Do the quick exercises in part I to help you zero in on what is most important to you in a major and a career. Tables that accompany the exercises will help you assemble a "Hot List" of majors that may offer what you want.

- Browse the book for quick and effective information. This is easy because the description of each major begins with a "Career Snapshot" that quickly defines the major and explains its relationship to various career tracks.

- Use the Introduction for suggestions on how to follow the link from a career to a major and then to a different career.

- See specific and up-to-date facts about careers, derived from the databases of the U.S. Department of Labor's databases.

- Easily compare majors and careers with the consistent naming scheme used for work-related skills, values, and environments (derived from the Department of Labor's databases).

- Quickly locate more information sources through the handy appendix. It links the college majors to standard coding schemes used for majors and careers—so the book can serve as a jumping-off point for exploring other reference works.

How to Make This Book Work for You

Different people will use this book differently. The following section explains how you can use this book to serve several different functions, depending on your particular needs.

Use it as a complete guide. Starting with part I, work your way through the exercises and assemble your Hot List of majors. Then move into part II to explore the majors and annotate your Hot List with notes about the related careers. This method is particularly useful for people who are undecided and like to do things in an orderly way. Or you can merely do one or two exercises to quickly generate majors to investigate.

Use it as an evaluation tool. Go directly to part II to review a major and its related careers. Take note of the required courses and skills, the value rewards, and the work environment. Then you may want to do some or all of the exercises in part I to see whether your choice is a good fit for your personality. Or create a Hot List for a more thorough evaluation; then compare your tentative choice to other majors on that list. This method is particularly useful to those who are decided but not 100 percent committed to a major.

Use it as a skill identifier. Use the index to locate a major you have already taken or that corresponds to your career. If it is not there, use the "Your Interests" exercise in part I to find the appropriate work group for your career, then go to the majors listed in part II to find the closest equivalent(s) to your experience. Jot down the skill requirements for the major(s). Then use the "Your Skills" exercise to find majors and careers that use those skills. This method is particularly useful for people who wish to make a career change.

Use it as a major/career linker. Jump directly to part II to see which careers are associated with specific majors. The "Related Job Titles, Projected Growth, and Earnings" table lists the careers most commonly linked to the major. The "Career Snapshot" may suggest additional career paths to consider.

If you really want to open up your thinking, make a note of the GOE codes (work groups) listed in the "Other Information Sources" box, then go to the "Your Interests" exercise in part I to see what other majors are associated with that work group. Then see which careers are linked to those majors. This method is particularly useful for people who want see which careers "use" a major that they have already completed (or will soon).

Use it as a resume stimulus. Go to part II and look at the major you have completed (or will soon). Make note of the skills listed for the related careers. If you have these skills, use those terms on your resume—or in cover letters and job interviews. Also, look at "Related Specialties and Careers" and "Typical College Courses." This method is most useful for people who are looking for a job.

Where Does This Information Come From?

The information in this book comes from the best and most current sources available.

The U.S. Department of Labor (DOL) is the nation's number-one source of information about careers. For valuable facts about the skills, values, satisfactions, and working environments of careers, the *Quick Guide to College Majors and Careers* draws on the DOL's O*NET database. The information about whether job openings in a career are growing, shrinking, or holding steady is from the DOL's Office of Employment Projections. The information regarding the average earnings in the careers is from another office of the DOL, Occupational Employment Statistics. Finally, much of the information about career paths and opportunities is from the DOL's best-selling *Occupational Outlook Handbook.* Taken together, these facts give you a good introduction to the wide range of careers linked to the majors in this book.

The information for "Typical College Courses" is derived from research in actual college catalogs. The author examined and compared several catalogs and identified commonly required courses. You may notice some variation in the number of courses listed. Some majors have fairly standard requirements that can be listed in detail; in some cases, a professional association mandates that certain courses be included. For other majors, notably the interdisciplinary subjects, requirements are either so minimal or so varied that it is difficult to list more than a handful of typical courses.

The "Some Suggested High School Courses" sections are based on a general understanding of which high school courses are considered prerequisites for the college-level courses required by the major. They are "suggestions" because often they are helpful for entering the major but not required.

When you read the information in this book about a major or career, keep in mind that the description covers what is *average* or *typical*—but in the real world plenty of exceptions exist. For example, one college may offer a major with an unusual emphasis not mentioned here. And if you start looking at "help wanted" advertisements, you may learn about jobs that require a somewhat different mix of skills than the ones listed here. Use this book as an introduction to the majors and careers. When you've found some choices that interest you, explore them in greater detail. You may be able to find a way to carve out a niche within a major or career to suit your particular abilities and interests.

Part I

What Majors and Careers Might Suit You?

Before you can figure out where you're going, it helps to understand who you are. This section will help you do that. With the help of some quick and easy exercises, you'll take a look at yourself and what matters most to you. You'll examine your priorities from several different angles:

- Your interests

- Your skills

- Your favorite high school courses

- Your work-related values

Each time you draw conclusions about your priorities, you'll get immediate feedback in terms of **college majors** and **work groups** (families of careers) that you should consider.

Then in **"Your Hot List of College Majors and Careers,"** you'll put together the suggestions from all four factors to create a Hot List of college majors that you should explore in part II.

As you do the exercises in the following sections, keep in mind that for exercises about career planning there are no "right" or "wrong" answers. The most important thing they require is honesty.

Your Interests

Surely you have been in a situation where someone you knew, perhaps even a close friend, was bored by something that you found fascinating. Different people have different interests. Becoming aware of your interests is an important first step in career planning.

It is important not to exaggerate the importance of interests. In the past, people have attempted to base career guidance entirely on interests. Yet most of us are happy enough with jobs that fail to satisfy all of our interests because we can compensate by pursuing those extra interests in our spare time as *hobbies*. Therefore, the *Quick Guide to College Majors and Careers* does not let interests alone determine your choices. You will have the chance to look at majors and careers from three other perspectives: skills, high school courses, and work-related values.

We're not discussing just any kind of interests here, but *work-related* interests. Consider the interests described in the *Guide for Occupational Exploration,* Third Edition (JIST Works, 2001), which expands and updates the work originally done by a government task force. Under this interest classification, the world of work is divided into 14 broad areas of interest. Each interest area is further divided into 83 work groups.

The following table lists and defines the 14 interest areas and the 52 work groups that are closely associated with college majors found in this book. Read over the table and find the work groups that interest you most. They may all be in the same interest area, or they may be from two or even three different interest areas. Note the majors that are related to the work groups that interest you. At the end of this section, you can list the three areas of your greatest interest.

Interest Areas with Job Descriptions and Related College Majors

1   **Arts, Entertainment, and Media:** An interest in creatively expressing feelings or ideas, in communicating news or information, or in performing.

Interest Area with Work Groups (GOE)	Workers in This Field...	College Majors
Managerial Work in Arts, Entertainment, and Media, 01.01	Manage people who work in the fields of arts, entertainment, and media.	Advertising, drama/theater arts, graphic design, commercial art and illustration, public relations
Writing and Editing, 01.02	Write or edit prose or poetry.	Advertising, drama/theater arts, journalism and mass communications
News, Broadcasting, and Public Relations, 01.03	Write, edit, translate, and report factual or persuasive information.	Journalism and mass communications, modern foreign language, public relations
Visual Arts, 01.04	Draw, paint, or sculpt works of art, or design consumer goods in which visual appeal is important.	Art, drama/theater arts, graphic design, commercial art and illustration, industrial design
Performing Arts, 01.05	Direct or perform for the public in works of drama, music, dance, or spectacle.	Dance, drama/theater arts, music, parks and recreation management
Craft Arts, 01.06	Create visually appealing objects from clay, glass, fabric, and other materials.	Art
Graphic Arts, 01.07	Produce printed materials, specializing in text, in pictures, or in combining both.	Graphic design, commercial art and illustration
Media Technology, 01.08	Perform the technical tasks that create photographs, movies and videos, radio and television broadcasts, and sound recordings.	Film/cinema studies
Sports: Coaching, Instructing, Officiating, and Performing, 01.10	Participate in professional sporting events such as football, baseball, and horse racing.	Physical education

2 Science, Math, and Engineering: An interest in discovering, collecting, and analyzing information about the natural world; in applying scientific research findings; in imagining and manipulating quantitative data; and in applying technology.

Interest Area with Work Groups (GOE)	Workers in This Field...	College Majors
Managerial Work in Science, Math, and Engineering, 02.01	Manage scientists who do research and engineers who apply scientific principles to solve real-world problems.	Civil engineering, environmental science/studies, management information systems
Physical Sciences, 02.02	Are mostly concerned with non-living things, such as chemicals, rocks, metals, and movements of the earth and stars.	Anthropology, astronomy, chemistry, geography, geology, oceanography, materials science, physics
Life Sciences, 02.03	Research and conduct experiments to find out more about plants, animals, and other living things.	Agronomy and crop science, animal science, biochemistry, environmental science/studies, food science, forestry, microbiology/bacteriology, soil science, zoology
Social Sciences, 02.04	Gather, study, and analyze information about individuals, groups, or entire societies.	Agricultural business and economics, anthropology, archeology, business management, criminology, drama/theater arts, economics, history, international relations, political science, psychology, sociology
Laboratory Technology, 02.05	Use special laboratory techniques and equipment to perform tests in such fields as chemistry, biology, and physics; then they record information resulting from their experiments and tests.	Agronomy and crop science, animal science, food science
Mathematics and Computers, 02.06	Use advanced math, statistics, and computer programs to solve problems and conduct research.	Actuarial science, computer science, economics, finance, management information systems, mathematics, physics, statistics

(continues)

(continued)

Interest Areas with Job Descriptions and Related College Majors

2 Science, Math, and Engineering, continued

Interest Area with Work Groups (GOE)	Workers in This Field...	College Majors
Engineering, 02.07	Plan, design, and direct the development and construction of buildings, bridges, roads, airports, dams, sewage systems, air-conditioning systems, mining machinery, and other structures and equipment.	Aeronautical/aerospace engineering, architecture, chemical engineering, civil engineering, computer engineering, electrical engineering, agricultural engineering, industrial engineering, landscape architecture, materials science, mechanical engineering, petroleum engineering
Engineering Technology, 02.08	Perform a variety of technical tasks in support of engineering.	Business management, geography, management information systems

3 Plants and Animals: An interest in working with plants and animals, usually outdoors.

Interest Area with Work Groups (GOE)	Workers in This Field...	College Majors
Managerial Work in Plants and Animals, 03.01	Operate or manage farms, ranches, hatcheries, nurseries, forests, and other plant and animal businesses.	Agricultural business and economics, animal science
Animal Care and Training, 03.02	Care for and train animals of many kinds.	Veterinary medicine

4 Law, Law Enforcement, and Public Safety: An interest in upholding people's rights, or in protecting people and property by using authority, inspecting, or monitoring.

Interest Area with Work Groups (GOE)	Workers in This Field...	College Majors
Managerial Work in Law, Law Enforcement, and Public Safety, 04.01	Manage fire and police departments.	Public administration

Interest Area with Work Groups (GOE)	Workers in This Field...	College Majors
Law, 04.02	Provide legal advice and representation to clients, hear and make decisions on court cases, help individuals and groups reach agreements, and conduct investigations into legal matters.	Business management, law, social work
Law Enforcement, 04.03	Enforce laws and regulations to protect people, animals, and property.	Criminology, law enforcement, social work, wildlife management
Public Safety, 04.04	Protect the public by responding to emergencies and by ensuring that people are not exposed to unsafe products or facilities.	Civil engineering, finance, food science, human resources management, law enforcement, public administration

5 Mechanics, Installers, and Repairers: An interest in applying mechanical and electrical/electronic principles to practical situations by use of machines or hand tools.

Interest Area with Work Groups (GOE)	Workers in This Field...	College Majors
Managerial Work in Mechanics, Installers, and Repairers, 05.01	Directly supervise and coordinate activities of mechanics, repairers, and installers and their helpers.	Business management

6 Construction, Mining, and Drilling: An interest in assembling components of buildings and other structures, or in using mechanical devices to drill or excavate.

Interest Area with Work Groups (GOE)	Workers in This Field...	College Majors
Managerial Work in Construction, Mining, and Drilling, 06.01	Directly supervise and coordinate activities of the workers who construct buildings, roads, or other structures, or who drill or dig for oil and minerals.	Business management

(continues)

(continued)

Interest Areas with Job Descriptions and Related College Majors

7 Transportation: An interest in operations that move people or materials.

Interest Area with Work Groups (GOE)	Workers in This Field...	College Majors
Managerial Work in Transportation, 07.01	Manage transportation services.	Business management

8 Industrial Production: An interest in repetitive, concrete, organized activities most often done in a factory setting.

Interest Area with Work Groups (GOE)	Workers in This Field...	College Majors
Managerial Work in Industrial Production, 08.01	Manage industrial processing and manufacturing plants.	Business management, food science
Production Technology, 08.02	Perform highly skilled hand and/or machine work requiring special techniques, training, and experience.	Food science, forestry
Production Work, 08.03	Use hands and hand tools with skill to make or process materials, products, and parts.	Graphic design, commercial art and illustration

9 Business Detail: An interest in organized, clearly defined activities requiring accuracy and attention to details, primarily in an office setting.

Interest Area with Work Groups (GOE)	Workers in This Field...	College Majors
Managerial Work in Business Detail, 09.01	Supervise and coordinate certain high-level business activities: contracts for buying or selling goods and services, office support services, facilities planning and maintenance, customer service, and administrative support.	Business management, hotel/motel and restaurant management, management information systems
Administrative Detail, 09.02	Perform high-level clerical work requiring special skills and knowledge, as well as some low-level managerial work.	Business management, finance, human resources management, public administration, social work

Interest Area with Work Groups (GOE)	Workers in This Field…	College Majors
Mathematical Detail, 09.03	Collect, organize, compute, and record the numerical information used in business and financial transactions.	Finance
Material Control, 09.04	Monitor the production of a business or the use of utilities.	Business management, management information systems
Customer Service, 09.05	Deal with people in person, often standing behind a window or in a booth.	Finance
Records Processing, 09.07	Prepare, review, file, and coordinate recorded information.	Finance, human resources management
Clerical Machine Operation, 09.09	Use business machines to record or process data.	Finance, management information systems

10 Sales and Marketing: An interest in bringing others to a particular point of view by personal persuasion, using sales and promotional techniques.

Interest Area with Work Groups (GOE)	Workers in This Field…	College Majors
Managerial Work in Sales and Marketing, 10.01	Direct or manage various kinds of selling and/or advertising operations, either a department within a business or a specialized business firm that contracts to provide selling and/or advertising services.	Advertising, hotel/motel and restaurant management, marketing
Sales Technology, 10.02	Sell products such as industrial machinery, data-processing equipment, and pharmaceuticals, plus services such as investment counseling, insurance, and advertising.	Advertising, animal science, finance, insurance

(continues)

(continued)

Interest Areas with Job Descriptions and Related College Majors

11   Recreation, Travel, and Other Personal Services: An interest in catering to the personal wishes and needs of others, so that they may enjoy cleanliness, good food and drink, comfortable lodging away from home, and enjoyable recreation.

Interest Area with Work Groups (GOE)	Workers in This Field...	College Majors
Managerial Work in Recreation, Travel, and Other Personal Services, 11.01	Manage, through lower-level personnel, all or part of the activities in restaurants, hotels, resorts, and other places where people expect good personal service.	Hotel/motel and restaurant management, business management
Recreational Services, 11.02	Provide services to help people enjoy their leisure activities.	Parks and recreation management

12   Education and Social Service: An interest in teaching people or improving their social or spiritual well-being.

Interest Area with Work Groups (GOE)	Workers in This Field...	College Majors
Managerial in Education and Social Service, 12.01	Are employed at colleges, school districts, corporations, parks, and social-service agencies.	Business management, early childhood education, home economics education, hospital/health facilities administration, public administration, social work, special education
Social Services, 12.02	Help people deal with their problems and major life events.	Philosophy, psychology, religion/religious studies, social work
Educational Services, 12.03	Do general and specialized teaching, vocational training, and advising about education, career planning, or finances.	Actuarial science, aeronautical/aerospace engineering, African-American studies, agricultural business and economics, agricultural engineering, gronomy and crop science, American studies, animal science, anthropology, archeology, area studies, art, bio-

Interest Area with Work Groups (GOE)	Workers in This Field...	College Majors
Educational Services, 12.03		chemistry, biology, botany, business education, chemical engineering, chemistry, Chinese, chiropractic, civil engineering, classics, computer engineering, computer science, criminology, dance, dentistry, dietetics, drama/theater arts, early childhood education, economics, electrical engineering, elementary education, English, environmental science/studies, film/cinema studies, finance, food science, forestry, French, German, history, home economics education, hospital/health facilities administration, human resources management, industrial engineering, industrial/technology education, international relations, Japanese, journalism and mass communications, law enforcement, library science, management information systems, materials science, mathematics, mechanical engineering, medical technology, medicine, metallurgical engineering, microbiology/bacteriology, modern foreign language, nursing (RN training), occupational health and industrial hygiene, occupational therapy, optometry, orthotics/prosthetics, petroleum engineering, pharmacy,

(continues)

(continued)

Interest Areas with Job Descriptions and Related College Majors

12 Education and Social Service, continued

Interest Area with Work Groups (GOE)	Workers in This Field...	College Majors
Educational Services, 12.03		physical education, physical therapy, physician assisting, physics, podiatry, political science, psychology, Russian, secondary education, sociology, sociology, soil science, Spanish, special education, speech pathology and audiology, statistics, veterinary medicine, wildlife management, women's studies, zoology

13 General Management and Support: An interest in making an organization run smoothly.

Interest Area with Work Groups (GOE)	Workers in This Field...	College Majors
General Management and Management of Support Functions, 13.01	Are top-level and middle-level administrators who direct, through lower-level personnel, all or part of the activities in business establishments, government agencies, and labor unions.	Business management, economics, environmental science/studies, finance, human resources management, international relations, law enforcement, parks and recreation management, public administration, wildlife management
Management Support, 13.02	Plan, manage, analyze, evaluate, and make decisions about personnel, purchases, and financial transactions and records.	Accounting, business management, economics, finance, human resources management, insurance, public administration

14 Medical and Health Services: An interest in helping people be healthy.		
Interest Area with Work Groups (GOE)	**Workers in This Field...**	**College Majors**
Managerial Work in Medical and Health Services, 14.01	Manage medical activities.	Business management, health information systems administration, hospital/health facilities administration
Medicine and Surgery, 14.02	Diagnose and treat human diseases, disorders, and injuries.	Medicine, nursing, pharmacy, physician assisting
Dentistry, 14.03	Provide health care for patients' teeth and mouth tissues.	Dentistry
Health Specialties, 14.04	Are health professionals and technicians who specialize in certain parts of the human body.	Chiropractic, optometry, podiatry
Medical Technology, 14.05	Use technology, mostly to detect signs of disease.	Medical technology, orthotics/prosthetics
Medical Therapy, 14.06	Care for, treat, or train people to improve their physical and emotional well-being.	Occupational therapy, physical therapy, speech pathology and audiology
Health Protection and Promotion, 14.08	Help people maintain good health and fitness.	Dietetics

Write down the three areas in which you have the greatest interest in the left column of the list that follows. In the right column, put the majors that are related to the work groups that interest you.

College Majors That Relate to My Interests

1. _____   _____

                             _____

                             _____

2. _____   _____

                             _____

                             _____

3. _____   _____

                             _____

                             _____

Your Skills

Different kinds of work demand different skills. Most people want to go into a kind of work where they will be able to handle the skill requirements. Of course, you don't yet *have* all the skills you will need for your career—that's why you are planning to get further education. Nevertheless, based on your experience in school, you probably have a good idea of which skills you learn easily and which come harder. You may also have work experience that indicates some of your skills.

The following chart lists and defines 29 skills that the U.S. Department of Labor (USDOL) describes in the O*NET database. For each skill in the chart, ask yourself, "What things have I done in which I've used this skill at a high level and *enjoyed* using it?" If you can think of several good examples, mark the name of the skill with a plus sign or an underline; otherwise, move on to another skill.

Which Skills Are Most Important to You?

Skill	Description
Active Learning	Working with new material or information to grasp its implications
Active Listening	Listening to what other people are saying and asking questions as appropriate
Coordination	Adjusting actions in relation to others' actions
Critical Thinking	Using logic and analysis to identify the strengths and weaknesses of different approaches
Idea Evaluation	Evaluating the likely success of an idea in relation to the demands of the situation
Idea Generation	Generating a number of different approaches to problems
Information Gathering	Knowing how to find information and identify essential information
Information Organization	Finding ways to structure or classify multiple pieces of information
Instructing	Teaching others how to do something
Judgment and Decision Making	Weighing the relative costs and benefits of a potential action
Learning Strategies	Using multiple approaches when learning or teaching new things
Management of Personnel Resources	Motivating, developing, and directing people as they work, identifying the best people for the job
Mathematics	Using mathematics to solve problems
Operations Analysis	Analyzing needs and product requirements to create a design
Problem Identification	Identifying the nature of problems
Product Inspection	Inspecting and evaluating the quality of products
Reading Comprehension	Understanding written sentences and paragraphs in work-related documents
Science	Using scientific methods to solve problems
Service Orientation	Actively looking for ways to help people
Social Perceptiveness	Being aware of others' reactions and understanding why they react the way they do

(continues)

(continued)

Which Skills Are Most Important to You?	
Skill	**Description**
Solution Appraisal	Observing and evaluating the outcomes of a problem solution to identify lessons learned or redirect efforts
Speaking	Talking to others to effectively convey information
Synthesis/Reorganization	Reorganizing information to get a better approach to problems or tasks
Systems Evaluation	Looking at many indicators of system performance, taking into account their accuracy
Systems Perception	Determining when important changes have occurred in a system or are likely to occur
Technology Design	Generating or adapting equipment and technology to serve user needs
Testing	Conducting tests to determine whether equipment, software, or procedures are operating as expected
Visioning	Developing an image of how a system should work under ideal conditions
Writing	Communicating effectively with others in writing as indicated by the needs of the audience

Now that you've looked at all the skills, determine the three skills that you would most like to use in your career and list them below.

The Most Desirable Skills for My Career

1. _____

2. _____

3. _____

The following table relates these 29 skills to college majors and to the *Guide for Occupational Exploration (GOE)* work groups. Using the three skills that you listed above, find the corresponding college majors and work groups. At the end of this section, enter the college majors and work groups that match your skills.

> **Note** A skill applies to a college major because it is required by the occupations to which the major is linked. You do not necessarily need this skill in the college major, but it is likely that learning this skill will be part of what you do in the major.

Relationship of Skills to College Majors and Work Groups

Skill	College Majors	Work Groups (GOE)
Active Learning	Actuarial science, aeronautical/aerospace engineering, African-American studies, agricultural business and economics, agricultural engineering, American studies, anthropology, archeology, area studies, astronomy, biochemistry, biology, botany, chemical engineering, chemistry, computer engineering, computer science, criminology, dentistry, earth sciences, economics, electrical engineering, environmental science/ studies, forestry, geography, geology, geophysics, history, industrial design, industrial engineering, international relations, materials science, mathematics, mechanical engineering, medical technology, medicine, metallurgical engineering, microbiology/bacteriology, modern foreign language, oceanography, petroleum engineering, pharmacy, physical therapy, physics,	Engineering, 02.07 Law, 04.02 Life Sciences, 02.03 Managerial Work in Science, Math, and Engineering, 02.01 Physical Sciences, 02.02

(continues)

(continued)

Relationship of Skills to College Majors and Work Groups

Skill	College Majors	Work Groups (GOE)
Active Learning	podiatry, political science, psychology, sociology, soil science, statistics, urban studies, veterinary medicine, wildlife management, women's studies, zoology	
Active Listening	Archeology, area studies, chiropractic, classics, criminology, earth sciences, interior design, law, law enforcement, modern foreign language, occupational therapy, optometry, orthotics/prosthetics, physical therapy, podiatry, psychology, social work, transportation and logistics management, women's studies	Administrative Detail, 09.02 Educational Services, 12.03 General Management Work and Management of Support Functions, 13.01 Health Specialties, 14.04 Law, 04.02 Law Enforcement, 04.03 Managerial Work in Education and Social Service, 12.01 Medical Technology, 14.05 Medical Therapy, 14.06 Public Safety, 04.04 Social Sciences, 02.04 Social Services, 12.02
Coordination	Architecture, interior design, hotel/motel and restaurant management, marketing, music, parks and recreation	Engineering, 02.07 Managerial Work in Business Detail, 09.01

Skill	College Majors	Work Groups (GOE)
Coordination	management, transportation and logistics management	Managerial Work in Recreation, Travel, and Other Personal Services, 11.01 Managerial Work in Sales and Marketing, 10.01 Performing Arts, Drama, 01.05 Recreational Services, 11.02
Critical Thinking	Actuarial science, aeronautical/aerospace engineering, agricultural engineering, anthropology, archeology, area studies, astronomy, bioengineering, biology, botany, chemical engineering, civil engineering, classics, computer engineering, computer science, criminology, dentistry, earth sciences, electrical engineering, environmental science/studies, film/cinema studies, industrial engineering, landscape architecture, law, mathematics, mechanical engineering, medicine, metallurgical engineering, modern foreign language, petroleum engineering, podiatry, soil science, statistics, wildlife management, zoology	Engineering, 02.07 Law, 04.02 Managerial Work in Science, Math, and Engineering, 02.01 Physical Sciences, 02.02 Social Sciences, 02.04
Idea Evaluation	Chemistry, podiatry	Managerial Work in Science, Math, and Engineering, 02.01
Idea Generation	African-American studies, agricultural engineering, American studies, area	Managerial Work in Science, Math, and Engineering, 02.01

(continues)

(continued)

Relationship of Skills to College Majors and Work Groups		
Skill	**College Majors**	**Work Groups (GOE)**
Idea Generation	studies, art, astronomy, biology, chiropractic, landscape architecture, metallurgical engineering, petroleum engineering, podiatry, sociology, speech pathology and audiology, statistics, women's studies, zoology	
Information Gathering	Accounting, actuarial science, anthropology, archeology, area studies, astronomy, biochemistry, biology, chemistry, chiropractic, civil engineering, classics, computer science, criminology, earth sciences, economics, environmental science/studies, forestry, geology, geophysics, history, insurance, international relations, law, library science, marketing, mathematics, medical technology, modern foreign language, occupational health and industrial hygiene, oceanography, physician assisting, physics, political science, sociology, speech pathology and audiology, statistics, veterinary medicine	Engineering, 02.07 Law, 04.02 Life Sciences, 02.03 Management Support, 13.02 Managerial Work in Education and Social Service, 12.01 Managerial Work in Medical and Health Services, 14.01 Managerial Work in Science, Math, and Engineering, 02.01 Physical Sciences, 02.02 Social Sciences, 02.04
Information Organization	Accounting, archeology, astronomy, classics, English, environmental science/studies, Japanese, law, modern foreign	Managerial Work in Science, Math, and Engineering, 02.01

Skill	College Majors	Work Groups (GOE)
Information Organization	language, physics, Russian, Spanish, statistics	Mathematics and Computers, 02.06 Physical Sciences, 02.02 Social Sciences, 02.04
Instructing	African-American studies, agricultural business and economics, American studies, archeology, area studies, bio-engineering, biology, botany, business education, Chinese, classics, criminology, dance, earth sciences, English, film/cinema studies, French, German, home economics education, industrial/tech-nology education, Japanese, microbiology/bacteriology, modern foreign language, nursing (RN training), occu-pational health and industrial hygiene, occupational therapy, optometry, orthotics/prosthe-tics, pharmacy, physical therapy, psychology, Russian, secondary education, sociology, Spanish, special education, speech pathology and audiology, urban studies, wildlife management, women's studies	Educational Services, 12.03
Judgment and Decision Making	Accounting, computer engineering, landscape architecture, law, marketing	Engineering, 02.07 Law, 04.02 Managerial Work in Science, Math, and Engineering, 02.01

(continues)

(continued)

Relationship of Skills to College Majors and Work Groups

Skill	College Majors	Work Groups (GOE)
Learning Strategies	Archeology, area studies, biology, botany, business education, Chinese, classics, criminology, early childhood education, economics, elementary education, English, film/cinema studies, French, German, home economics education, industrial/technology education, Japanese, medical technology, modern foreign language, nursing (RN training), physical education, Russian, secondary education, soil science, Spanish, special education, statistics	Educational Services, 12.03
Management of Personnel Resources	Industrial and labor relations, transportation and logistics management	General Management Work and Management of Support Functions, 13.01 Managerial Work in Arts, Entertainment, and Media, 01.01 Managerial Work in Business Detail, 09.01 Managerial Work in Construction, Mining, and Drilling, 06.01 Managerial Work in Industrial Production, 08.01 Managerial Work in Mechanics, Installers, and Repairers, 05.01

Skill	College Majors	Work Groups (GOE)
Management of Personnel Resources		Managerial Work in Recreation, Travel, and Other Personal Services, 11.01 Managerial Work in Law, Law Enforcement, and Public Safety, 04.01
Mathematics	Accounting, actuarial science, aeronautical/aerospace engineering, agricultural engineering, astronomy, bioengineering, botany, chemical engineering, computer engineering, criminology, electrical engineering, forestry, geography, geology, geophysics, industrial engineering, industrial/ technology education, materials science, mathematics, mechanical engineering, medicine, metallurgical engineering, oceanography, petroleum engineering, physics, statistics	Engineering, 02.07 Managerial Work in Science, Math, and Engineering, 02.01 Mathematics and Computers, 02.06 Physical Sciences, 02.02
Operations Analysis	Civil engineering	Engineering, 02.07 Managerial Work in Science, Math, and Engineering, 02.01
Problem Identification	Accounting, chiropractic, industrial and labor relations, marketing, microbiology/ bacteriology, occupational health and industrial hygiene, physician assisting, veterinary medicine	Engineering, 02.07 General Management Work and Management of Support Functions, 13.01 Managerial Work in Science, Math, and Engineering, 02.01

(continues)

(continued)

Relationship of Skills to College Majors and Work Groups		
Skill	**College Majors**	**Work Groups (GOE)**
Product Inspection	Graphic design, commercial art, and illustration	[No GOE group is rated high on this skill.]
Reading Comprehension	Accounting, actuarial science, advertising, aeronautical/ aerospace engineering, African-American studies, agricultural business and economics, agricultural engineering, agronomy and crop science, American studies, animal science, anthropology, archeology, architecture, area studies, astronomy, biochemistry, bioengineering, biology, botany, business education, business management, chemical engineering, chemistry, Chinese, chiropractic, civil engineering, classics, computer engineering, computer science, criminology, dentistry, drama/theater arts, earth sciences, economics, electrical engineering, English, environmental science/studies, finance, food science, forestry, French, geography, German, history, home economics education, hospital/health facilities management administration, human resources management, humanities, industrial design, industrial engineering, industrial/technology education, insurance, interior design, international relations, Japanese, journalism and mass	Dentistry, 14.03 Educational Services, 12.03 Engineering, 02.07 Health Specialties, 14.04 Law, 04.02 Life Sciences, 02.03 Managerial Work in Education and Social Service, 12.01 Managerial Work in Medical and Health Services, 14.01 Managerial Work in Science, Math, and Engineering, 02.01 Mathematics and Computers, 02.06 Medicine and Surgery, 14.02 News, Broadcasting, and Public Relations, 01.03 Physical Sciences, 02.02 Social Sciences, 02.04

Skill	College Majors	Work Groups (GOE)
Reading Comprehension	communications, law, library science, management information systems, marketing, materials science, mathematics, mechanical engineering, medical technology, medicine, metallurgical engineering, microbiology/bacteriology, modern foreign language, nursing (RN training), occupational health and industrial hygiene, occupational therapy, optometry, orthotics/prosthetics, petroleum engineering, pharmacy, philosophy, physical therapy, physician assisting, physics, podiatry, political science, psychology, public administration, religion/religious studies, Russian, secondary education, social work, sociology, soil science, Spanish, special education, speech pathology and audiology, statistics, transportation and logistics management, urban studies, veterinary medicine, wildlife management, women's studies, zoology	Social Services, 12.02 Writing and Editing, 01.02
Science	Astronomy, biochemistry, bioengineering, biology, chemical engineering, chemistry, chiropractic, computer engineering, dentistry, geology, geophysics, industrial engineering, materials science, medical technology, medicine, metallurgical engineering, microbiology/bacteriology,	Engineering, 02.07 Life Sciences, 02.03 Physical Sciences, 02.02

(continues)

(continued)

Relationship of Skills to College Majors and Work Groups

Skill	College Majors	Work Groups (GOE)
Science	occupational health and industrial hygiene, oceanography, optometry, petroleum engineering, pharmacy, physical therapy, physician assisting, soil science, veterinary medicine, zoology	
Service Orientation	Philosophy, religion/religious studies	[No GOE group is rated high on this skill.]
Social Perceptiveness	Philosophy, religion/religious studies, social work	Social Services, 12.02
Solution Appraisal	Landscape architecture, marketing, statistics	Engineering, 02.07 Managerial Work in Science, Math, and Engineering, 02.01
Speaking	Aeronautical/aerospace engineering, African-American studies, agricultural business and economics, agricultural engineering, American studies, archeology, area studies, biology, business education, Chinese, classics, criminology, earth sciences, economics, English, film/cinema studies, French, German, history, home economics education, hospital/health facilities administration, industrial/technology education, international relations, Japanese, modern foreign language, nursing (RN training), occupational therapy, orthotics/prosthetics, philosophy, political science,	Educational Services, 12.03 Law, 04.02 Managerial Work in Education and Social Service, 12.01 Managerial Work in Science, Math, and Engineering, 02.01

Skill	College Majors	Work Groups (GOE)
Speaking	psychology, public relations, religion/religious studies, Russian, secondary education, Spanish, special education, speech pathology and audiology, veterinary medicine, wildlife management, women's studies	
Synthesis/Reorganization	Astronomy, Chinese, classics, French, German, landscape architecture, modern foreign language	[No GOE group is rated high on this skill.]
Systems Evaluation	Health information systems administration	Managerial Work in Science, Math, and Engineering, 02.01
Systems Perception	Health information systems administration	Managerial Work in Science, Math, and Engineering, 02.01
Technology Design	Chemical engineering, mechanical engineering	[No GOE group is rated high on this skill.]
Testing	Computer science	[No GOE group is rated high on this skill.]
Visioning	Interior design, landscape architecture	Managerial Work in Science, Math, and Engineering, 02.01
Writing	Aeronautical/aerospace engineering, African-American studies, agricultural business and economics, American studies, anthropology, archeology, area studies, biochemistry, biology, chemistry, Chinese, civil engineering, classics, computer science, criminology, dentistry, dietetics, earth	Educational Services, 12.03 Engineering, 02.07 Law, 04.02 Life Sciences, 02.03 Managerial Work in Education and Social Service, 12.01

(continues)

(continued)

Relationship of Skills to College Majors and Work Groups

Skill	College Majors	Work Groups (GOE)
Writing	sciences, economics, electrical engineering, English, environmental science/studies, film/cinema studies, forestry, French, geography, geology, geophysics, German, history, hospital/health facilities administration, international relations, Japanese, journalism and mass communications, materials science, mathematics, medical technology, medicine, microbiology/bacteriology, modern foreign language, occupational health and industrial hygiene, occupational therapy, oceanography, optometry, orthotics/prosthetics, pharmacy, philosophy, physical therapy, physician assisting, physics, political science, psychology, religion/religious studies, Russian, sociology, soil science, Spanish, special education, speech pathology and audiology, statistics, transportation and logistics management, wildlife management, zoology	Managerial Work in Science, Math, and Engineering, 02.01 News, Broadcasting, and Public Relations, 01.03 Physical Sciences, 02.02 Social Sciences, 02.04 Writing and Editing, 01.02

Write down the college majors and work groups that correspond with the three skills you listed earlier in this section. If there are many, try to find college majors and work groups that are linked to *more than one* of your important skills. Write these names in the following box.

College Majors That Relate to My Skills

_____   _____

_____   _____

_____   _____

_____   _____

_____   _____

_____   _____

_____   _____

_____   _____

_____   _____

_____   _____

_____   _____

Your Favorite High School Courses

A good way to predict how well people will like college courses is to ask them how much they liked similar high school courses. Also, most people earn their highest grades in college courses similar to the high school courses in which they did well. Therefore, it can be useful to take note and write down the names of three high school courses that you liked and in which you earned high grades.

My Best High School Courses

1. _____

2. _____

3. _____

Next, with those courses in mind, look over the information in the following table and find related college majors and work groups from the Work Groups (GOE) column. As you review this information, mark the items that most closely match your best high school courses. At the end of this section, you can make a list of the best matches.

 Note Many of the math courses listed in the following table are commonly required for a large number of college majors. For example, if you did well in math, you should look for a high school course that represents a *high level* of math, such as pre-calculus or calculus rather than algebra or geometry. Similarly, if you did well in English, it might help to look for what is related to literature.

The Relationship of High School Courses to College Majors and Work Groups

High School Course	College Majors	Work Groups (GOE)
Algebra	Accounting, actuarial science, advertising, aeronautical/ aerospace engineering, African-American studies, agricultural business and economics, agricultural engineering, agronomy and crop science, American studies, animal science, anthropology, archeology, architecture, area studies, astronomy, biochemistry, bioengineering, biology, botany, business education, business management, chemical engineering, chemistry, chiropractic, civil engineering, computer engineering, computer science, criminology, dentistry, dietetics, early childhood education, earth sciences, economics,	Administrative Detail, 09.02 Air Vehicle Operation, 07.03 Animal Care and Training, 03.02 Clerical Machine Operation, 09.09 Customer Service, 09.05 Educational Services, 12.03 General Management, 13.01 General Sales, 10.03 Hands-on Work: Loading, Moving, Hoisting, and Conveying, 08.07

High School Course	College Majors	Work Groups (GOE)
Algebra	electrical engineering, elementary education, environmental science/studies, finance, food science, forestry, geology, geophysics, graphic design, commercial art and illustration, health information systems administration, history, home economics education, hospital/health facilities administration, hotel/motel and restaurant management, human resources management, humanities, industrial design, industrial engineering, industrial and labor relations, industrial/technology education, insurance, interior design, international relations, journalism and mass communications, landscape architecture, law, law enforcement, library science, management information systems, marketing, materials science, mathematics, mechanical engineering, medical technology, medicine, metallurgical engineering, microbiology/bacteriology, nursing (RN training), occupational health and industrial hygiene, occupational therapy, oceanography, optometry, orthotics/prosthetics, petroleum engineering, pharmacy, philosophy, physical education, physical therapy,	Health Protection and Promotion, 14.08

Management Support, 13,02

Managerial Work, 01.01, 04.01, 05.01, 07.01, 08.01, 09.01, 10.01, 11.01

Managerial, 12.01, 14.01

Material Control, 09.04

Mechanical Work, 05.03

Media Technology, 01.08

Metal and Plastics Machining Technology, 08.04

Other Services Requiring Driving, 07.07

Patient Care and Assistance, 14.07

Production Technology, 08.02

Production Work, 08.03

Public Safety, 04.04

Rail Vehicle Operation, 07.06

Records and Materials Processing, 09.08 |

(continues)

(continued)

The Relationship of High School Courses to College Majors and Work Groups

High School Course	College Majors	Work Groups (GOE)
Algebra	physician assisting, physics, podiatry, political science, psychology, public administration, public relations, religion/religious studies, secondary education, social work, sociology, soil science, special education, speech pathology and audiology, statistics, transportation and logistics management, urban studies, veterinary medicine, wildlife management, women's studies, zoology	Recreational Services, 11.02 Sales Technology, 10.02 Social Sciences, 02.04 Social Services, 12.02 Systems Operation, 08.06 Truck Driving, 07.05 Vehicle Expediting and Coordinating, 07.02 Water Vehicle Operation, 07.04 Woodworking Technology, 08.05
Art	Advertising, architecture, art, geography, graphic design, commercial art and illustration, industrial design, interior design, journalism and mass communications, landscape architecture, public relations	Barber and Beauty Services, 11.04 Craft Arts, 01.06 Educational Services, 12.03 Graphic Arts, 01.07 Medical Therapy, 14.06 Visual Arts, 01.04
Biology	Agricultural business and economics, agricultural engineering, agronomy and	Animal Care and Training, 03.02

High School Course	College Majors	Work Groups (GOE)
Biology	crop science, animal science, anthropology, archeology, biochemistry, bioengineering, biology, botany, chiropractic, dance, dentistry, dietetics, environmental science/studies, food science, forestry, health information systems administration, hospital/health facilities administration, landscape architecture, medical technology, medicine, microbiology/bacteriology, nursing (RN training), occupational therapy, oceanography, optometry, orthotics/prosthetics, parks and recreation management, pharmacy, physical therapy, physician assisting, podiatry, psychology, social work, soil science, speech pathology and audiology, veterinary medicine, wildlife management, zoology	Dentistry, 14.03 Educational Services, 12.03 Hands-on Work, 03.03 Health Protection and Promotion, 14.08 Health Specialties, 14.04 Laboratory Technology, 02.05 Life Sciences, 02.03 Managerial Work, 02.01, 03.01, 11.01 Managerial, 12.01, 14.01 Medical Technology, 14.05 Medical Therapy, 14.06 Medicine and Surgery, 14.02 Other Personal Services, 11.08 Patient Care and Assistance, 14.07 Public Safety, 04.04 Social Services, 12.02 Sports: Coaching, Instructing, Officiating, and Performing, 01.10

(continues)

(continued)

The Relationship of High School Courses to College Majors and Work Groups

High School Course	College Majors	Work Groups (GOE)
Calculus	Actuarial science, aeronautical/aerospace engineering, agricultural engineering, architecture, astronomy, biochemistry, bioengineering, biology, botany, chemical engineering, chemistry, civil engineering, computer engineering, computer science, earth sciences, electrical engineering, geology, geophysics,industrial engineering, landscape architecture, materials science, mathematics, mechanical engineering, metallurgical engineering, microbiology/bacteriology, oceanography, optometry, petroleum engineering, pharmacy, physics, statistics, zoology	Educational Services, 12.03 Engineering, 02.07 Engineering Technology, 02.08 Life Sciences, 02.03 Management Support, 13.02 Mathematics and Computers, 02.06 Physical Sciences, 02.02
Chemistry	Aeronautical/aerospace engineering, agricultural business and economics, agricultural engineering, agronomy and crop science, animal science, anthropology, astronomy, biochemistry, bioengineering, biology, botany, chemical engineering, chemistry, chiropractic, civil engineering, computer engineering, computer science, dentistry, dietetics, earth sciences, electrical engineering, environmental science/ studies, food science, forestry,	Animal Care and Training, 03.02 Craft Arts, 01.06 Dentistry, 14.03 Engineering, 02.07 Engineering Technology, 02.08 Health Specialties, 14.04 Laboratory Technology, 02.05

High School Course	College Majors	Work Groups (GOE)
Chemistry	geology, geophysics, health information systems administration, hospital/health facilities administration, industrial engineering, materials science, mechanical engineering, medical technology, medicine, metallurgical engineering, microbiology/bacteriology, nursing (RN training), occupational health and industrial hygiene, occupational therapy, oceanography, optometry, orthotics/prosthetics, parks and recreation management, petroleum engineering, pharmacy, physical therapy, physician assisting, physics, podiatry, soil science, speech pathology and audiology, veterinary medicine, wildlife management, zoology	Life Sciences, 02.03 Managerial Work, 02.01 Managerial, 14.01 Medical Technology, 14.05 Medical Therapy, 14.06 Medicine and Surgery, 14.02 Other Personal Services, 11.08 Physical Sciences, 02.02 Public Safety, 04.04 Systems Operation, 08.06
Computer Science	Accounting, actuarial science, aeronautical/aerospace engineering, agricultural business and economics, agricultural engineering, agronomy and crop science, animal science, architecture, astronomy, biochemistry, bioengineering, biology, botany, business management, chemical engineering, chemistry, chiropractic, civil engineering, computer engineering, computer science, dentistry, earth sciences, electrical engineering, environmental science/studies, finance, food	Air Vehicle Operation, 07.03 Construction, 06.02 Educational Services, 12.03 Electrical and Electronic Systems, 05.02 Engineering Technology, 02.08 Engineering, 02.07 General Management, 13.01

(continues)

(continued)

The Relationship of High School Courses to College Majors and Work Groups		
High School Course	**College Majors**	**Work Groups (GOE)**
Computer Science	science, forestry, geography, geology, graphic design, commercial art and illustration, geophysics, health information systems administration, hospital/health facilities administration, hotel/motel and restaurant management, human resources management, industrial and labor relations, industrial design, industrial engineering, insurance, interior design, landscape architecture, law enforcement, library science, management information systems, marketing, materials science, mathematics, mechanical engineering, medical technology, medicine, metallurgical engineering, microbiology/bacteriology, nursing (RN training), occupational health and industrial hygiene, occupational therapy, oceanography optometry, orthotics/prosthetics, petroleum engineering, pharmacy, physical therapy, physician assisting physics, podiatry, public administration, soil science, speech pathology and audiology, statistics, transportation and logistics management, veterinary medicine, wildlife management, zoology	Graphic Arts, 01.07 Laboratory Technology, 02.05 Life Sciences, 02.03 Management Support, 13.02 Managerial 14.01 Managerial Work, 01.01, 02.01, 03.01, 04.01, 05.01, 06.01, 07.01, 08.01, 09.01, 10.01, 11.01 Mathematical Detail, 09.03 Mathematics and Computers, 02.06 Media Technology, 101.08 Physical Sciences, 02.02 Public Safety, 04.04 Systems Operation, 08.06 Vehicle Expediting and Coordinating, 07.02 Water Vehicle Operation, 07.04
Dance	Dance, drama/theater arts	Educational Services, 12.03 Performing Arts, 01.05

High School Course	College Majors	Work Groups (GOE)
English	All majors listed in part II	Administrative Detail, 09.02
		Educational Services, 12.03
		Engineering, 02.07
		General Management, 13.01
		Law Enforcement, 04.03
		Law, 04.02
		Managerial Work, 01.01, 03.01, 04.01, 05.01, 06.01, 07.01, 08.01, 09.01, 10.01, 11.01
		Managerial, 12.01, 14.01
		News, Broadcasting, and Public Relations, 01.03
		Performing Arts, 01.05
		Public Safety, 04.04
		Social Sciences, 02.04
		Social Services, 12.02
		Writing and Editing, 01.02
Foreign Language	Accounting, advertising, African-American studies, American studies, anthropology, archeology, area studies, art, business education, business management, Chinese, chiropractic, classics, criminology, dance, dentistry, drama/theater arts, early childhood education, economics, elementary	Craft Arts, 01.06
		Educational Services, 12.03
		Law Enforcement, 04.03
		Law, 04.02
		Managerial Work, 04.01

(continues)

(continued)

The Relationship of High School Courses to College Majors and Work Groups

High School Course	College Majors	Work Groups (GOE)
Foreign Language	education, English, film/cinema studies, finance, geography, health information systems administration, history, home economics education, hospital/ health facilities administration, hotel/motel and restaurant management, human resources management, humanities, industrial and labor relations, industrial/technology educa- tion, insurance, international relations, Japanese, journalism and mass communications, law, law enforcement, library science, management informa- tion systems, marketing, medi- cine, modern foreign language, music, nursing (RN training), occupational therapy, optom- etry, orthotics/prosthetics, pharmacy	Military, 04.05 News, Broadcasting, and Public Relations, 01.03 Performing Arts, 01.05 Social Sciences, 02.04 Social Services, 12.02 Visual Arts, 01.04 Writing and Editing, 01.02
French	Accounting, advertising, African-American studies, American studies, anthropology, archeology, area studies, art, business education, business management, chiropractic, classics, criminology, dance, dentistry, drama/theater arts, early childhood education, economics, elementary edu- cation, English, French, film/cinema studies, finance, geography, health information systems administration, history,	Craft Arts, 01.06 Educational Services, 12.03 Law Enforcement, 04.03 Law, 04.02 Managerial Work, 04.01 Military, 04.05 News, Broadcasting, and Public Relations, 01.03

High School Course	College Majors	Work Groups (GOE)
French	home economics education, hospital/health facilities administration, hotel/motel and restaurant management, human resources management, humanities, industrial and labor relations, industrial/technology education, insurance, international relations, journalism and mass communications, law, law enforcement, library science, management information systems, marketing, medicine, modern foreign language, music, nursing (RN training), occupational therapy, optometry, orthotics/prosthetics, pharmacy, philosophy, physical education, physical therapy, physician assisting, podiatry, political science, psychology, public relations, religious studies, secondary education, social work, sociology, special education, transportation and logistics management, urban studies, veterinary medicine, women's studies	Performing Arts, 01.05 Social Sciences, 02.04 Social Services, 12.02 Visual Arts, 01.04 Writing and Editing, 01.02
Geography	Environmental science/studies, forestry, geography, wildlife management	Air Vehicle Operation, 07.03 Educational Services, 12.03 Managerial Work, 07.01, 11.01 Military, 04.05 Mining and Drilling, 06.03

(continues)

(continued)

The Relationship of High School Courses to College Majors and Work Groups		
High School Course	**College Majors**	**Work Groups (GOE)**
Geography		News, Broadcasting, and Public Relations, 01.03 Rail Vehicle Operation, 07.06 Recreational Services, 11.02 Social Sciences, 02.04 Truck Driving, 07.05 Vehicle Expediting and Coordinating, 07.02 Water Vehicle Operation, 07.04
Geometry	Accounting, actuarial science, aeronautical/aerospace engineering, agricultural business and economics, agricultural engineering, agronomy and crop science, animal science, architecture, astronomy, biochemistry, bioengineering, biology, botany, business education, business management, chemical engineering, chemistry, chiropractic, civil engineering, computer engineering, computer science, dentistry, dietetics, early childhood education, earth sciences, electrical engineering, elementary education, environmental science/studies, finance, food	Construction, 06.02 Educational Services, 12.03 Graphic Arts, 01.07 Hands-on Work, 06.04 Managerial Work, 01.01 Mining and Drilling, 06.03

High School Course	College Majors	Work Groups (GOE)
Geometry	science, forestry, geology, geophysics, graphic design, commercial art and illustration, health information systems administration, home economics education, hospital/health facilities administration, hotel/motel and restaurant management, human resources management, industrial and labor relations, industrial design, industrial engineering, industrial/technology education, insurance, interior design, landscape architecture, law, management information systems, marketing, materials science, mathematics, mechanical engineering, medical technology, medicine, metallurgical engineering, microbiology/bacteriology, nursing (RN training), occupational health and industrial hygiene, occupational therapy, oceanography, optometry, orthotics/prosthetics, parks and recreation management, petroleum engineering, pharmacy, philosophy, physical education, physical therapy, physician assisting, physics, podiatry, religion/religious studies, secondary education, soil science, special education, speech pathology and audiology, statistics, transportation and logistics management, veterinary medicine, wildlife management, zoology	

(continues)

(continued)

The Relationship of High School Courses to College Majors and Work Groups		
High School Course	**College Majors**	**Work Groups (GOE)**
German	Accounting, advertising, African-American studies, American studies, anthropology, archeology, area studies, art, business education, business management, chiropractic, classics, criminology, dance, dentistry, drama/theater arts, early childhood education, economics, elementary education, English, film/cinema studies, finance, geography, German, health information systems administration, history, home economics education, hospital/health facilities administration, hotel/motel and restaurant management, human resources management, humanities, industrial and labor relations, industrial/technology education, insurance, international relations, journalism and mass communications, law, law enforcement, library science, management information systems, marketing, medicine, modern foreign language, music, nursing (RN training), occupational therapy, optometry, orthotics/prosthetics, pharmacy, philosophy, physical education, physical therapy, physician	Craft Arts, 01.06 Educational Services, 12.03 Law Enforcement, 04.03 Law, 04.02 Managerial Work, 04.01 Military, 04.05 News, Broadcasting, and Public Relations, 01.03 Performing Arts, 01.05 Social Sciences, 02.04 Social Services, 12.02 Visual Arts, 01.04 Writing and Editing, 01.02

High School Course	College Majors	Work Groups (GOE)
German	assisting, podiatry, political science, psychology, public relations, religious studies, secondary education, social work, sociology, special education, transportation and logistics management, urban studies, veterinary medicine, women's studies	
History	African-American studies, American studies, anthropology, archeology, area studies, art, Chinese, classics, English, film/cinema studies, French, geography, German, history, humanities, interior design, international relations, Japanese, law, law enforcement, modern foreign language, philosophy, political science, public administration, religion/ religious studies, Russian, Spanish, urban studies, women's studies	Educational Services, 12.03 Law, 04.02 Military, 04.05 News, Broadcasting, and Public Relations, 01.03 Performing Arts, 01.05 Social Sciences, 02.04 Writing and Editing, 01.02
Home Economics	Advertising, dietetics, food science, home economics education, hospital/health facilities administration, interior design, marketing, women's studies	Apparel, Shoes, Leather, and Fabric Care, 11.06 Cleaning and Building Services, 11.07 Educational Services, 12.03 Food and Beverage Services, 11.05 General Sales, 10.03 Health Protection and Promotion, 14.08

(continues)

(continued)

The Relationship of High School Courses to College Majors and Work Groups

High School Course	College Majors	Work Groups (GOE)
Home Economics		Management Support, 13.02
		Managerial Work, 10.01
		Modeling and Personal Appearance, 01.09
		Other Personal Services, 11.08
		Patient Care and Assistance, 14.07
		Sales Technology, 10.02
		Transportation and Lodging Services, 11.03
Industrial Arts	Business education, industrial/technology education	Apparel, Shoes, Leather, and Fabric Care, 11.06
		Craft Arts, 01.06
		Electrical and Electronic Systems, 05.02
		Hands-on Work, 05.04, 06.04
		Hands-on Work: Loading, Moving, Hoisting, and Conveying, 08.07
		Managerial Work, 05.01, 08.01
		Mechanical Work, 05.03

High School Course	College Majors	Work Groups (GOE)
Industrial Arts		Metal and Plastics Machining Technology, 08.04 Production Technology, 08.02 Production Work, 08.03 Support Work, 07.08 Woodworking Technology, 08.05
Keyboarding	Business education; graphic design, commercial art, and illustration, library science	Administrative Detail, 09.02 Clerical Machine Operation, 09.09 Communications, 09.06 Mathematical Detail, 09.03 News, Broadcasting, and Public Relations, 01.03 Records and Materials Processing, 09.08 Writing and Editing, 01.02
Literature	Advertising, African-American studies, American studies, area studies, art, Chinese, classics, drama/theater arts, English, film/cinema studies, French, German, humanities, interior design, Japanese, journalism and mass communications, public relations, Russian, Spanish, women's studies	Educational Services, 12.03 Law, 04.02 News, Broadcasting, and Public Relations, 01.03 Writing and Editing, 01.02

(continues)

(continued)

The Relationship of High School Courses to College Majors and Work Groups		
High School Course	**College Majors**	**Work Groups (GOE)**
Mechanical Drawing	Graphic design, commercial art and illustration, industrial design, industrial/technology education	Construction, 06.02
		Craft Arts, 01.06
		Electrical and Electronic Systems, 05.02
		Engineering, 02.07
		Graphic Arts, 01.07
		Hands-on Work, 05.04, 06.04
		Managerial Work, 05.01, 06.01, 08.01
		Mechanical Work, 05.03
		Metal and Plastics Machining Technology, 08.04
		Mining and Drilling, 06.03
		Production Technology, 08.02
		Production Work, 08.03
		Woodworking Technology, 08.05
Music	Dance, drama/theater arts, early childhood education, elementary education, music	Educational Services, 12.03
		Medical Therapy, 14.06
		Performing Arts, 01.05

High School Course	College Majors	Work Groups (GOE)
Office Computer Applications	Business education, health information systems administration, hospital/health facilities administration, library science	Administrative Detail, 09.02 Clerical Machine Operation, 09.09 Customer Service, 09.05 Educational Services, 12.03 General Sales, 10.03 Graphic Arts, 01.07 Law Enforcement, 04.03 Management Support, 13.02 Managerial Work, 09.01 Managerial, 14.01 Material Control, 09.04 Mathematical Detail, 09.03 Military, 04.05 Records and Materials Processing, 09.08 Records Processing, 09.07
Photography	Film/cinema studies, graphic design, commercial art and illustration, industrial design	Graphic Arts, 01.07 Media Technology, 01.08 Production Work, 08.03 Public Safety, 04.04 Visual Arts, 01.04

(continues)

(continued)

The Relationship of High School Courses to College Majors and Work Groups

High School Course	College Majors	Work Groups (GOE)
Physics	Aeronautical/aerospace engineering, architecture, astronomy, biochemistry, bioengineering, biology, botany, chemical engineering, chemistry, chiropractic, civil engineering, computer engineering, computer science, dentistry, dietetics, earth sciences, electrical engineering, geology, geo-physics, industrial engineering, interior design, landscape architecture, materials science, mathematics, mechanical engineering, medical tech-nology, medicine, metal-lurgical engineering, microbiology/bacteriology, occupational health and industrial hygiene, occupa-tional therapy, ocean-ography, optometry, orthotics/prosthetics, petroleum engineering, pharmacy, physical therapy, physics, podiatry, speech pathology and audiology, statistics, veterinary medicine, zoology	Construction, 06.02 Dentistry, 14.03 Educational Services, 12.03 Electrical and Electronic Systems, 05.02 Engineering Technology, 02.08 Engineering, 02.07 Health Specialties, 14.04 Laboratory Technology, 02.05 Life Sciences, 02.03 Managerial Work, 06.01 Mathematics and Computers, 02.06 Media Technology, 01.08 Medical Technology, 14.05 Medical Therapy, 14.06 Medicine and Surgery, 14.02 Physical Sciences, 02.02 Systems Operation, 08.06

High School Course	College Majors	Work Groups (GOE)
Pre-Calculus	Actuarial science, aeronautical/aerospace engineering, agricultural engineering, architecture, astronomy, biochemistry, bioengineering, biology, botany, chemical engineering, chemistry, chiropractic, civil engineering, computer engineering, computer science, dentistry, earth sciences, economics, electrical engineering, geology, geophysics, graphic design, commercial art and illustration, health information systems administration, hospital/health facilities administration, industrial design, industrial engineering, interior design, landscape architecture, materials science, mathematics, mechanical engineering, medicine, metallurgical engineering, microbiology/bacteriology, occupational health and industrial hygiene, oceanography, optometry, petroleum engineering, physician assisting, physics, podiatry, speech pathology and audiology, statistics, transportation and logistics management, veterinary medicine, zoology	Dentistry, 14.03 Educational Services, 12.03 Electrical and Electronic Systems, 05.02 Health Specialties, 14.04 Laboratory Technology, 02.05 Management Support, 13.02 Managerial Work, 02.01, 03.01, 06.01 Managerial, 14.01 Mathematical Detail, 09.03 Medical Technology, 14.05 Medical Therapy, 14.06 Medicine and Surgery, 14.02 Sales Technology, 10.02
Public Speaking	Advertising, African-American studies, agronomy and crop science, American studies, animal science, anthropology, archeology, business educa-	Administrative Detail, 09.02 Barber and Beauty Services, 11.04

(continues)

(continued)

The Relationship of High School Courses to College Majors and Work Groups

High School Course	College Majors	Work Groups (GOE)
Public Speaking	tion, business management, Chinese, chiropractic, classics, dentistry, drama/theater arts, early childhood education, elementary education, English, environmental science/studies, food science, forestry, French, German, graphic design, commercial art and illustration, health information systems administration, home economics education, hospital/health facilities administration, hotel/motel and restaurant management, human resources management, humanities, industrial and labor relations, industrial design, industrial/technology education, Japanese, journalism and mass communications, law, law enforcement, library science, medicine, modern foreign language, nursing (RN training), occupational health and industrial hygiene, optometry, parks and recreation management, pharmacy, physical education, physician assisting, podiatry, public administration, public relations, religion/religious studies, Russian, secondary education, soil science, Spanish, special education, speech pathology	Communications, 09.06 Customer Service, 09.05 Educational Services, 12.03 Food and Beverage Services, 11.05 General Management, 13.01 General Sales, 10.03 Health Protection and Promotion, 14.08 Law Enforcement, 04.03 Law, 04.02 Management Support, 13.02 Managerial, 12.01, 14.01 Managerial Work, 01.01, 02.01, 03.01, 04.01, 05.01, 06.01, 07.01, 08.01, 09.01, 10.01, 10.01, 11.01 Modeling and Personal Appearance, 01.09 News, Broadcasting, and Public Relations, 01.03 Other Services Requiring Driving, 07.07

High School Course	College Majors	Work Groups (GOE)
Public Speaking	and audiology, transportation and logistics management, veterinary medicine, wildlife management, women's studies	Performing Arts, 01.05 Personal Soliciting, 10.04 Records Processing, 09.07 Recreational Services, 11.02 Sales Technology, 10.02 Social Services, 12.02 Sports: Coaching, Instructing, Officiating, and Performing, 01.10 Transportation and Lodging Services, 11.03 Vehicle Expediting and Coordinating, 07.02
Science	Accounting, actuarial science, business education, business management, early childhood education, elementary education, finance, home economics education, hotel/motel and restaurant management, human resources management, industrial/technology education, insurance, management information systems, marketing, physical education, secondary education, special education	Air Vehicle Operation, 07.03 Construction, 06.02 Dentistry, 14.03 Educational Services, 12.03 Health Specialties, 14.04 Managerial Work, 01.01, 11.01 Mathematics and Computers, 02.06 Mechanical Work, 05.03

(continues)

(continued)

The Relationship of High School Courses to College Majors and Work Groups		
High School Course	**College Majors**	**Work Groups (GOE)**
Science		Medical Technology, 14.05
		Medical Therapy, 14.06
		Medicine and Surgery, 14.02
		Mining and Drilling, 06.03
		Production Technology, 08.02
		Sales Technology, 10.02
		Sports: Coaching, Instructing, Officiating, and Performing, 01.10
		Water Vehicle Operation, 07.04
Social Science	Advertising, African-American studies, American studies, anthropology, archeology, area studies, Chinese, classics, criminology, dietetics, economics, English, French, geography, German, health information systems administration, history, hospital/health facilities administration, humanities, industrial and labor relations, international relations, Japanese, journalism and mass communications, law, law enforcement, library science,	Administrative Detail, 09.02
		Dentistry, 14.03
		Educational Services, 12.03
		General Management, 13.01
		General Sales, 10.03
		Health Specialties, 14.04
		Law Enforcement, 04.03
		Law, 04.02

High School Course	College Majors	Work Groups (GOE)
Social Science	modern foreign language, parks and recreation management, philosophy, political science, psychology, public administration, public relations, religion/religious studies, Russian, social work, sociology, Spanish, speech pathology and audiology, urban studies, women's studies	Managerial, 12.01, 14.01 Managerial Work, 01.01, 02.01, 03.01, 04.01, 05.01, 06.01, 07.01, 08.01, 09.01, 10.01, 11.01 Medical Technology, 14.05 Medical Therapy, 14.06 Medicine and Surgery, 14.02 Other Personal Services, 11.08 Patient Care and Assistance, 14.07 Performing Arts, 01.05 Public Safety, 04.04 Sales Technology, 10.02 Social Sciences, 02.04 Social Services, 12.02 Sports: Coaching, Instructing, Officiating, and Performing, 01.10 Writing and Editing, 01.02
Spanish	Accounting, advertising, African-American studies, American studies, anthropology, archeology, area studies, art, business education, business management,	Craft Arts, 01.06 Educational Services, 12.03 Law Enforcement, 04.03

(continues)

(continued)

The Relationship of High School Courses to College Majors and Work Groups

High School Course	College Majors	Work Groups (GOE)
Spanish	chiropractic, classics, criminology, dance, dentistry, drama/theater arts, early childhood education, economics, elementary education, English, film/cinema studies, finance, geography, health information systems administration, history, home economics education, hospital/health facilities administration, hotel/motel and restaurant management, human resources management, humanities, industrial and labor relations, industrial/technology education, insurance, international relations, journalism and mass communications, law, law enforcement, library science, management information systems, marketing, medicine, modern foreign language, music, nursing (RN training), occupational therapy, optometry, orthotics/prosthetics, pharmacy, philosophy, physical education, physical therapy, physician assisting, podiatry, political science, psychology, public relations, religious studies, secondary education, social work, sociology, Spanish, special education, transportation and logistics management, urban	Law, 04.02 Managerial Work, 04.01 Military, 04.05 News, Broadcasting, and Public Relations, 01.03 Performing Arts, 01.05 Social Sciences, 02.04 Social Services, 12.02 Visual Arts, 01.04 Writing and Editing, 01.02

High School Course	College Majors	Work Groups (GOE)
Spanish	studies, veterinary medicine, women's studies	
Trigonometry	Accounting, actuarial science, aeronautical/aerospace engineering, agricultural business and economics, agricultural engineering, agronomy and crop science, animal science, architecture, astronomy, biochemistry, bioengineering, biology, botany, business education, business management, chemical engineering, chemistry, chiropractic, civil engineering, computer engineering, computer science, criminology, dentistry, dietetics, earth sciences, economics, electrical engineering, elementary education, environmental science/studies, finance, food science, forestry, geography, geology, geophysics, graphic design, commercial art and illustration, health information systems administration, home economics education, hospital/health facilities administration, human resources management, industrial and labor relations, industrial design, industrial engineering, industrial/technology education, insurance, interior design, international relations, landscape architecture, management information systems, marketing, materials science, mathematics,	Managerial Work, 01.01

(continues)

(continued)

The Relationship of High School Courses to College Majors and Work Groups		
High School Course	**College Majors**	**Work Groups (GOE)**
Trigonometry	mechanical engineering, medical technology, medicine, metallurgical engineering, microbiology/bacteriology, nursing (RN training), occupational health and industrial hygiene, occupational therapy, oceanography, optometry, orthotics/prosthetics, petroleum engineering, pharmacy, physical education, physical therapy, physician assisting, physics, podiatry, political science, psychology, public administration, secondary education, sociology, soil science, special education, speech pathology and audiology, statistics, transportation and logistics management, urban studies, veterinary medicine, wildlife management, zoology	

Look over the items that you marked in the table. Determine the courses and work groups that best fit with the high school courses you listed at the beginning of this section. Then write them in the following box. If there are many, try to find college majors and work groups that are linked to *more than one* of your best high school courses.

Similar College Majors and Work Groups

_____

_____

_____

_____

_____

_____

_____

Your Work-Related Values

People rarely talk about values, except occasionally when politicians boast about their "family values." Yet values affect every decision we make. A value is something that we consider desirable to gain or keep. When we choose between two things that we have the chance to gain or keep, we base our preference on our values. Sometimes it is obvious that one choice is better aligned with our values than another one. But a lot of the time we have to make *trade-offs,* accepting less of one thing that we value to get something else that we value more.

For example, when choosing what to have for lunch, we make trade-offs among several values: good taste, good nutrition, reasonable price, convenient location, something different from what we had yesterday, and perhaps trying to impress our lunch date. It may be impossible to find one meal that will fit *all* of these values perfectly, but we usually can find a compromise choice that will satisfy our most important values. Note that our lunch-related values may change over time, as we might become more nutrition-conscious or short on lunch money. Most important of all, consider that there is no one "right" set of lunch-related values for all people. Some people *enjoy* having the same lunch every day, and others don't care what their lunch date thinks of their choice. Lunch-related values are a matter of personal preference.

The same applies to *work-related values*. People have their own unique preferences; they often need to make trade-offs; and they may find that their values change over time. But in fact most people don't actually know consciously what their work-related values are. If you ask them, "What makes one job better than another?" they usually can name only one or two things—such as the salary or the working conditions.

This is where this section can help you: by making you more aware of your work-related values. In the following chart, look over the names and definitions of work-related values, which the U.S. Department of Labor (USDOL) uses to describe jobs in its O*NET database. (The work-related values in this book are particular to the listed college majors. The USDOL uses additional values that are unrelated.) When you compare the importance of two values, ask yourself, "Would I quit a job that had a lot of Value X if I could get a job with a lot of Value Y?"

Work-Related Values	
Value	**Description**
Ability Utilization	Making use of your individual abilities
Achievement	Getting a feeling of accomplishment
Authority	Giving directions and instructions to others
Autonomy	Planning your work with little supervision
Coworkers	Having coworkers who are easy to get along with
Creativity	Getting chances to try out your own ideas
Moral Values	Never being pressured to do things that go against your sense of right and wrong
Recognition	Receiving recognition for the work you do
Responsibility	Making decisions on your own
Security	Having steady employment
Social Service	Having work where you do things to improve other people's lives

Value	Description
Social Status	Being looked up to by others in your company and your community
Working Conditions	Having good working conditions

When you've decided which three of these values are most important for you to get from your work, list them here:

Work Values for My Career

1. _____

2. _____

3. _____

In the following table, start by drawing a large box around each row that contains the work-related values that you listed above as your most important. Now look in the second and third columns of these rows and circle any college majors and work groups that appear in two or more of your selected rows. At the end of this section you can list the names of those college majors and work groups, because they correspond well to your three most important work-related values. If *none* of them appears more than once in the selected rows, list some of the majors and work groups that correspond to your number-one value.

 Note The work-related values are related to college majors in that they characterize the occupations to which the majors are linked. They do not necessarily reflect the experience of *being in* the major.

Work-Related Values and Their Relationship to College Majors and Work Groups

Work-Related Values	College Majors	Work Groups (GOE)
Ability Utilization—making use of your individual abilities	Aeronautical/aerospace engineering, African-American studies, agricultural	Air Vehicle Operation, 07.03 Dentistry, 14.03

(continues)

(continued)

Work-Related Values and Their Relationship to College Majors and Work Groups

Work-Related Values	College Majors	Work Groups (GOE)
Ability Utilization	engineering, American studies, anthropology, archeology, architecture, area studies, art, astronomy, biochemistry, bioengineering, biology, botany, chemical engineering, chemistry, Chinese, chiropractic, civil engineering, classics, computer engineering, criminology, dance, dentistry, drama/theater arts, earth sciences, economics, electrical engineering, English, environmental science/studies, film/cinema studies, French, geology, geophysics, German, humanities, industrial and labor relations, industrial design, industrial engineering, interior design, international relations, Japanese, journalism and mass communications, landscape architecture, materials science, mathematics, mechanical engineering, medical technology, medicine, metallurgical engineering, microbiology/bacteriology, modern foreign language, music, nursing (RN training), occupational health and industrial hygiene, occupational therapy, oceanography, orthotics/prosthetics, petroleum engineering, pharmacy, physical therapy, physician assisting, physics, podiatry,	Engineering, 02.07 Health Specialties, 14.04 Medicine and Surgery, 14.02 Performing Arts, 01.05 Physical Sciences, 02.02 Visual Arts, 01.04 Writing and Editing, 01.02

Work-Related Values	College Majors	Work Groups (GOE)
Ability Utilization	political science, psychology, Russian, sociology, Spanish, special education, speech pathology and audiology, statistics, urban studies, veterinary medicine, women's studies, zoology	
Achievement—getting a feeling of accomplishment	African-American studies, agronomy and crop science, American studies, anthropology, archeology, architecture, area studies, art, biochemistry, botany, bioengineering, biology, business education, chemistry, Chinese, chiropractic, dance, dentistry, drama/theater arts, economics, elementary education, English, film/cinema studies, forestry, French, German, history, home economics education, humanities, industrial design, industrial/technology education, interior design, international relations, Japanese, journalism and mass communications, medicine, metallurgical engineering, microbiology/bacteriology, modern foreign language, music, nursing (RN training), occupational health and industrial hygiene, occupational therapy, optometry, orthotics/prosthetics, pharmacy, philosophy, physical education, physical therapy, physician assisting, physics, podiatry, political science, psychology, religion/religious studies, Russian, secondary	Dentistry, 14.03 Educational Services, 12.03 Health Specialties, 14.04 Managerial Work in Arts, Entertainment, and Media, 01.01 Managerial Work in Law, Law Enforcement, and Public Safety, 04.01 Medicine and Surgery, 14.02 Performing Arts, 01.05 Visual Arts, 01.04 Writing and Editing, 01.02

(continues)

(continued)

Work-Related Values and Their Relationship to College Majors and Work Groups		
Work-Related Values	**College Majors**	**Work Groups (GOE)**
Achievement	education, sociology, Spanish, special education, speech pathology and audiology, statistics, urban studies, veterinary medicine, wildlife management, women's studies, zoology	
Authority—giving directions and instructions to others	African-American studies, agricultural business and economics, American studies, area studies, bioengineering, biology, botany, business education, Chinese, classics, early childhood education, elementary education, English, film/cinema studies, French, German, home economics education, hospital/health facilities administration, hotel/motel and restaurant management, industrial and labor relations, industrial/technology education, Japanese, metallurgical engineering, modern foreign language, occupational health and industrial hygiene, physical education, Russian, secondary education, Spanish, speech pathology and audiology, transportation and logistics management, women's studies	General Management Work and Management of Support Functions, 13.01

Managerial Work in Construction, Mining, and Drilling, 06.01

Managerial Work in Industrial Production, 08.01

Managerial Work in Law, Law Enforcement, and Public Safety, 04.01

Managerial Work in Mechanics, Installers, and Repairers, 05.01 |
| Autonomy—planning your work with little supervision | Actuarial science, African-American studies, agricultural business and economics, American studies, animal | Health Specialties, 14.04

Managerial Work in Arts, Entertainment, and Media, 01.01 |

Work-Related Values	College Majors	Work Groups (GOE)
Autonomy	science, anthropology, archeology, area studies, art, astronomy, biochemistry, biology, business management, chemistry, Chinese, chiropractic, classics, computer science, criminology, dentistry, drama/theater arts, earth sciences, economics, English, film/cinema studies, food science, French, geography, geology, geophysics, German, humanities, industrial and labor relations, industrial engineering, interior design, international relations, Japanese, law, materials science, mathematics, medicine, metallurgical engineering, microbiology/bacteriology, modern foreign language, music, occupational health and industrial hygiene, oceanography, optometry, parks and recreation management, petroleum engineering, philosophy, physics, podiatry, political science, psychology, religion/religious studies, Russian, sociology, soil science, Spanish, statistics, transportation and logistics management, urban studies, veterinary medicine, women's studies, zoology	Physical Sciences, 02.02 Social Sciences, 02.04
Creativity—trying out your own ideas	Advertising, archeology, architecture, area studies, art, astronomy, biology, chemistry, computer engineering, criminology, dance, drama/theater arts, industrial design, interior design, landscape architecture, music, physics, psychology	Writing and Editing, 01.02 Visual Arts, 01.04

(continues)

(continued)

Work-Related Values and Their Relationship to College Majors and Work Groups		
Work-Related Values	**College Majors**	**Work Groups (GOE)**
Moral Values—never being pressured to do things that go against your sense of right and wrong	Geology, graphic design, commercial art and illustration, geophysics, library science, music, oceanography	Apparel, Shoes, Leather, and Fabric Care, 11.06 Construction, 06.02 Craft Arts, 01.06 Electrical and Electronic Systems, 05.02 Graphic Arts, 01.07 Hands-on Work, 05.04 Mechanical Work, 05.03 Metal and Plastics Machining Technology, 08.04 Production Technology, 08.02 Production Work, 08.03 Woodworking Technology, 08.05
Recognition—receiving recognition for the work you do	Architecture	[No GOE work group has a high average for this value.]
Responsibility—making decisions on your own	African-American studies, American studies, anthropology, archeology, area studies, biochemistry, biology, business education, computer engineering, criminology, dentistry, geology, geophysics,	Health Specialties, 14.04 Managerial Work in Law, Law Enforcement, and Public Safety, 04.01

Work-Related Values	College Majors	Work Groups (GOE)
Responsibility	humanities, industrial/ technology education, law, medicine, metallurgical engineering, occupational health and industrial hygiene, oceanography, optometry, petroleum engineering, physical education, podiatry, psychology, secondary education, sociology, statistics, transportation and logistics management, urban studies, veterinary medicine, women's studies	
Security—having steady employment	Law, law enforcement, philosophy, religion/religious studies	Health Specialties, 14.04 Medicine and Surgery, 14.02
Social Service—having work where you do things for other people	Area studies, business education, chiropractic, dentistry, dietetics, elementary education, medicine, modern foreign language, nursing (RN training), occupational therapy, optometry, orthotics/ prosthetics, philosophy, physical education, physical therapy, physician assisting, podiatry	Barber and Beauty Services, 11.04 Dentistry, 14.03 Health Specialties, 14.04 Medical Therapy, 14.06 Medicine and Surgery, 14.02 Patient Care and Assistance, 14.07 Social Services, 12.02
Social Status—being looked up to by others in your company and your community	Architecture, area studies, biology, chiropractic, dentistry, medicine, microbiology/ bacteriology, optometry, philosophy, podiatry, religion/ religious studies, veterinary medicine	Health Specialties, 14.04 Managerial Work in Law, Law Enforcement, and Public Safety, 04.01

(continues)

(continued)

Work-Related Values and Their Relationship to College Majors and Work Groups		
Work-Related Values	**College Majors**	**Work Groups (GOE)**
Working Conditions— having good working conditions	Accounting, area studies, biology, computer engineering, film/cinema studies, finance, health information systems administration, human resources management, industrial and labor relations, law, library science, management information systems, marketing, mathematics, metallurgical engineering, modern foreign language, optometry, psychology, public administration, public relations, statistics	[No GOE work group has a high average for this value.]

In the following box, write the college majors and work groups that most closely correspond to the three values you listed at the beginning of this section.

College Majors That Relate to My Values

_____

_____

_____

_____

_____

_____

_____

_____

_____

Your Hot List of College Majors and Careers

Now that you've done the four exercises in this part of the book, it's time for you to assemble a "Hot List" of college majors and careers that deserve your active consideration in part II.

At the end of each of the four exercises in part I—interests, skills, high school courses, and work-related values—you'll find a list of the college majors and work groups that were most strongly suggested by each exercise. Look these over now and decide which of the following statements best characterizes what you see:

- **Certain majors and work groups appear at the end of all four, or three of the four, exercises.** If this is what you find, congratulations! These majors obviously correspond well to your personality, and you should write them in your Hot List below.

- **Certain majors and work groups appear in two outputs of the exercises, but none appear in three or four.** This is still a meaningful finding; these majors probably belong on your Hot List below. If many majors fit this description, you might ask yourself whether you feel more confident about one kind of exercise than another. For example, do you feel you have a more clear notion of your interests and high school courses than of your skills and values? In that case, you might want to give greater weight to the majors that are shared by the outputs of the exercises relating to your interests and high school courses.

- **There's no pattern at all—no majors or work groups appear in more than one output of the exercises.** In this case, you need to decide which exercise you trust the most. Different people have different styles of thinking about themselves; for example, some have a much keener awareness of their interests than their values. Or perhaps the terms used in one exercise seem easier to understand than the terms in the others. Go with the results of the exercise that you feel most confident about. Write those majors in your Hot List.

- **One of the preceding three statements applies to you, but you have a *very* large number of majors on your Hot List.** Here's where the work groups can help you. Find the work group that appears most often in the results of the exercises for skills, high school courses, and values. Then go back to the interest exercise and see which majors are linked to that work group. These are strong candidates for your Hot List.

After you have filled in your Hot List below and have started investigating these majors in part II, you can also use the Hot List as an informal way of recording your impressions:

- If a major appeals to you when you read about it, put a few stars next to the name on the Hot List. The stars can serve to remind you which majors are the hottest of the hot!

- One of the important facts you'll read about the major is what jobs it is linked to. When you see a job that looks interesting to you, write its name next to the name of the major on the Hot List. Later you can use other resources to investigate these jobs in greater detail.

My Hot List

_____

_____

_____

_____

_____

_____

_____

_____

_____

_____

Part II

Facts About College Majors and Careers

I n this section you can get the facts about 118 college majors and the careers related to them. You may learn new things about majors that you thought you knew all about. You may also encounter majors that you never heard of before, or that you don't know well.

The Hot List you created in part I can help you choose majors to explore here. But even if you just browse at random, the facts are organized in a way that makes it easy for you to get an understanding of the major and related careers.

Here's what you'll find for each major:

- **Career Snapshot:** What the subject is and what careers are related
- **Related Specialties and Careers:** Common areas of concentration
- **Related Job Titles, Projected Growth, and Earnings:** Specific facts about the jobs, from the U.S. Department of Labor (earnings reflect the national average for all workers in the occupation)
- **Typical College Courses:** Courses often required for this major (each college varies)
- **Some Suggested High School Courses:** High school coursework that is considered good preparation
- **Essential Knowledge and Skills:** Skills that are most important for the careers related to this major
- **Values/Work Environment:** The rewards of being in the related jobs; also, the typical work setting and physical demands
- **Other Information Sources:** Where to look in other reference materials for additional facts

Accounting

Career Snapshot

Accountants maintain the financial records of an organization and supervise the recording of transactions. They provide information about the fiscal condition and trends of the organization, and figures for tax forms and financial reports. They advise management and therefore need good communication skills. A bachelor's degree is sufficient preparation for many entry-level jobs, but some employers prefer a master's degree. Accountants with diverse skills may advance to management after a few years. The job outlook is generally good.

Related Specialties and Careers

Accounting computer systems, auditing, cost accounting, financial reporting, forensic accounting, taxation.

Related Job Titles, Projected Growth, and Earnings		
Job Title	Projected Growth	Average Earnings
Accountants (O*NET code 13-2011.01)	Average	$37,860
Auditors (O*NET code 13-2011.02)	Average	$37,860
Budget Analysts (O*NET code 13-2031.00)	Average	$44,950
Tax Examiners, Collectors, and Revenue Agents (O*NET code 13-2081.00)	Little or none	$39,540

Typical College Courses

Auditing; business finance; business writing; calculus for business and social sciences; cost accounting; English composition; introduction to accounting; introduction to management information systems; introduction to marketing; introduction to psychology; legal environment of business; operations management; principles of macroeconomics; principles of management and organization; principles of microeconomics; statistics for business and social sciences; strategic management; taxation of corporations, partnerships and estates; taxation of individuals.

Some Suggested High School Courses

Algebra, computer science, English, foreign language, geometry, science, trigonometry.

Essential Knowledge and Skills

Problem identification, information gathering, mathematics, judgment and decision-making, reading comprehension, critical thinking, solution appraisal, systems evaluation, information organization. **Values/Work Environment:** Good working conditions, sitting.

Other Information Sources

Many career and education information sources use the standard cross-referencing systems noted below. You can use the codes to obtain substantial additional information on the major (via CIP code) and related occupations (via GOE code). The O*NET codes on the opposite page refer to another major career information system. See this book's Introduction for details on obtaining additional information.

Classification of Instructional Programs (CIP) code: 520301 Accounting

Guide for Occupational Exploration (GOE) code: 13.02 Management Support

---

Actuarial Science

Career Snapshot

Actuarial science is the analysis of mathematical data to predict the likelihood of certain events, such as death, accident, or disability. Insurance companies are the main employers of actuaries; actuaries determine how much the insurers charge for policies. The usual entry route is a bachelor's degree, but actuaries continue to study and sit for exams to upgrade their professional standing over the course of 5 to 10 years. Although the occupation is not expected to grow much, there will probably be many openings for those who are able to pass the series of exams.

Related Specialties and Careers

Insurance, investment.

Related Job Titles, Projected Growth, and Earnings		
Job Title	**Projected Growth**	**Average Earnings**
Actuaries (O*NET code 15-2011.00)	Little or none	$65,560
Mathematical Science Teachers, Postsecondary (O*NET code 25-1022.00)	Faster than average	(No salary data available)

Typical College Courses

Actuarial models, advanced calculus, applied regression, calculus, financial management, income and employment theory, introduction to accounting, introduction to actuarial mathematics, introduction to computer science, introduction to probability, investment analysis, linear algebra, mathematical statistics, price theory, principles of macroeconomics, principles of microeconomics, programming in C.

Some Suggested High School Courses

Algebra, calculus, computer science, English, geometry, pre-calculus, science, trigonometry.

Essential Knowledge and Skills

Mathematics, reading comprehension, information gathering, critical thinking, active learning, information organization, writing. **Values/Work Environment:** Autonomy, working indoors, sitting.

Other Information Sources

Many career and education information sources use the standard cross-referencing systems noted below. You can use the codes to obtain substantial additional information on the major (via CIP code) and related occupations (via GOE code). The O*NET codes on the opposite page refer to another major career information system. See the Introduction for details on obtaining additional information.

Classification of Instructional Programs (CIP) code: 520802 Actuarial Science

Guide for Occupational Exploration (GOE) codes: 02.06 Mathematics and Computers, 12.03 Educational Services

 **Advertising**

Career Snapshot

Advertising is a combination of writing, art, and business. Graduates with a bachelor's degree in advertising often go on to jobs in advertising agencies, mostly in large cities. Competition can be keen because the industry is considered glamorous. A knowledge of how to advertise on the Internet can be an advantage.

Related Specialties and Careers

Creative process, management.

Related Job Titles, Projected Growth, and Earnings		
Job Title	Projected Growth	Average Earnings
Advertising and Promotions Managers (O*NET code 11-2011.00)	Faster than average	$57,300
Sales Managers (O*NET code 11-2022.00)	Faster than average	$57,300
Art Directors (O*NET code 27-1011.00)	Faster than average	$31,690
Copy Writers (O*NET code 27-3043.04)	Faster than average	$34,570
Advertising Sales Agents (O*NET code 41-3011.00)	Average	$31,850

Typical College Courses

Advertising account planning and research, advertising campaign management, advertising copy and layout, advertising media, advertising message strategy, communication ethics, communications theory, English composition, introduction to advertising, introduction to communication research, introduction to marketing, mass communication law, oral communication, statistics for business and social sciences.

Some Suggested High School Courses

Algebra, art, English, foreign language, home economics, literature, public speaking, social science.

Essential Knowledge and Skills

Reading comprehension. **Values/Work Environment:** Creativity, working indoors, sitting.

Other Information Sources

Many career and education information sources use the standard cross-referencing systems noted below. You can use the codes to obtain substantial additional information on the major (via CIP code) and related occupations (via GOE code). The O*NET codes on the opposite page refer to another major career information system. See the Introduction for details on obtaining additional information.

Classification of Instructional Programs (CIP) code: 090201 Advertising

Guide for Occupational Exploration (GOE) codes: 01.01 Managerial Work in Arts, Entertainment, and Media; 01.02 Writing and Editing; 10.01 Managerial Work in Sales and Marketing; 10.02 Sales Technology

Aeronautical/Aerospace Engineering

Career Snapshot

Engineers apply scientific principles to real-world problems, finding the optimal solution that balances elegant technology with realistic cost. Aeronautical/aerospace engineers need to learn the specific principles of air flow and resistance, and the workings of various kinds of propulsion systems. Most enter the job market with a bachelor's degree. Some later move into managerial positions. Job outlook is not as good as for some other engineering fields because of cutbacks in defense spending.

Related Specialties and Careers

Airframes and aerodynamics, propulsion, spacecraft, testing.

Related Job Titles, Projected Growth, and Earnings		
Job Title	**Projected Growth**	**Average Earnings**
Aerospace Engineers (O*NET code 17-2011.00)	Little or none	$66,950
Engineering Teachers, Postsecondary (O*NET code 25-1032.00)	Faster than average	(No salary data available)
Sales Engineers (O*NET code 41-9031.00)	Average	$54,600

Typical College Courses

Aerodynamics, aircraft stability and control, aircraft structural design, aircraft systems and propulsion, calculus, differential equations, dynamics, English composition, experimental aerodynamics, flight control systems, fluid mechanics, general chemistry, general physics, introduction to aerospace engineering, introduction to computer science, introduction to electric circuits, materials engineering, senior design project, statics, technical writing, thermodynamics.

Some Suggested High School Courses

Algebra, calculus, chemistry, computer science, English, geometry, physics, pre-calculus, trigonometry.

Essential Knowledge and Skills

Mathematics, active learning, reading comprehension, writing, critical thinking, technology design, science, solution appraisal, operations analysis, speaking. **Values/ Work Environment:** Ability utilization, working indoors, sitting, standing.

Other Information Sources

Many career and education information sources use the standard cross-referencing systems noted below. You can use the codes to obtain substantial additional information on the major (via CIP code) and related occupations (via GOE code). The O*NET codes on the opposite page refer to another major career information system. See the Introduction for details on obtaining additional information.

Classification of Instructional Programs (CIP) code: 140201 Aerospace, Aeronautical, and Astronautical Engineering

Guide for Occupational Exploration (GOE) codes: 02.07 Engineering, 12.03 Educational Services

African-American Studies

Career Snapshot

African-American studies draws on a number of disciplines, including history, sociology, literature, linguistics, and political science. Usually you can shape the program to emphasize whichever appeals most to you. Graduates frequently pursue higher degrees as a means of establishing a career in a field such as college teaching or the law.

Related Specialties and Careers

Behavioral and social inquiry, history and culture, literature, language and the arts.

Related Job Titles, Projected Growth, and Earnings		
Job Title	**Projected Growth**	**Average Earnings**
Anthropology and Archeology Teachers, Postsecondary (O*NET code 25-1061.00)	Faster than average	(No salary data available)
Area, Ethnic, and Cultural Studies Teachers, Postsecondary (O*NET code 25-1062.00)	Faster than average	(No salary data available)
Political Science Teachers, Postsecondary (O*NET code 25-1065.00)	Faster than average	(No salary data available)
Sociology Teachers, Postsecondary (O*NET code 25-1067.00)	Faster than average	(No salary data available)
History Teachers, Postsecondary (O*NET code 25-1125.00)	Faster than average	(No salary data available)

Typical College Courses

African-American history, African-American literature, African diaspora studies, American history, English composition, foreign language, introduction to African-American studies, research methods in African American studies, seminar (reporting on research).

Some Suggested High School Courses

Algebra, English, foreign language, history, literature, public speaking, social science.

Essential Knowledge and Skills

Reading comprehension, instructing, active learning, speaking, writing, learning strategies, active listening, information gathering, critical thinking, idea generation.

Values/Work Environment: Achievement, ability utilization, authority, autonomy, responsibility, working indoors, sitting, standing.

Other Information Sources

Many career and education information sources use the standard cross-referencing systems noted below. You can use the codes to obtain substantial additional information on the major (via CIP code) and related occupations (via GOE code). The O*NET codes on the opposite page refer to another major career information system. See the Introduction for details on obtaining additional information.

Classification of Instructional Programs (CIP) code: 050201 African-American (Black) Studies

Guide for Occupational Exploration (GOE) code: 12.03 Educational Services

---

Agricultural Business and Economics

Career Snapshot

Agriculture is a major business in the United States, and graduates of agricultural business and economics programs often work far away from a farm or ranch. They may be employed by a bank that lends to farmers, by a food company that purchases large amounts of agricultural products, by a government agency that sets agricultural policies, or by a manufacturer that sells agricultural equipment, chemicals, or seed. They need to know how agricultural products are produced and how the markets for these products (increasingly global) behave. A bachelor's degree is a common entry route, although a graduate degree is useful for teaching or research positions.

Related Specialties and Careers

Agricultural economics, agricultural finance, agricultural marketing and sales, computer applications and data management, farm business management, natural resources management, public policy, ranch business management.

Related Job Titles, Projected Growth, and Earnings		
Job Title	**Projected Growth**	**Average Earnings**
Nursery and Greenhouse Managers (O*NET code 11-9011.01)	Average	$25,360
Agricultural Crop Farm Managers (O*NET code 11-9011.02)	Declining	$25,360
Fish Hatchery Managers (O*NET code 11-9011.03)	Little or none	$49,157
Economists (O*NET code 19-3011.00)	Average	$48,330
Economics Teachers, Postsecondary (O*NET code 25-1063.00)	Faster than average	(No salary data available)
Farm and Home Management Advisors (O*NET code 25-9021.00)	Declining	$37,200

Typical College Courses

Agribusiness financial management, agricultural policy, business math, computer applications in agriculture, English composition, farm/ranch management, general biology, introduction to agricultural economics and business, introduction to accounting, introduction to economics, introduction to marketing, legal and social environment of agriculture, macroeconomic theory, marketing and pricing agricultural products, microeconomic theory, natural resource economics, oral communication, quantitative methods in agricultural business, statistics for business and social sciences, technical writing.

Some Suggested High School Courses

Algebra, biology, chemistry, computer science, English, geometry, trigonometry.

Essential Knowledge and Skills

Reading comprehension, speaking, instructing, writing, active learning, information gathering. **Values/Work Environment:** Autonomy, authority, working indoors, sitting, standing.

Other Information Sources

Many career and education information sources use the standard cross-referencing systems noted below. You can use the codes to obtain substantial additional information on the major (via CIP code) and related occupations (via GOE code). The O*NET codes on the opposite page refer to another major career information system. See the Introduction for details on obtaining additional information.

Classification of Instructional Programs (CIP) code: 010101 Agricultural Business and Management, General

Guide for Occupational Exploration (GOE) codes: 03.01 Managerial Work: Nursery, Groundskeeping, and Logging; 12.03 Educational Services; 02.04 Social Sciences

---

Agricultural Engineering

Career Snapshot

Agricultural engineers use scientific knowledge to solve problems of growing food and fiber crops, building and maintaining agricultural equipment and structures, and processing agricultural products. A bachelor's degree is usually sufficient preparation to enter this field. Often an engineering job can be a springboard for a managerial position. Job outlook is much better than for most other engineering fields, especially in specializations related to biological engineering and environmental protection.

Related Specialties and Careers

Agricultural machinery, agricultural structures, environmental engineering, food and fiber processing, irrigation.

Related Job Titles, Projected Growth, and Earnings		
Job Title	**Projected Growth**	**Average Earnings**
Agricultural Engineers (O*NET code 17-2021.00)	Faster than average	$52,510
Engineering Teachers, Postsecondary (O*NET code 25-1032.00)	Faster than average	(No salary data available)
Sales Engineers (O*NET code 41-9031.00)	Average	$54,600

Typical College Courses

Agricultural power and machines, biological materials processing, calculus, differential equations, dynamics, engineering properties of biological materials, English composition, fluid mechanics, general biology, general chemistry, general physics, introduction to agricultural engineering, introduction to computer science, introduction to electric circuits, materials engineering, microcomputer applications, numerical analysis, senior design project, soil and water engineering, statics, technical writing, thermodynamics.

Some Suggested High School Courses

Algebra, biology, calculus, chemistry, computer science, English, geometry, precalculus, trigonometry.

Essential Knowledge and Skills

Mathematics, active learning, reading comprehension, critical thinking, speaking, operations analysis, technology design, science, solution appraisal, idea generation. **Values/Work Environment:** Ability utilization; working indoors; sitting; standing; using hands on objects, tools, or controls.

Other Information Sources

Many career and education information sources use the standard cross-referencing systems noted below. You can use the codes to obtain substantial additional information on the major (via CIP code) and related occupations (via GOE code). The O*NET codes on the opposite page refer to another major career information system. See the Introduction for details on obtaining additional information.

Classification of Instructional Programs (CIP) code: 140301 Agricultural Engineering

Guide for Occupational Exploration (GOE) codes: 02.07 Engineering, 12.03 Educational Services

---

Agronomy and Crop Science

Career Snapshot

Agronomists and crop scientists look for ways to improve the production and quality of food, feed, and fiber crops. They need to understand the chemical requirements of soils and growing plants and the genetic basis of plant development—especially now that genetic engineering is growing in importance. Those with a bachelor's degree may work in applied research, but a graduate degree is useful to do basic research. Because agriculture is a vital U.S. industry supported by agricultural extension programs, a large number of agronomists and crop scientists work for federal, state, and local governments.

Related Specialties and Careers

Agro-industry, soil and crop management, turfgrass management.

Related Job Titles, Projected Growth, and Earnings		
Job Title	**Projected Growth**	**Average Earnings**
Plant Scientists (O*NET code 19-1013.01)	Average	$42,340
Agricultural Technicians (O*NET code 19-4011.01)	Little or none	$27,430
Biological Technicians (O*NET code 19-4021.00)	Little or none	$27,430
Agricultural Sciences Teachers, Postsecondary (O*NET code 25-1041.00)	Faster than average	(No salary data available)
Biological Science Teachers, Postsecondary (O*NET code 25-1042.00)	Faster than average	(No salary data available)
Forestry and Conservation Science Teachers, Postsecondary (O*NET code 25-1043.00)	Faster than average	(No salary data available)

Typical College Courses

Botany, college algebra, computer applications in agriculture, crop production, English composition, general biology, general chemistry, general entomology, genetics, introduction to agricultural economics and business, introduction to soil science, organic chemistry, plant breeding, plant pathology, seed production, soil fertility, plant nutrition and fertilizers, weed control.

Some Suggested High School Courses

Algebra, biology, chemistry, computer science, English, geometry, public speaking, trigonometry.

Essential Knowledge and Skills

Reading comprehension. **Values/Work Environment:** Achievement, working indoors, sitting, standing.

Other Information Sources

Many career and education information sources use the standard cross-referencing systems noted below. You can use the codes to obtain substantial additional information on the major (via CIP code) and related occupations (via GOE code). The O*NET codes on the opposite page refer to another major career information system. See the Introduction for details on obtaining additional information.

Classification of Instructional Programs (CIP) code: 020402 Agronomy and Crop Science

Guide for Occupational Exploration (GOE) codes: 02.03 Life Sciences, 02.05 Laboratory Technology, 12.03 Educational Services

---

American Studies

Career Snapshot

American studies is an interdisciplinary major that allows you to concentrate on the aspect of American culture that is of greatest interest to you. Many, perhaps most, graduates use this major as a springboard to postgraduate or professional training to prepare for a career in college teaching, business, law, the arts, politics, or some other field.

Related Specialties and Careers

History and political science, literature, language and the arts, popular culture.

Related Job Titles, Projected Growth, and Earnings		
Job Title	Projected Growth	Average Earnings
Anthropology and Archeology Teachers, Postsecondary (O*NET code 25-1061.00)	Faster than average	(No salary data available)
Area, Ethnic, and Cultural Studies Teachers, Postsecondary (O*NET code 25-1062.00)	Faster than average	(No salary data available)
Economics Teachers, Postsecondary (O*NET code 25-1063.00)	Faster than average	(No salary data available)
Political Science Teachers, Postsecondary (O*NET code 25-1065.00)	Faster than average	(No salary data available)
Sociology Teachers, Postsecondary (O*NET code 25-1067.00)	Faster than average	(No salary data available)
History Teachers, Postsecondary (O*NET code 25-1125.00)	Faster than average	(No salary data available)

Typical College Courses

American government, American history, American literature, American popular culture, English composition, seminar (reporting on research).

Some Suggested High School Courses

Algebra, English, foreign language, history, literature, public speaking, social science.

Essential Knowledge and Skills

Reading comprehension, instructing, speaking, active learning, writing, learning strategies, active listening, critical thinking, information gathering, idea generation.
Values/Work Environment: Achievement, authority, ability utilization, responsibility, autonomy, working indoors, sitting, standing.

Other Information Sources

Many career and education information sources use the standard cross-referencing systems noted below. You can use the codes to obtain substantial additional information on the major (via CIP code) and related occupations (via GOE code). The O*NET codes on the opposite page refer to another major career information system. See the Introduction for details on obtaining additional information.

Classification of Instructional Programs (CIP) code: 050102 American Studies/Civilization

Guide for Occupational Exploration (GOE) code: 12.03 Educational Services

Animal Science

Career Snapshot

Animal science graduates may work directly for farms and ranches that raise animals, or they may work in research, marketing, or sales for pharmaceutical or feed companies that supply farmers, ranchers, and veterinarians. About one-third go on to veterinary school, medical school, or another post-graduate scientific field.

Related Specialties and Careers

Production, veterinary research.

Related Job Titles, Projected Growth, and Earnings		
Job Title	**Projected Growth**	**Average Earnings**
Animal Scientists (O*NET code 19-1011.00)	Average	$42,340
Plant Scientists (O*NET code 19-1013.01)	Average	$42,340
Agricultural Technicians (O*NET code 19-4011.01)	Little or none	$27,430
Biological Technicians (O*NET code 19-4021.00)	Little or none	$27,430
Agricultural Sciences Teachers, Postsecondary (O*NET code 25-1041.00)	Faster than average	(No salary data available)
Biological Science Teachers, Postsecondary (O*NET code 25-1042.00)	Faster than average	(No salary data available)
Forestry and Conservation Science Teachers, Postsecondary (O*NET code 25-1043.00)	Faster than average	(No salary data available)
Farm and Home Management Advisors (O*NET code 25-9021.00)	Declining	$37,200
Sales Representatives, Agricultural (O*NET code 41-4011.01)	Average	$44,690
First-Line Supervisors and Manager/ Supervisors—Animal Husbandry Workers (O*NET code 45-1011.02)	Little or none	$27,410

Job Title	Projected Growth	Average Earnings
First-Line Supervisors and Manager/Supervisors—Animal Care Workers, Except Livestock (O*NET code 45-1011.03)	Little or none	$27,410

Typical College Courses

Anatomy and physiology of farm animals, animal breeding, animal nutrition and nutritional diseases, college algebra, English composition, feeds and feeding, general biology, general chemistry, genetics, introduction to agricultural economics and business, introduction to animal science, marking and grading of livestock and meats, meats and other animal products, organic chemistry, plant physiology, reproduction of farm animals, statistics.

Some Suggested High School Courses

Algebra, biology, chemistry, computer science, English, geometry, public speaking, trigonometry.

Essential Knowledge and Skills

Reading comprehension. **Values/Work Environment:** Autonomy; working indoors; standing; sitting; using hands on objects, tools, or controls.

Other Information Sources

Many career and education information sources use the standard cross-referencing systems noted below. You can use the codes to obtain substantial additional information on the major (via CIP code) and related occupations (via GOE code). The O*NET codes on the opposite page refer to another major career information system. See the Introduction for details on obtaining additional information.

Classification of Instructional Programs (CIP) code: 020201 Animal Sciences, General

Guide for Occupational Exploration (GOE) codes: 02.03 Life Sciences; 02.05 Laboratory Technology; 03.01 Managerial Work: Nursery, Groundskeeping, and Logging; 10.02 Sales Technology; 12.03 Educational Services

Anthropology

Career Snapshot

Some anthropologists study the social and cultural behavior of people. They investigate communities throughout the world, focusing on their arts, religions, and economic and social institutions. A graduate degree is usually needed to do research or college teaching in this field, but some graduates with bachelor's degrees find their skills useful in business, such as in marketing research. Other anthropologists specialize in human physical characteristics and may study human remains to understand history or evolution, or to provide evidence in criminal investigations. A graduate degree is usually required for this specialization.

Related Specialties and Careers

Archeology, biological/forensic anthropology, cultural anthropology.

Related Job Titles, Projected Growth, and Earnings		
Job Title	**Projected Growth**	**Average Earnings**
Sociologists (O*NET code 19-3041.00)	Average	$38,990
Anthropologists (O*NET code 19-3091.01)	Average	$38,990
Archeologists (O*NET code 19-3091.02)	Average	$38,990
Anthropology and Archeology Teachers, Postsecondary (O*NET code 25-1061.00)	Faster than average	(No salary data available)
Area, Ethnic, and Cultural Studies Teachers, Postsecondary (O*NET code 25-1062.00)	Faster than average	(No salary data available)

Typical College Courses

Archeology, cultural anthropology, current issues in anthropology, English composition, foreign language, general biology, history of anthropological theory, human growth and development, introduction to sociology, language and culture, physical anthropology, research methods in anthropology, statistics for business and social sciences.

Some Suggested High School Courses

Algebra, biology, chemistry, English, foreign language, history, public speaking, social science.

Essential Knowledge and Skills

Reading comprehension, active learning, writing, information gathering, critical thinking, information organization, speaking. **Values/Work Environment:** Achievement, autonomy, ability utilization, responsibility, working indoors, sitting, standing.

Other Information Sources

Many career and education information sources use the standard cross-referencing systems noted below. You can use the codes to obtain substantial additional information on the major (via CIP code) and related occupations (via GOE code). The O*NET codes on the opposite page refer to another major career information system. See the Introduction for details on obtaining additional information.

Classification of Instructional Programs (CIP) code: 450201 Anthropology

Guide for Occupational Exploration (GOE) codes: 02.04 Social Sciences, 12.03 Educational Services

---

Archeology

Career Snapshot

Archeology (also spelled *archaeology*) is the study of prehistoric and historic cultures through the discovery, preservation, and interpretation of their material remains. As a major, it is sometimes offered as a specialization within anthropology or classics. Students work with languages as well as physical objects, so they develop a number of skills that are appreciated in the business world. They may also get higher degrees in archeology in order to do museum work, field work, or college teaching.

Related Specialties and Careers

Ancient civilizations, field work, prehistoric archeology, preservation.

Related Job Titles, Projected Growth, and Earnings		
Job Title	**Projected Growth**	**Average Earnings**
Anthropologists (O*NET code 19-3091.01)	Average	$38, 990
Anthropology and Archeology Teachers, Postsecondary (O*NET code 25-1061.00)	Faster than average	(No salary data available)
Archeologists (O*NET code 19-3091.02)	Average	$38, 990
Area, Ethnic, and Cultural Studies Teachers, Postsecondary (O*NET code 25-1062.00)	Faster than average	(No salary data available)
History Teachers, Postsecondary (O*NET code 25-1125.00)	Faster than average	(No salary data available)
Sociology Teachers, Postsecondary (O*NET code 25-1067.00)	Faster than average	(No salary data available)

Typical College Courses

Ancient literate civilizations, English composition, field methods in archeology, foreign language, introduction to archeology, new world archeology, statistics for business and social sciences, world prehistory.

Some Suggested High School Courses

Algebra, biology, English, foreign language, history, public speaking, social science.

Essential Knowledge and Skills

Reading comprehension, active learning, writing, information gathering, speaking, critical thinking, instructing, information organization, active listening, learning strategies. **Values/Work Environment:** Achievement, ability utilization, autonomy, responsibility, creativity, working indoors, sitting, standing.

Other Information Sources

Many career and education information sources use the standard cross-referencing systems noted below. You can use the codes to obtain substantial additional information on the major (via CIP code) and related occupations (via GOE code). The O*NET codes on the opposite page refer to another major career information system. See the Introduction for details on obtaining additional information.

Classification of Instructional Programs (CIP) code: 450301 Archeology

Guide for Occupational Exploration (GOE) codes: 02.04 Social Sciences, 12.03 Educational Services

---

Architecture

Career Snapshot

Architects design buildings and the spaces between them. They must have a combination of artistic, technical, and business skills. In order to be licensed, they must obtain a professional degree in architecture (sometimes a five-year bachelor's degree, sometimes a master's degree after a bachelor's in another field), get some on-the-job training, and pass a licensing exam. About one-third are self-employed, and most architectural firms are quite small. Computer skills can be a big advantage for new graduates.

Related Specialties and Careers

Architectural engineering, design, history, theory and criticism, urban studies.

Related Job Titles, Projected Growth, and Earnings		
Job Title	Projected Growth	Average Earnings
Architects, Except Landscape and Naval (O*NET code 17-1011.00)	Average	$47,710

Typical College Courses

Architectural computer graphics, architectural design, architectural graphics, art history: Renaissance to modern, basic drawing, building science, calculus, English composition, general physics, history of architecture, introduction to computer science, introduction to urban planning, site analysis, structures, visual analysis of architecture.

Some Suggested High School Courses

Algebra, art, calculus, computer science, English, geometry, physics, pre-calculus, trigonometry.

Essential Knowledge and Skills

Coordination, reading comprehension. **Values/Work Environment:** Ability utilization; creativity; recognition; achievement; social status; working indoors; sitting; using hands on objects, tools, or controls.

Other Information Sources

Many career and education information sources use the standard cross-referencing systems noted below. You can use the codes to obtain substantial additional information on the major (via CIP code) and related occupations (via GOE code). The O*NET codes on the opposite page refer to another major career information system. See the Introduction for details on obtaining additional information.

Classification of Instructional Programs (CIP) code: 040201 Architecture

Guide for Occupational Exploration (GOE) codes: 01.01 Managerial Work in Arts, Entertainment, and Media; 01.04 Visual Arts; 01.06 Craft Arts

Area Studies

Career Snapshot

Certain very popular area studies—African-American studies, American studies, and women's studies—are described elsewhere in this book. But many colleges offer other area studies majors, usually defined in terms of a region of the world: East Asian studies, European studies, Latin American studies, and so on. These are interdisciplinary majors that may involve some combination of linguistics, literature, history, sociology, political science, economic development, or other disciplines. Usually you can emphasize whichever aspects interest you most. Graduates of area studies may go into a business or government career where knowledge of a foreign culture is an advantage. Many get higher degrees to prepare for a career in law or college teaching.

Related Specialties and Careers

Economics and trade, history and culture, language and literature, political science.

Related Job Titles, Projected Growth, and Earnings		
Job Title	**Projected Growth**	**Average Earnings**
Anthropology and Archeology Teachers, Postsecondary (O*NET code 25-1061.00)	Faster than average	(No salary data available)
Area, Ethnic, and Cultural Studies Teachers, Postsecondary (O*NET code 25-1062.00)	Faster than average	(No salary data available)
Economics Teachers, Postsecondary (O*NET code 25-1063.00)	Faster than average	(No salary data available)
Political Science Teachers, Postsecondary (O*NET code 25-1065.00)	Faster than average	(No salary data available)
Psychology Teachers, Postsecondary (O*NET code 25-1066.00)	Faster than average	(No salary data available)
Sociology Teachers, Postsecondary (O*NET code 25-1067.00)	Faster than average	(No salary data available)
History Teachers, Postsecondary (O*NET code 25-1125.00)	Faster than average	(No salary data available)

Typical College Courses

Comparative governments, English composition, foreign language, foreign literature and culture, international economics, introduction to economics, seminar (reporting on research).

Some Suggested High School Courses

Algebra, English, foreign language, history, literature, social science.

Essential Knowledge and Skills

Reading comprehension, instructing, active learning, speaking, active listening, learning strategies, writing, critical thinking, information gathering, idea generation. **Values/Work Environment:** Achievement, ability utilization, authority, autonomy, responsibility, creativity, social service, social status, good working conditions, working indoors, sitting, standing.

Other Information Sources

Many career and education information sources use the standard cross-referencing systems noted below. You can use the codes to obtain substantial additional information on the major (via CIP code) and related occupations (via GOE code). The O*NET codes on the opposite page refer to another major career information system. See the Introduction for details on obtaining additional information.

Classification of Instructional Programs (CIP) codes: 050102 American Studies/Civilization, 050103 Asian Studies, 050104 East Asian Studies, 050105 Eastern European Area Studies, 050106 European Studies, 050107 Latin American Studies, 050108 Middle Eastern Studies, 050109 Pacific Area Studies, 050110 Russian and Slavic Area Studies, 050111 Scandinavian Area Studies, 050115 Canadian Studies

Guide for Occupational Exploration (GOE) code: 12.03 Educational Services

---

Art

Career Snapshot

Only a few highly talented and motivated artists are able to support themselves by producing and selling their artworks. But many other graduates of art programs find work in education—as private instructors, school teachers, and university instructors of art and art history. Some apply their artistic skills to crafts or to commercial applications such as illustration or cartooning.

Related Specialties and Careers

Art conservation, art education, art history, ceramics, painting, screen printing, sculpture, studio art.

Related Job Titles, Projected Growth, and Earnings		
Job Title	Projected Growth	Average Earnings
Art, Drama, and Music Teachers, Postsecondary (O*NET code 25-1121.00)	Faster than average	(No salary data available)
Art Directors (O*NET code 27-1011.00)	Faster than average	$31,690
Art, Drama, and Music Teachers, Postsecondary (O*NET code 25-1121.00)	Faster than average	$41,870
Cartoonists (O*NET code 27-1013.03)	Faster than average	$31,690
Painters and Illustrators (O*NET code 27-1013.01)	Faster than average	$31,690
Sculptors (O*NET code 27-1013.04)	Faster than average	$31,690
Sketch Artists (O*NET code 27-1013.02)	Faster than average	$31,690

Typical College Courses

A medium (such as painting, sculpture, or ceramics), art and culture, art history: prehistoric to Renaissance, art history: Renaissance to modern, art practicum, basic drawing, color and design, English composition, figure drawing, foreign language, three-dimensional design, two-dimensional design.

Some Suggested High School Courses

Art, English, foreign language, history, literature.

Essential Knowledge and Skills

Reading comprehension, instructing, active learning, speaking, active listening, learning strategies, writing, critical thinking, information gathering, idea generation. **Values/Work Environment:** Achievement, ability utilization, authority, autonomy, responsibility, creativity, social service, social status, working conditions, working indoors, sitting, standing.

Other Information Sources

Many career and education information sources use the standard cross-referencing systems noted below. You can use the codes to obtain substantial additional information on the major (via CIP code) and related occupations (via GOE code). The O*NET codes on the opposite page refer to another major career information system. See the Introduction for details on obtaining additional information.

Classification of Instructional Programs (CIP) code: 360110 Art

Guide for Occupational Exploration (GOE) codes: 01.04 Visual Arts, 01.06 Craft Arts, 12.03 Educational Services

---

Astronomy

Career Snapshot

Almost every year, astronomers make important discoveries that challenge existing theories about the planets, stars, and galaxies and the forces that formed them. Astronomers typically spend only a small fraction of their time actually observing, and much more time analyzing data and comparing it to theoretical models. Many are college faculty members with teaching responsibilities. A Ph.D. is the usual requirement for astronomers, and many new Ph.D.s find a postdoctoral research appointment helpful for future employment. Competition in this field is expected to remain intense for the foreseeable future.

Related Specialties and Careers

Astrophysics, cosmology.

Related Job Titles, Projected Growth, and Earnings		
Job Title	Projected Growth	Average Earnings
Astronomers (O*NET code 19-2012.00)	Little or none	$73,240
Physicists (O*NET code 19-2012.00)	Little or none	$73,240

Typical College Courses

Astrophysical processes, calculus, differential equations, electricity and magnetism, English composition, general chemistry, general physics, introduction to astrophysics, introduction to computer science, mechanics, observational astronomy, quantum and atomic physics, thermal physics.

Some Suggested High School Courses

Algebra, calculus, chemistry, computer science, English, geometry, physics, pre-calculus, trigonometry.

Essential Knowledge and Skills

Mathematics, science, information gathering, reading comprehension, critical thinking, active learning, information organization, idea generation, synthesis and reorganization. **Values/Work Environment:** Autonomy; ability utilization; creativity; working outdoors; working indoors; using hands on objects, tools, or controls.

Other Information Sources

Many career and education information sources use the standard cross-referencing systems noted below. You can use the codes to obtain substantial additional information on the major (via CIP code) and related occupations (via GOE code). The O*NET codes on the opposite page refer to another major career information system. See the Introduction for details on obtaining additional information.

Classification of Instructional Programs (CIP) code: 400201 Astronomy

Guide for Occupational Exploration (GOE) code: 02.02 Physical Sciences

Biochemistry

Career Snapshot

Biochemistry studies the fundamental chemical processes that support life. The recent growth of the pharmaceutical industry and of genetic engineering technology has fueled the demand for biochemistry majors, especially at the graduate level. Those with bachelor's degrees may find work in non-research jobs such as clinical laboratory testing.

Related Specialties and Careers

Forensic chemistry, pharmacological chemistry, recombinant DNA, research.

Related Job Titles, Projected Growth, and Earnings		
Job Title	**Projected Growth**	**Average Earnings**
Biochemists (O*NET code 19-1021.01)	Faster than average	$46,140
Biophysicists (O*NET code 19-1021.02)	Faster than average	$46,140
Microbiologists (O*NET code 19-1022.00)	Faster than average	$46,140
Epidemiologists (O*NET code 19-1041.00)	Faster than average	$50,410
Medical Scientists, Except Epidemiologists (O*NET code 19-1042.00)	Faster than average	$50,410
Agricultural Sciences Teachers, Postsecondary (O*NET code 25-1041.00)	Faster than average	(No salary data available)
Biological Science Teachers, Postsecondary (O*NET code 25-1042.00)	Faster than average	(No salary data available)
Forestry and Conservation Science Teachers, Postsecondary (O*NET code 25-1043.00)	Faster than average	(No salary data available)

Typical College Courses

Analytical chemistry, calculus, cell biology, English composition, general biology, general chemistry, general microbiology, general physics, genetics, introduction to biochemistry, introduction to computer science, molecular biology, organic chemistry, physical chemistry.

Some Suggested High School Courses

Algebra, biology, calculus, chemistry, computer science, English, geometry, physics, pre-calculus, trigonometry.

Essential Knowledge and Skills

Reading comprehension, science, writing, active learning, information gathering, critical thinking, mathematics, problem identification, idea evaluation. **Values/Work Environment:** Ability utilization; autonomy; achievement; responsibility; working indoors; sitting; using hands on objects, tools, or controls.

Other Information Sources

Many career and education information sources use the standard cross-referencing systems noted below. You can use the codes to obtain substantial additional information on the major (via CIP code) and related occupations (via GOE code). The O*NET codes on the opposite page refer to another major career information system. See the Introduction for details on obtaining additional information.

Classification of Instructional Programs (CIP) code: 260202 Biochemistry

Guide for Occupational Exploration (GOE) codes: 02.03 Life Sciences, 12.03 Educational Services

---

Bioengineering

Career Snapshot

Bioengineering uses engineering principles of analysis and design to solve problems in medicine and biology. It finds ways to improve health care, agriculture, and industrial processes. Graduates with a bachelor's may work in industry, but many get an advanced degree to enter industry at a higher professional level, or to prepare for a career in research or college teaching. Others go on to medical school. This is one of the fastest-moving fields in engineering, so people in this field need to learn continuously to keep up with new technologies.

Related Specialties and Careers

Biomedical engineering, biomechanics, computational bioengineering, controlled drug delivery, engineered biomaterials, medical imaging, molecular bioengineering, prosthetics and artificial organs.

Related Job Titles, Projected Growth, and Earnings		
Job Title	Projected Growth	Average Earnings
Engineering Teachers, Postsecondary (O*NET code 25-1032.00)	Faster than average	(No salary data available)

Typical College Courses

Bioinstrumentation, biomaterials, biomechanics, business information processing, calculus, differential equations, English composition, general biology, general chemistry, general physics, introduction to bioengineering, introduction to computer science, introduction to electric circuits, mechanics, technical writing.

Some Suggested High School Courses

Algebra, biology, calculus, chemistry, computer science, English, geometry, physics, pre-calculus, trigonometry.

Essential Knowledge and Skills

Mathematics, reading comprehension, critical thinking, science, instructing.
Values/Work Environment: Ability utilization, achievement, authority, working indoors, sitting, standing.

Other Information Sources

Many career and education information sources use the standard cross-referencing systems noted below. You can use the codes to obtain substantial additional information on the major (via CIP code) and related occupations (via GOE code). The O*NET codes on the opposite page refer to another major career information system. See the Introduction for details on obtaining additional information.

Classification of Instructional Programs (CIP) code: 140501 Bioengineering and Biomedical Engineering

Guide for Occupational Exploration (GOE) code: 12.03 Educational Services

 **Biology**

Career Snapshot

Although it is often possible to study a specialization—such as botany, zoology, or biochemistry—many colleges offer a major in the general field of biology. With a bachelor's degree in biology, one may work as a technician or entry-level researcher in a medical, pharmaceutical, or governmental regulatory setting, or as a sales representative in a technical field such as pharmaceuticals. Teaching biology in high school or middle school almost always requires additional coursework (perhaps a master's) in teaching theory and methods, plus supervised classroom experience. A large number of biology majors go on to pursue graduate or professional degrees and thus prepare for careers as researchers, college teachers, physicians, dentists, and veterinarians.

Related Specialties and Careers

Botany, biochemistry, cell biology, ecology, genetics, microbiology, zoology.

Related Job Titles, Projected Growth, and Earnings		
Job Title	**Projected Growth**	**Average Earnings**
Agricultural Sciences Teachers, Postsecondary (College and University Faculty) (O*NET code 25-1041.00)	Faster than average	(No salary data available)
Biological Science Teachers, Postsecondary (College and University Faculty) (O*NET code 25-1042.00)	Faster than average	(No salary data available)
Forestry and Conservation Science Teachers, Postsecondary (College and University Faculty) (O*NET code 25-1043.00)	Faster than average	(No salary data available)

Typical College Courses

Animal anatomy and physiology, calculus, cell biology, ecology, English composition, general biology, general chemistry, general microbiology, general physics, genetics, introduction to biochemistry, introduction to computer science, organic chemistry, organisms and populations, plant anatomy, statistics.

Some Suggested High School Courses

Algebra, biology, calculus, chemistry, computer science, English, geometry, physics, pre-calculus, trigonometry.

Essential Knowledge and Skills

Reading comprehension, instructing, speaking, science, active learning, writing, critical thinking, information gathering, learning strategies, idea generation.

Values/Work Environment: Achievement, ability utilization, authority, social status, autonomy, creativity, responsibility, good working conditions, working indoors, sitting, standing.

Other Information Sources

Many career and education information sources use the standard cross-referencing systems noted below. You can use the codes to obtain substantial additional information on the major (via CIP code) and related occupations (via GOE code). The O*NET codes on the opposite page refer to another major career information system. See the Introduction for details on obtaining additional information.

Classification of Instructional Programs (CIP) code: 260101 Biology, General

Guide for Occupational Exploration (GOE) code: 12.03 Educational Services

---

 **Botany**

Career Snapshot

Botany is the science of plants. Since all of our food resources and the very air we breathe ultimately depend on the growth of plants, botany is a vital field of knowledge. A bachelor's degree in this field prepares you for some non-research jobs in industry, agriculture, forestry, and environmental protection. Best opportunities are in agricultural research, where a graduate degree is expected.

Related Specialties and Careers

Forestry, phytopathology (plant disease), plant genetics.

Related Job Titles, Projected Growth, and Earnings		
Job Title	**Projected Growth**	**Average Earnings**
Agricultural Sciences Teachers, Postsecondary (O*NET code 25-1041.00)	Faster than average	(No salary data available)
Biological Science Teachers, Postsecondary (O*NET code 25-1042.00)	Faster than average	(No salary data available)
Forestry and Conservation Science Teachers, Postsecondary (O*NET code 25-1043.00)	Faster than average	(No salary data available)

Typical College Courses

Calculus, cell biology, ecology, English composition, general biology, general chemistry, general microbiology, general physics, genetics, introduction to biochemistry, introduction to computer science, organic chemistry, plant anatomy, plant physiology, statistics, taxonomy of flowering plants.

Some Suggested High School Courses

Algebra, biology, calculus, chemistry, computer science, English, geometry, physics, pre-calculus, trigonometry.

Essential Knowledge and Skills

Reading comprehension, instructing, learning strategies, critical thinking, active learning, writing, science, information gathering, speaking, mathematics. **Values/ Work Environment:** Achievement, ability utilization, authority, working indoors, sitting, standing.

Other Information Sources

Many career and education information sources use the standard cross-referencing systems noted below. You can use the codes to obtain substantial additional information on the major (via CIP code) and related occupations (via GOE code). The O*NET codes on the opposite page refer to another major career information system. See the Introduction for details on obtaining additional information.

Classification of Instructional Programs (CIP) code: 260301 Botany, General

Guide for Occupational Exploration (GOE) code: 12.03 Educational Services

Business Education

Career Snapshot

Business educators teach secondary school students skills and knowledge they will need to succeed in the business world. Therefore, they must know about one or more specific business fields—such as bookkeeping, retailing, or office computer applications—as well as about techniques for teaching and for managing the classroom. A bachelor's degree is often an entry route to the first teaching job, but job security and pay raises often require a master's degree.

Related Specialties and Careers

Distributive education, office skills.

Related Job Titles, Projected Growth, and Earnings		
Job Title	**Projected Growth**	**Average Earnings**
Vocational Education Teachers Postsecondary (O*NET code 25-1194.00)	Average	$34,430
Middle School Teachers, Except Special and Vocational Education (O*NET code 25-2022.00)	Faster than average	$37,890
Vocational Education Teachers, Middle School (O*NET code 25-2023.00)	Faster than average	$34,430
Secondary School Teachers, Except Special and Vocational Education (O*NET code 25-2031.00)	Faster than average	$37,890
Vocational Education Teachers, Secondary School (O*NET code 25-2032.00)	Faster than average	$34,430

Typical College Courses

Business information processing, business math, business reports and communication, English composition, history and philosophy of education, human growth and development, introduction to accounting, introduction to business management, introduction to marketing, introduction to psychology, keyboarding, legal environment of business, methods of teaching business subjects, oral communication, statistics, student teaching.

Some Suggested High School Courses

Algebra, English, foreign language, geometry, industrial arts, keyboarding, office computer applications, public speaking, science, trigonometry.

Essential Knowledge and Skills

Learning strategies, speaking, reading comprehension, instructing. **Values/Work Environment:** Authority, social service, achievement, responsibility, working indoors, standing, sitting.

Other Information Sources

Many career and education information sources use the standard cross-referencing systems noted below. You can use the codes to obtain substantial additional information on the major (via CIP code) and related occupations (via GOE code). The O*NET codes on the opposite page refer to another major career information system. See the Introduction for details on obtaining additional information.

Classification of Instructional Programs (CIP) code: 131303 Business Teacher Education

Guide for Occupational Exploration (GOE) code: 12.03 Educational Services

---

Business Management

Career Snapshot

Students of business management learn about the principles of economics, the legal and social environment in which business operates, and quantitative methods for measuring and projecting business activity. Graduates may enter the business world directly or pursue a master's degree. Some get a bachelor's degree in a non-business field and enter a master's of business administration program after getting some entry-level work experience.

Related Specialties and Careers

International business, management, marketing, operations.

Related Job Titles, Projected Growth, and Earnings		
Job Title	Projected Growth	Average Earnings
Government Service Executives (O*NET code 11-1011.01)	Average	$55,030
Private-Sector Executives (O*NET code 11-1011.02)	Average	$55,890
Administrative Services Managers (O*NET code 11-3011.00)	Average	$44,370
Industrial Production Managers (O*NET code 11-3051.00)	Declining	$56,320
Purchasing Managers (O*NET code 11-3061.00)	Little or none	$41,830
Transportation Managers (O*NET code 11-3071.01)	Average	$52,810
Storage and Distribution Managers (O*NET code 11-3071.02)	Average	$52,810
Gaming Managers (O*NET code 11-9071.00)	Average	$49,220
Medical and Health Services Managers (O*NET code 11-9111.00)	Faster than average	$48,870
Postmasters and Mail Superintendents (O*NET code 11-9131.00)	Little or none	$44,730

Job Title	Projected Growth	Average Earnings
Social and Community Service Managers (O*NET code 11-9151.00)	Average	$49,220
Purchasing Agents, Except Wholesale, Retail, and Farm Products (O*NET code 13-1023.00)	Average	$38,040
Cost Estimators (O*NET code 13-1051.00)	Average	$40,590
Management Analysts (O*NET code 13-1111.00)	Faster than average	$49,470

Typical College Courses

Business finance, business writing, calculus for business and social sciences, English composition, human resource management, international management, accounting, management information systems, marketing, psychology, legal environment of business, operations management, organizational behavior, organizational theory, macroeconomics, management and organization, microeconomics, statistics for business and social sciences, strategic management.

Some Suggested High School Courses

Algebra, computer science, English, foreign language, geometry, public speaking, science, trigonometry.

Essential Knowledge and Skills

Reading comprehension. **Values/Work Environment:** Autonomy, working indoors.

Other Information Sources

Many career and education information sources use the standard cross-referencing systems noted below. You can use the codes to obtain substantial additional information on the major (via CIP code) and related occupations (via GOE code). The O*NET codes on the opposite page refer to another major career information system. See the Introduction for details on obtaining additional information.

Classification of Instructional Programs (CIP) code: 520201 Business Administration and Management, General

Guide for Occupational Exploration (GOE) codes: 07.01 Managerial Work in Transportation; 08.01 Managerial Work in Industrial Production; 09.01 Managerial Work; 11.01 Managerial Work in Recreation, Travel, and Other Personal Services; 12.01 Managerial Work in Education and Social Service; 13.01 General Management Work and Management of Support Functions; 13.02 Management Support; 14.01 Managerial Work in Medical and Health Services

Chemical Engineering

Career Snapshot

Chemical engineers apply principles of chemistry to solve engineering problems, such as how to prepare large batches of chemical compounds economically, with uniform consistency and quality. A bachelor's degree is the usual entry route for this field. Keen competition is expected for entry-level jobs, with best opportunities in the manufacture of specialty chemicals, plastics, pharmaceuticals, and electronics, plus in some non-manufacturing industries. Engineers often move on to managerial jobs.

Related Specialties and Careers

Bioengineering, nuclear engineering, pharmaceuticals, quality control.

Related Job Titles, Projected Growth, and Earnings		
Job Title	**Projected Growth**	**Average Earnings**
Chemical Engineers (O*NET code 17-2041.00)	Little or none	$64,760
Engineering Teachers, Postsecondary (O*NET code 25-1032.00)	Faster than average	(No salary data available)
Sales Engineers (O*NET code 41-9031.00)	Average	$54,600

Typical College Courses

Calculus, chemical engineering thermodynamics, differential equations, English composition, general chemistry, general physics, introduction to chemical engineering, introduction to computer science, introduction to electric circuits, kinetics and reactor design, mass transfer operations, materials engineering, numerical analysis, organic chemistry, plant design, process design and optimization, process dynamics and controls, senior design project, technical writing, thermodynamics.

Some Suggested High School Courses

Algebra, calculus, chemistry, computer science, English, geometry, physics, pre-calculus, trigonometry.

Essential Knowledge and Skills

Reading comprehension, active learning, mathematics, science, critical thinking, operations analysis, speaking, writing, solution appraisal, technology design. **Values/Work Environment:** Ability utilization; working indoors; sitting; standing; using hands on objects, tools, or controls.

Other Information Sources

Many career and education information sources use the standard cross-referencing systems noted below. You can use the codes to obtain substantial additional information on the major (via CIP code) and related occupations (via GOE code). The O*NET codes on the opposite page refer to another major career information system. See the Introduction for details on obtaining additional information.

Classification of Instructional Programs (CIP) code: 140701 Chemical Engineering

Guide for Occupational Exploration (GOE) codes: 02.07 Engineering, 12.03 Educational Services

---

 **Chemistry**

Career Snapshot

Everything around us and within us is composed of chemicals, and chemists search for and put to use new knowledge about the nature and properties of matter. Chemists develop new fibers, paints, pharmaceuticals, solvents, fuels, and countless other materials that are used in industry and the home. A bachelor's degree is usually required for entry to this field, but a Ph.D. is often needed for research or college teaching. Job opportunities are good, especially in companies that manufacture pharmaceuticals or do chemical testing.

Related Specialties and Careers

Forensic chemistry, geological/ocean chemistry, quality control, research.

Related Job Titles, Projected Growth, and Earnings		
Job Title	Projected Growth	Average Earnings
Chemists (O*NET code 19-2031.00)	Average	$46,220
Chemistry Teachers, Postsecondary (O*NET code 25-1052.00)	Faster than average	(No salary data available)

Typical College Courses

Calculus, English composition, general chemistry, general physics, inorganic chemistry, introduction to computer science, molecular structure and bonding, organic chemistry, physical chemistry, qualitative analysis, quantitative analysis, statistics, undergraduate research project.

Some Suggested High School Courses

Algebra, calculus, chemistry, computer science, English, geometry, physics, pre-calculus, trigonometry.

Essential Knowledge and Skills

Writing, reading comprehension, science, active learning, information gathering, mathematics, critical thinking, information organization, idea generation, idea evaluation. **Values/Work Environment:** Ability utilization; autonomy; achievement; creativity; working indoors; sitting; standing; hazardous conditions; using hands on objects, tools, or controls.

Other Information Sources

Many career and education information sources use the standard cross-referencing systems noted below. You can use the codes to obtain substantial additional information on the major (via CIP code) and related occupations (via GOE code). The O*NET codes on the opposite page refer to another major career information system. See the Introduction for details on obtaining additional information.

Classification of Instructional Programs (CIP) code: 400501 Chemistry, General

Guide for Occupational Exploration (GOE) codes: 02.02 Physical Sciences; 12.03 Educational Services

 **Chinese**

Career Snapshot

Because Chinese is spoken by more people than any other language, there is a growing need for Americans with knowledge of the Chinese language and culture, especially now that U.S. trade with China is increasing. A bachelor's degree in Chinese, perhaps with additional education in business or law, may lead to an Asia-centered career in business or government. A graduate degree is good preparation for translation or college teaching.

Related Specialties and Careers

History and culture, language education, literature, translation.

Related Job Titles, Projected Growth, and Earnings		
Job Title	Projected Growth	Average Earnings
Foreign Language and Literature Teachers, Postsecondary (O*NET code 25-1124.00)	Faster than average	(No salary data available)
Interpreters and Translators (O*NET code 27-3091.00)	(No job growth data available)	(No salary data available)

Typical College Courses

Chinese language, Chinese literature, composition, conversation, east Asian literature, east Asian studies, grammar, linguistics, phonetics.

Some Suggested High School Courses

English, foreign language, history, literature, public speaking, social science.

Essential Knowledge and Skills

Reading comprehension, speaking, instructing, learning strategies, writing, information gathering, critical thinking, active listening, information organization, synthesis/reorganization. **Values/Work Environment:** Achievement, authority, ability utilization, autonomy, working indoors, sitting, standing.

Other Information Sources

Many career and education information sources use the standard cross-referencing systems noted below. You can use the codes to obtain substantial additional information on the major (via CIP code) and related occupations (via GOE code). The O*NET codes on the opposite page refer to another major career information system. See the Introduction for details on obtaining additional information.

Classification of Instructional Programs (CIP) code: 160301 Chinese Language and Literature

Guide for Occupational Exploration (GOE) codes: 01.01 News, Broadcasting, and Public Relations; 12.03 Educational Services

Chiropractic

Career Snapshot

Chiropractors are health practitioners who specialize in health problems associated with the muscular, nervous, and skeletal systems, especially the spine. They learn a variety of specialized diagnostic and treatment techniques but also tend to emphasize the patient's overall health and wellness, recommending changes in diet and lifestyle that can help the body's own healing powers. The educational program includes not only theory and laboratory work, but also a lot of supervised clinical work with patients. With the aging of the population and increased acceptance of chiropractic medicine, job opportunities for graduates are expected to be good.

Related Specialties and Careers

Diagnostic imaging, orthopedics, sports medicine.

Related Job Titles, Projected Growth, and Earnings		
Job Title	Projected Growth	Average Earnings
Health Specialties Teachers, Postsecondary (O*NET code 25-1071.00)	Faster than average	(No salary data available)
Chiropractors (O*NET code 29-1011.00)	Faster than average	$63,930

Typical College Courses

Biomechanics, calculus, chiropractic manipulative therapeutics, clinical experience in geriatrics, clinical experience in obstetrics/gynecology, clinical experience in pediatrics, college algebra, emergency care, English composition, ethics in health care, general biology, general chemistry, general microbiology, genetics, histology, human anatomy and physiology, introduction to biochemistry, introduction to computer science, introduction to psychology, introduction to sociology, mental health, minor surgery, neuroanatomy, neuromusculoskeletal diagnosis and treatment, neurophysiology, nutrition, oral communication, organic chemistry, pathology, patient examination and evaluation, pharmacology, physical diagnosis, professional practice management, public health, radiographic anatomy, spinal anatomy, veterinary gross anatomy.

Some Suggested High School Courses

Algebra, biology, chemistry, computer science, English, foreign language, geometry, physics, pre-calculus, public speaking, trigonometry.

Essential Knowledge and Skills

Reading comprehension, information gathering, problem identification, active listening, science, active learning, idea evaluation, critical thinking, writing, idea generation. **Values/Work Environment:** Achievement, autonomy, ability utilization, social service, social status, working indoors, standing, sitting.

Other Information Sources

Many career and education information sources use the standard cross-referencing systems noted below. You can use the codes to obtain substantial additional information on the major (via CIP code) and related occupations (via GOE code). The O*NET codes on the opposite page refer to another major career information system. See the Introduction for details on obtaining additional information.

Classification of Instructional Programs (CIP) code: 510101 Chiropractic (D.C., D.C.M.)

Guide for Occupational Exploration (GOE) codes: 12.03 Educational Services, 14.04 Health Specialties

---

Civil Engineering

Career Snapshot

Civil engineers design and supervise construction of roads, buildings, bridges, dams, airports, water-supply systems, and many other projects that affect the quality of our environment. They apply principles of physics and other sciences to devise engineering solutions that are technically effective, as well as being economically and environmentally sound. A bachelor's degree is the usual way to enter the field. Engineering is also a good way to prepare for a later position in management. Employment opportunities tend to rise and fall with the economy.

Related Specialties and Careers

Environmental engineering, geotechnical engineering, structural engineering, transportation engineering, water resources.

Related Job Titles, Projected Growth, and Earnings		
Job Title	**Projected Growth**	**Average Earnings**
Engineering Managers (O*NET code 11-9041.00)	Much faster than average	$75,320
Civil Engineers (O*NET code 17-2051.00)	Faster than average	$53,450
Nuclear Engineers (O*NET code 17-2161.00)	Little or none	$71,310
Engineering Teachers, Postsecondary (O*NET code 25-1032.00)	Faster than average	(No salary data available)
Public Transportation Inspectors (O*NET code 53-6051.02)	Average	$39,560

Typical College Courses

Analysis of structures, calculus, differential equations, dynamics, engineering economics, engineering graphics, engineering surveying and measurement, English composition, environmental engineering and design, fluid mechanics, general chemistry, general physics, highway and transportation engineering, introduction to civil engineering, introduction to computer science, introduction to electric circuits, materials engineering, numerical analysis, reinforced concrete design, senior design project, soil mechanics, statics, steel design, technical writing, water resources and hydraulic engineering.

Some Suggested High School Courses

Algebra, calculus, chemistry, computer science, English, geometry, physics, pre-calculus, trigonometry.

Essential Knowledge and Skills

Reading comprehension, operations analysis, information gathering, writing, critical thinking, mathematics, solution appraisal, problem identification, active learning. **Values/Work Environment:** Ability utilization, working indoors, sitting, standing.

Other Information Sources

Many career and education information sources use the standard cross-referencing systems noted below. You can use the codes to obtain substantial additional information on the major (via CIP code) and related occupations (via GOE code). The O*NET codes on the opposite page refer to another major career information system. See the Introduction for details on obtaining additional information.

Classification of Instructional Programs (CIP) code: 140801 Civil Engineering, General

Guide for Occupational Exploration (GOE) codes: 02.01 Managerial Work in Science, Math, and Engineering; 02.07 Engineering; 04.04 Public Safety; 12.03 Educational Services

---

Classics

Career Snapshot

The classical languages—Latin and Greek—may be dead, but students who study them often end up in very lively careers. The mental discipline and critical-thinking skills learned in the classics can be first-rate preparation for law school and medical school, and business recruiters report that classics graduates have an exceptional breadth of view. The demand for Latin teachers in secondary schools is strong. A classics major is also a good first step to graduate training in archeology, history, or theology.

Related Specialties and Careers

Archeology, classical civilization, classical linguistics, classical literature/mythology, Greek, Latin.

Related Job Titles, Projected Growth, and Earnings		
Job Title	**Projected Growth**	**Average Earnings**
English Language and Literature Teachers, Postsecondary (O*NET code 25-1123.00)	Faster than average	(No salary data available)
Foreign Language and Literature Teachers, Postsecondary (O*NET code 25-1124.00)	Faster than average	(No salary data available)

Typical College Courses

Grammar, Greek, history of the ancient world, Latin, linguistics, literature in ancient Greek, literature of the Roman empire.

Some Suggested High School Courses

English, foreign language, history, literature, public speaking, social science.

Essential Knowledge and Skills

Reading comprehension, speaking, instructing, writing, learning strategies, information gathering, critical thinking, active listening, information organization, synthesis/reorganization. **Values/Work Environment:** Achievement, ability utilization, authority, autonomy, working indoors, sitting, standing.

Other Information Sources

Many career and education information sources use the standard cross-referencing systems noted below. You can use the codes to obtain substantial additional information on the major (via CIP code) and related occupations (via GOE code). The O*NET codes on the opposite page refer to another major career information system. See the Introduction for details on obtaining additional information.

Classification of Instructional Programs (CIP) code: 161201 Classics and Classical Languages and Literatures

Guide for Occupational Exploration (GOE) code: 12.03 Educational Services

Computer Engineering

Career Snapshot

Computer engineers use their knowledge of scientific principles to design computers, networks of computers, and systems (such as telecommunications) that include computers. They need to understand both hardware and software, and they may build prototypes of new systems. The usual entry route is via a bachelor's degree. Opportunities for employment are excellent, as there seems to be no end to the boom in computer use. Some engineers go into management, and the computer industry provides many opportunities for creative and motivated engineers to become entrepreneurs.

Related Specialties and Careers

Hardware design, software/systems design, systems analysis.

Related Job Titles, Projected Growth, and Earnings		
Job Title	**Projected Growth**	**Average Earnings**
Computer Software Engineers, Applications (O*NET code 15-1031.00)	Much faster than average	$61,910
Computer Software Engineers, Systems Software (O*NET code 15-1032.00)	Much faster than average	$62,093
Computer Hardware Engineers (O*NET code 17-2061.00)	Much faster than average	$62,093
Electronics Engineers, Except Computer (O*NET code 17-2072.00)	Faster than average	$62,260
Engineering Teachers, Postsecondary (O*NET code 25-1032.00)	Faster than average	(No salary data available)

Typical College Courses

Algorithms and data structures, calculus, computer architecture, differential equations, digital system design, electrical networks, electronics, engineering circuit analysis, English composition, senior design project, general chemistry, general physics, introduction to computer science, introduction to electric circuits, introduction to engineering, microcomputer systems, numerical analysis, operating systems, software engineering, technical writing.

Some Suggested High School Courses

Algebra, calculus, chemistry, computer science, English, geometry, physics, pre-calculus, trigonometry.

Essential Knowledge and Skills

Mathematics, active learning, reading comprehension, science, critical thinking, operations analysis, information gathering, information organization, writing, judgment and decision-making. **Values/Work Environment:** Ability utilization; good working conditions; responsibility; creativity; working indoors; sitting; using hands on objects, tools, or controls.

Other Information Sources

Many career and education information sources use the standard cross-referencing systems noted below. You can use the codes to obtain substantial additional information on the major (via CIP code) and related occupations (via GOE code). The O*NET codes on the opposite page refer to another major career information system. See the Introduction for details on obtaining additional information.

Classification of Instructional Programs (CIP) code: 140901 Computer Engineering

Guide for Occupational Exploration (GOE) codes: 02.07 Engineering, 12.03 Educational Services

---

Computer Science

Career Snapshot

Computer science is among the hottest fields now, especially with the explosion of Internet sites, and it is likely to continue to offer many job openings. The major teaches you not only specific languages, but the principles by which languages are created, the structures used to store data, and the logical structures by which programs solve problems. You may want to concentrate more on business or scientific programming needs and procedures.

Related Specialties and Careers

Business programming, database programming, programming for the Internet, scientific programming, security and disaster recovery, systems programming.

Related Job Titles, Projected Growth, and Earnings		
Job Title	Projected Growth	Average Earnings
Computer Support Specialists (O*NET code 15-1041.00)	Much faster than average	$37,120
Computer Science Teachers, Postsecondary (O*NET code 25-1021.00)	Faster than average	(No salary data available)

Typical College Courses

Algorithms and data structures, artificial intelligence, calculus, computer architecture, database systems, English composition, introduction to computer science, introduction to economics, operating systems, programming in a language (such as C++ or Java), software engineering, statistics for business and social sciences, theory of computer languages.

Some Suggested High School Courses

Algebra, calculus, chemistry, computer science, English, geometry, physics, pre-calculus, trigonometry.

Essential Knowledge and Skills

Testing, reading comprehension, writing, active learning, information gathering, programming, instructing, information organization, learning strategies, critical thinking. **Values/Work Environment:** Autonomy; working indoors; sitting; using hands on objects, tools, or controls.

Other Information Sources

Many career and education information sources use the standard cross-referencing systems noted below. You can use the codes to obtain substantial additional information on the major (via CIP code) and related occupations (via GOE code). The O*NET codes on the opposite page refer to another major career information system. See the Introduction for details on obtaining additional information.

Classification of Instructional Programs (CIP) code: 110701 Computer Science

Guide for Occupational Exploration (GOE) codes: 02.06 Mathematics and Computers, 12.03 Educational Services

Criminology

Career Snapshot

Criminology is a branch of sociology that specializes in crime—its causes, its methods, its effects on society and on criminals, and how society works to prevent and punish it. Graduates of criminology programs may go into careers in law enforcement or corrections, usually after completing a specialized training program. Other graduates get further education for careers in law, college teaching, social work, or administration of justice or corrections.

Related Specialties and Careers

Criminal behavior, criminal investigation, criminal justice system, penology.

Related Job Titles, Projected Growth, and Earnings		
Job Title	**Projected Growth**	**Average Earnings**
Sociologists (O*NET code 19-3041.00)	Average	(No salary data available)
Forensic Science Technicians (O*NET code 19-4092.00)	Declining	$31,250
Anthropology and Archeology Teachers, Postsecondary (O*NET code 25-1061.00)	Faster than average	(No salary data available)
Area, Ethnic, and Cultural Studies Teachers, Postsecondary (O*NET code 25-1062.00)	Faster than average	(No salary data available)
Economics Teachers, Postsecondary (O*NET code 25-1063.00)	Faster than average	(No salary data available)
Political Science Teachers, Postsecondary (O*NET code 25-1065.00)	Faster than average	(No salary data available)
Psychology Teachers, Postsecondary (O*NET code 25-1066.00)	Faster than average	(No salary data available)
Sociology Teachers, Postsecondary (O*NET code 25-1067.00)	Faster than average	(No salary data available)
History Teachers, Postsecondary (O*NET code 25-1125.00)	Faster than average	(No salary data available)

Typical College Courses

American government, contemporary social problems, criminal investigation, criminal law, English composition, introduction to criminology, introduction to criminal justice, introduction to economics, introduction to psychology, introduction to social research, introduction to sociology, seminar (reporting on research), social inequality, statistics.

Some Suggested High School Courses

Algebra, English, foreign language, social science, trigonometry.

Essential Knowledge and Skills

Reading comprehension, writing, speaking, active learning, information gathering, active listening, instructing, critical thinking, learning strategies, mathematics.

Values/Work Environment: Achievement, ability utilization, autonomy, responsibility, creativity, working indoors, sitting, standing.

Other Information Sources

Many career and education information sources use the standard cross-referencing systems noted below. You can use the codes to obtain substantial additional information on the major (via CIP code) and related occupations (via GOE code). The O*NET codes on the opposite page refer to another major career information system. See the Introduction for details on obtaining additional information.

Classification of Instructional Programs (CIP) code: 450401 Criminology

Guide for Occupational Exploration (GOE) codes: 02.04 Social Sciences, 04.03 Law Enforcement, 12.03 Educational Services

 **Dance**

Career Snapshot

Dance is one of the most basic arts of all because the medium is the dancer's own body. This means that dance is also a physical discipline as demanding as any sport. Most dancers start training at a very early age and often must give up performing as their bodies age. However, many find continuing satisfaction and employment in dance instruction and choreography. This is a very competitive field, and only the most talented find regular employment as dancers or choreographers. Job opportunities are better for dance teachers.

Related Specialties and Careers

Ballet, ballroom dance, composite dance, dance education, folk dance, modern dance.

Related Job Titles, Projected Growth, and Earnings		
Job Title	**Projected Growth**	**Average Earnings**
Art, Drama, and Music Teachers, Postsecondary (O*NET code 25-1121.00)	Faster than average	(No salary data available)
Dancers (O*NET code 27-2031.00)	Average	$21,420
Choreographers (O*NET code 27-2032.00)	Average	$21,420

Typical College Courses

Anatomy and kinesiology for dance, dance composition, dance improvisation, dance notation, dance technique (such as ballet, tap, modern), history of dance, introduction to music, methods of teaching dance.

Some Suggested High School Courses

Biology, dance, foreign language, music.

Essential Knowledge and Skills

Instructing. **Values/Work Environment:** Ability utilization, achievement, creativity, working indoors, standing, walking, or running.

Other Information Sources

Many career and education information sources use the standard cross-referencing systems noted below. You can use the codes to obtain substantial additional information on the major (via CIP code) and related occupations (via GOE code). The O*NET codes on the opposite page refer to another major career information system. See the Introduction for details on obtaining additional information.

Classification of Instructional Programs (CIP) code: 500301 Dance

Guide for Occupational Exploration (GOE) codes: 01.05 Performing Arts, 12.03 Educational Services

Dentistry

Career Snapshot

Dentists generally get at least eight years of education beyond high school. Those who want to teach or do research usually must get additional education. Besides academic ability, students of dentistry need good eye-hand coordination and communication skills. Although it seems unlikely that a vaccine against decay germs will be developed anytime soon, tooth sealants and fluoridation have reduced the incidence of tooth decay among young people, which means that dentistry's emphasis has shifted to prevention and maintenance.

Related Specialties and Careers

Endodontics, oral and maxillofacial surgery, oral pathology, orthodontics, periodontics, public health dentistry.

Related Job Titles, Projected Growth, and Earnings		
Job Title	**Projected Growth**	**Average Earnings**
Health Specialties Teachers, Postsecondary (O*NET code 25-1071.00)	Faster than average	(No salary data available)
Dentists, General (O*NET code 29-1021.00)	Little or none	$110,160

Typical College Courses

Assessment and treatment planning, chronic orofacial pain, clinical experience in dentistry, college algebra, community dentistry programs, dental emergency diagnosis and treatment, dental materials, dental morphology and function, endodontics, English composition, dental anesthesia, ethics in health care, general biology, general chemistry, head and neck anatomy, introduction to accounting, introduction to biochemistry, introduction to business management, introduction to psychology, introduction to sociology, nutrition, occlusion, oral communication, oral implantology, oral pathology, oral radiology, organic chemistry, pediatric dentistry, pharmacology, professional practice management, prosthodontics (fixed/removable).

Some Suggested High School Courses

Algebra, biology, chemistry, computer science, English, foreign language, geometry, physics, pre-calculus, public speaking, trigonometry.

Essential Knowledge and Skills

Reading comprehension, science, writing, critical thinking, active learning, problem identification, active listening. **Values/Work Environment:** Achievement; ability utilization; responsibility; autonomy; social status; social service; working indoors; standing; sitting; using hands on objects, tools, or controls.

Other Information Sources

Many career and education information sources use the standard cross-referencing systems noted below. You can use the codes to obtain substantial additional information on the major (via CIP code) and related occupations (via GOE code). The O*NET codes on the opposite page refer to another major career information system. See the Introduction for details on obtaining additional information.

Classification of Instructional Programs (CIP) code: 510401 Dentistry (D.D.S., D.M.D.)

Guide for Occupational Exploration (GOE) codes: 12.03 Educational Services, 14.03 Dentistry

---

Dietetics

Career Snapshot

Dietitians plan food and nutrition programs and supervise the preparation and serving of food. They are concerned with creating diets that are healthful, appetizing, and within budget. They need to know about human nutritional needs in sickness and health, cultural preferences for foods, the nutritional properties of various foods and how they are affected by preparation techniques, and the business or health care environment in which food is prepared and served. A bachelor's degree is good preparation for entering this field; for research, teaching, advanced management, or public health, a graduate degree is helpful or required.

Related Specialties and Careers

Clinical dietetics, community dietetics, dietetics education, food service management, research dietetics.

Related Job Titles, Projected Growth, and Earnings		
Job Title	**Projected Growth**	**Average Earnings**
Farm and Home Management Advisors (O*NET code 25-9021.00)	Declining	$37,200
Dietitians and Nutritionists (O*NET code 29-1031.00)	Average	$35,040
Dietetic Technicians (O*NET code 29-2051.00)	Faster than average	$19,520

Typical College Courses

College algebra, community nutrition, diet therapy, English composition, food service operational management, general biology, general chemistry, home economics, human anatomy, human physiology, introduction to biochemistry, introduction to business management, introduction to computer science, introduction to economics, introduction to food science and technology, menu management, microbiology, nutrition through life, oral communication, organic chemistry, statistics.

Some Suggested High School Courses

Algebra, biology, chemistry, English, geometry, physics, social science, trigonometry.

Essential Knowledge and Skills

Writing. **Values/Work Environment:** Social service; working indoors; standing; sitting; using hands on objects, tools, or controls.

Other Information Sources

Many career and education information sources use the standard cross-referencing systems noted below. You can use the codes to obtain substantial additional information on the major (via CIP code) and related occupations (via GOE code). The O*NET codes on the opposite page refer to another major career information system. See the Introduction for details on obtaining additional information.

Classification of Instructional Programs (CIP) code: 190503 Dietetics/Human Nutritional Services

Guide for Occupational Exploration (GOE) codes: 12.03 Educational Services, 14.08 Health Protection and Promotion

Drama/Theater Arts

Career Snapshot

Drama is one of the most ancient art forms and continues to entertain audiences today. As in all performing arts, there are better opportunities for teachers than for performers. The technical aspects of theater—set design, lighting, costume design, and makeup—also offer jobs for non-performers. The academic program includes many opportunities to learn through student performances.

Related Specialties and Careers

Acting, design and technology, directing.

Related Job Titles, Projected Growth, and Earnings		
Job Title	Projected Growth	Average Earnings
Art, Drama, and Music Teachers, Postsecondary (O*NET code 25-1121.00)	Faster than average	(No salary data available)
Self-Enrichment Education Teachers (O*NET code 25-3021.00)	Faster than average	$24,790
Set Designers (O*NET code 27-1027.01)	Faster than average	$29,190
Actors (O*NET code 27-2011.00)	Faster than average	$27,370
Producers (O*NET code 27-2012.01)	Faster than average	$27,370
Directors—Stage, Motion Pictures, Television, and Radio (O*NET code 27-2012.02)	Faster than average	$27,370
Program Directors (O*NET code 27-2012.03)	Faster than average	$27,370
Talent Directors (O*NET code 27-2012.04)	Faster than average	$27,370

Typical College Courses

Acting technique, dramatic literature, English composition, foreign language, history of theater, performance techniques, theater practicum, theater technology (for example, set/costume/lighting).

Some Suggested High School Courses

Dance, English, foreign language, literature, music, public speaking.

Essential Knowledge and Skills

Reading comprehension. **Values/Work Environment:** Achievement, ability utilization, creativity, autonomy, working indoors, sitting, standing.

Other Information Sources

Many career and education information sources use the standard cross-referencing systems noted below. You can use the codes to obtain substantial additional information on the major (via CIP code) and related occupations (via GOE code). The O*NET codes on the opposite page refer to another major career information system. See the Introduction for details on obtaining additional information.

Classification of Instructional Programs (CIP) code: 500501 Drama/Theater Arts, General

Guide for Occupational Exploration (GOE) codes: 12.03 Educational Services; 01.05 Performing Arts; 01.01 Managerial Work in Arts, Entertainment, and Media; 01.04 Visual Arts

---

Early Childhood Education

Career Snapshot

Because very young children do not think exactly the same way as we do, an important part of an early childhood education major is learning effective educational techniques for this age group. As in any other teaching major, a bachelor's degree is the minimum requirement for employment, and a master's degree is often needed for job security and a pay raise. Although enrollments of very young students are expected to decline for some time, jobs will open to replace teachers who are retiring.

Related Specialties and Careers

Art education, bilingual education, music education, reading readiness.

Related Job Titles, Projected Growth, and Earnings		
Job Title	Projected Growth	Average Earnings
Education Administrators, Preschool and Child Care Center/Program (O*NET code 11-9031.00)	Average	$60,400
Education Administrators, Elementary and Secondary School (O*NET code 11-9032.00)	Average	$60,400
Preschool Teachers, Except Special Education (O*NET code 25-2011.00)	Faster than average	$17,310
Kindergarten Teachers, Except Special Education (O*NET code 25-2012.00)	Average	$33,590
Elementary School Teachers, Except Special Education (O*NET code 25-2021.00)	Average	$36,110

Typical College Courses

Art education, children's literature, educational alternatives for exceptional students, educational psychology, English composition, health education, history and philosophy of education, human growth and development, introduction to psychology, mathematics education, music education, oral communication, physical education, reading assessment and teaching, science education, student teaching, teaching methods.

Some Suggested High School Courses

Algebra, English, foreign language, geometry, music, public speaking, science, trigonometry.

Essential Knowledge and Skills

Learning strategies. **Values/Work Environment:** Authority; working indoors; sitting; standing.

Other Information Sources

Many career and education information sources use the standard cross-referencing systems noted below. You can use the codes to obtain substantial additional information on the major (via CIP code) and related occupations (via GOE code). The O*NET codes on the opposite page refer to another major career information system. See the Introduction for details on obtaining additional information.

Classification of Instructional Programs (CIP) code: 131204 Pre-Elementary/Early Childhood/Kindergarten Teacher Education

Guide for Occupational Exploration (GOE) codes: 12.01 Managerial Work in Education and Social Service, 12.03 Educational Services

---

Earth Sciences

Career Snapshot

The earth sciences major combines the disciplines of geology, oceanography, meteorology, and environmental science. Some graduates with a bachelor's degree go to work in environmental planning for consulting companies or government agencies, or find employment with mining or petroleum companies. Others go into secondary school teaching, with the addition of coursework (or perhaps a master's degree) in education. A higher degree in the field can lead to a career in college teaching or research.

Related Specialties and Careers

Climatology, earth science education, marine science, meteorology, watersheds and water resources.

Related Job Titles, Projected Growth, and Earnings		
Job Title	Projected Growth	Average Earnings
Astronomers (O*NET code 19-2011.00)	Declining	$73,240
Physicists (O*NET code 19-2012.00)	Little or none	$73,240

Typical College Courses

Calculus, English composition, general chemistry, general physics, geological oceanography, introduction to computer science, introduction to environmental science, introduction to geology, introduction to ground water/hydrology, mineralogy, stratigraphy, structural geology, summer field geology.

Some Suggested High School Courses

Algebra, calculus, chemistry, computer science, English, geometry, physics, pre-calculus, trigonometry.

Essential Knowledge and Skills

Reading comprehension, writing, speaking, active learning, information gathering, active listening, instructing, critical thinking. **Values/Work Environment:** Autonomy, ability utilization, working indoors, sitting.

Other Information Sources

Many career and education information sources use the standard cross-referencing systems noted below. You can use the codes to obtain substantial additional information on the major (via CIP code) and related occupations (via GOE code). The O*NET codes on the opposite page refer to another major career information system. See the Introduction for details on obtaining additional information.

Classification of Instructional Programs (CIP) code: 400703 Earth and Planetary Sciences

Guide for Occupational Exploration (GOE) code: 2.02 Physical Sciences

Economics

Career Snapshot

Economics is most basically the study of human needs and how they are satisfied. Therefore, it looks at how goods and services are produced, distributed, and consumed; how markets for these goods and services are created and behave; and how the actions of individuals, businesses, and governments affect these markets. Graduates of economics programs may work for business, government, or universities. The best job opportunities should be in the private sector for those with graduate degrees.

Related Specialties and Careers

Applied economics, econometrics, economic theory.

Related Job Titles, Projected Growth, and Earnings		
Job Title	**Projected Growth**	**Average Earnings**
Government Service Executives (O*NET code 11-1011.01)	Average	$55,030
Statisticians (O*NET code 15-2041.00)	Little or none	$48,540
Economists (O*NET code 19-3011.00)	Average	$48,330
Market Research Analysts (O*NET code 19-3021.00)	Average	$48,330
Economics Teachers, Postsecondary (O*NET code 25-1063.00)	Faster than average	(No salary data available)

Typical College Courses

American government, calculus, econometrics, English composition, foreign language, introduction to computer science, introduction to economics, introduction to psychology, introduction to sociology, macroeconomic theory, mathematical methods in economics, microeconomic theory, statistics, statistics for business and social sciences.

Some Suggested High School Courses

Algebra, English, foreign language, pre-calculus, social science, trigonometry.

Essential Knowledge and Skills

Reading comprehension, information gathering, active learning, writing, speaking, critical thinking, active listening, idea generation, solution appraisal, learning strategies. **Values/Work Environment:** Ability utilization, autonomy, achievement, working indoors, sitting, standing.

Other Information Sources

Many career and education information sources use the standard cross-referencing systems noted below. You can use the codes to obtain substantial additional information on the major (via CIP code) and related occupations (via GOE code). The O*NET codes on the opposite page refer to another major career information system. See the Introduction for details on obtaining additional information.

Classification of Instructional Programs (CIP) code: 450601 Economics, General

Guide for Occupational Exploration (GOE) codes: 02.04 Social Sciences, 02.06 Mathematics and Computers, 12.03 Educational Services, 13.01 General Management Work and Management of Support Functions, 13.02 Management Support

---

Electrical Engineering

Career Snapshot

Electrical engineers apply principles of physics, chemistry, and materials science to the generation, transmission, and use of electric power. They may develop huge dynamos or tiny chips. Usually they enter the field with a bachelor's degree. Management may be an option later in their careers. Electricity is not likely to be replaced as a power source anytime soon, and new electronic devices are being developed constantly, so the job outlook for electrical engineers is expected to be good.

Related Specialties and Careers

Aerospace applications, broadcasting, communications, computers, controls, power generation/transmission.

Related Job Titles, Projected Growth, and Earnings		
Job Title	**Projected Growth**	**Average Earnings**
Electrical Engineers (O*NET code 17-2071.00)	Faster than average	$62,260
Electronics Engineers, Except Computer (O*NET code 17-2072.00)	Faster than average	$62,260
Engineering Teachers, Postsecondary (O*NET code 25-1032.00)	Faster than average	(No salary data available)
Sales Engineers (O*NET code 41-9031.00)	Average	$54,600

Typical College Courses

Calculus, communication systems, control systems, differential equations, digital systems, electromagnetic fields, engineering circuit analysis, English composition, general chemistry, general physics, introduction to computer science, introduction to electric circuits, introduction to engineering, logic design, semiconductor devices, senior design project, signals and systems, technical writing.

Some Suggested High School Courses

Algebra, calculus, chemistry, computer science, English, geometry, physics, pre-calculus, trigonometry.

Essential Knowledge and Skills

Mathematics, reading comprehension, critical thinking, active learning, writing, science, speaking. **Values/Work Environment:** Ability utilization; working indoors; sitting; standing; using hands on objects, tools, or controls.

Other Information Sources

Many career and education information sources use the standard cross-referencing systems noted below. You can use the codes to obtain substantial additional information on the major (via CIP code) and related occupations (via GOE code). The O*NET codes on the opposite page refer to another major career information system. See the Introduction for details on obtaining additional information.

Classification of Instructional Programs (CIP) code: 141001 Electrical, Electronics, and Communication Engineering

Guide for Occupational Exploration (GOE) codes: 02.07 Engineering, 12.03 Educational Services

---

Elementary Education

Career Snapshot

In elementary education it is usually possible to specialize in a particular subject, such as reading or science, or to get a general background. Everyone in this field needs to learn general principles of how young people develop physically and mentally, as well as the teaching and classroom-management techniques that work best with children of this age. A bachelor's degree is often sufficient to enter this career, but in many school districts it is expected that you will continue your education as far as a master's degree. Enrollments in elementary schools are expected to decline for some time, but there will be job openings to replace teachers who retire.

Related Specialties and Careers

Art education, bilingual education, mathematics education, music education, reading, science education.

Related Job Titles, Projected Growth, and Earnings		
Job Title	Projected Growth	Average Earnings
Kindergarten Teachers, Except Special Education (O*NET code 25-2012.00)	Average	$33,590
Elementary School Teachers, Except Special Education (O*NET code 25-2021.00)	Average	$36,110

Typical College Courses

Art education, educational alternatives for exceptional students, educational psychology, English composition, health education, history and philosophy of education, human growth and development, introduction to psychology, language arts and literature, mathematics education, oral communication, physical education, reading assessment and teaching, science education, social studies education, student teaching, teaching methods.

Some Suggested High School Courses

Algebra, English, foreign language, geometry, music, public speaking, science, trigonometry.

Essential Knowledge and Skills

Learning strategies. **Values/Work Environment:** Authority, social service, achievement, working indoors, standing, sitting.

Other Information Sources

Many career and education information sources use the standard cross-referencing systems noted below. You can use the codes to obtain substantial additional information on the major (via CIP code) and related occupations (via GOE code). The O*NET codes on the opposite page refer to another major career information system. See the Introduction for details on obtaining additional information.

Classification of Instructional Programs (CIP) code: 131202 Elementary Teacher Education

Guide for Occupational Exploration (GOE) code: 12.03 Educational Services

---

English

Career Snapshot

English majors not only learn about a great literary tradition, but they also develop first-rate writing and critical-thinking skills that can be valuable in a variety of careers. Besides teaching, many of them go into business, law, and library science. They are said to make excellent trainees in computer programming. In a wide range of careers, their humanistic skills often allow them to advance higher than those who prepare through more specifically career-oriented curricula.

Related Specialties and Careers

Creative writing, English education, language, literature.

Related Job Titles, Projected Growth, and Earnings		
Job Title	Projected Growth	Average Earnings
English Language and Literature Teachers, Postsecondary (O*NET code 25-1123.00)	Faster than average	(No salary data available)
Editors (O*NET code 27-3041.00)	Faster than average	$36,325
Creative Writers (O*NET code 27-3043.02)	Faster than average	$34,570

Typical College Courses

A genre (such as drama, short story, poetry), a major writer (such as Shakespeare, the romantic poets), comparative literature, creative writing, English composition, foreign language, history of the English language, introduction to literary study, survey of American literature, survey of British literature.

Some Suggested High School Courses

English, foreign language, history, literature, public speaking, social science.

Essential Knowledge and Skills

Reading comprehension, instructing, speaking, learning strategies, writing, information gathering, critical thinking, active listening, synthesis/reorganization, information organization. **Values/Work Environment:** Achievement, authority, ability utilization, autonomy, working indoors, sitting, standing.

Other Information Sources

Many career and education information sources use the standard cross-referencing systems noted below. You can use the codes to obtain substantial additional information on the major (via CIP code) and related occupations (via GOE code). The O*NET codes on the opposite page refer to another major career information system. See the Introduction for details on obtaining additional information.

Classification of Instructional Programs (CIP) code: 230101 English Language and Literature, General

Guide for Occupational Exploration (GOE) codes: 01.01 Writing and Editing, 12.03 Educational Services

Environmental Science

Career Snapshot

Environmental science/studies is a multidisciplinary subject that involves a number of sciences such as biology, geology, and chemistry, as well as social sciences such as economics and geography. It also touches on urban/regional planning and on law and public policy. Those with a bachelor's degree may work for an environmental consulting business or a government planning agency, or may go on to get a graduate or professional degree in one of these related fields.

Related Specialties and Careers

Environmental education, environmental policy, environmental technology, land resources, natural history.

Related Job Titles, Projected Growth, and Earnings		
Job Title	Projected Growth	Average Earnings
Government Service Executives (O*NET code 11-1011.01)	Average	$55,030
Natural Sciences Managers (O*NET code 11-9121.00)	Much faster than average	$75,320
Environmental Scientists and Specialists, Including Health (O*NET code 19-2041.00)	Average	(No salary data available)
Agricultural Sciences Teachers, Postsecondary (O*NET code 25-1041.00)	Faster than average	(No salary data available)
Biological Science Teachers, Postsecondary (O*NET code 25-1042.00)	Faster than average	(No salary data available)
Forestry and Conservation Science Teachers, Postsecondary (O*NET code 25-1043.00)	Faster than average	(No salary data available)

Typical College Courses

College algebra, ecology, English composition, environmental chemistry, environmental economics, environmental impact assessment, environmental law, general biology, general chemistry, introduction to computer science, introduction to economics, introduction to environmental science, introduction to geology, introduction to ground water/hydrology, microbiology, natural resource management and water quality, oral communication, organic chemistry, regional planning and environmental protection, statistics.

Some Suggested High School Courses

Algebra, biology, chemistry, computer science, English, geography, geometry, public speaking, trigonometry.

Essential Knowledge and Skills

Reading comprehension, active learning, information gathering, critical thinking, writing, mathematics, idea generation, problem identification, speaking, information organization. **Values/Work Environment:** Ability utilization, working indoors, sitting, standing.

Other Information Sources

Many career and education information sources use the standard cross-referencing systems noted below. You can use the codes to obtain substantial additional information on the major (via CIP code) and related occupations (via GOE code). The O*NET codes on the opposite page refer to another major career information system. See the Introduction for details on obtaining additional information.

Classification of Instructional Programs (CIP) code: 030102 Environmental Science/Studies

Guide for Occupational Exploration (GOE) codes: 02.01 Managerial Work in Science, Math, and Engineering; 02.03 Life Sciences; 12.03 Educational Services; 13.01 General Management Work and Management of Support Functions

Film/Cinema Studies

Career Snapshot

Film is one of the newest art forms and still straddles the borderline between popular culture and high art. The American film and video industry continues to grow as it increasingly dominates the world market, but there is keen competition for creative jobs in this field. Some graduates of film programs become critics or work in industrial or educational film production. Students can usually tailor the academic program to emphasize the aspect of film that interests them; therefore, they may do a lot of writing about film or a lot of hands-on work producing film.

Related Specialties and Careers

Criticism, directing/producing, editing, screenwriting.

Related Job Titles, Projected Growth, and Earnings		
Job Title	**Projected Growth**	**Average Earnings**
Art, Drama, and Music Teachers, Postsecondary (O*NET code 25-1121.00)	Faster than average	(No salary data available)
Creative Writers (O*NET code 27-3043.02)	Faster than average	$34,570
Directors—Stage, Motion Pictures, Television, and Radio (O*NET code 27-2012.02)	Faster than average	$27,370
Producers (O*NET code 27-2012.01)	Faster than average	$27,370

Typical College Courses

English composition, film as a narrative art, film styles and genres, film theory and criticism, foreign language, gender and film, history of film, introduction to psychology, literature and media, major film directors, seminar (reporting on research), world history in the modern era.

Some Suggested High School Courses

English, foreign language, history, literature, photography.

Essential Knowledge and Skills

Instructing, learning strategies, speaking, writing, information gathering, information organization, idea evaluation, synthesis/reorganization, critical thinking.
Values/Work Environment: Achievement; ability utilization; authority; autonomy; good working conditions; working indoors; sitting; using hands on objects, tools, or controls; standing.

Other Information Sources

Many career and education information sources use the standard cross-referencing systems noted below. You can use the codes to obtain substantial additional information on the major (via CIP code) and related occupations (via GOE code). The O*NET codes on the opposite page refer to another major career information system. See the Introduction for details on obtaining additional information.

Classification of Instructional Programs (CIP) code: 500601 Film/Cinema Studies

Guide for Occupational Exploration (GOE) codes: 01.01 Managerial Work in Arts, Entertainment, and Media; 01.02 Writing and Editing; 01.05 Performing Arts; 12.03 Educational Services

---

Finance

Career Snapshot

Finance is the study of how organizations acquire funds and use them in ways that maximize their value. The banking and insurance industries, as well as investment service companies, employ graduates of this field. A bachelor's degree is good preparation for entry-level jobs.

Related Specialties and Careers

Corporate finance, public finance, securities analysis.

Related Job Titles, Projected Growth, and Earnings		
Job Title	**Projected Growth**	**Average Earnings**
Private-Sector Executives (O*NET code 11-1011.02)	Average	$55,890
Treasurers, Controllers, and Chief Financial Officers (O*NET code 11-3031.01)	Average	$55,070
Financial Managers, Branch or Department (O*NET code 11-3031.02)	Average	$55,070
Budget Analysts (O*NET code 13-2031.00)	Average	$44,950
Financial Analysts (O*NET code 13-2051.00)	Average	$40,534
Personal Financial Advisors (O*NET code 13-2052.00)	Much faster than average	$39,490
Financial Examiners (O*NET code 13-2061.00)	Average	$36,820
Mathematical Science Teachers, Postsecondary (O*NET code 25-1022.00)	Faster than average	(No salary data available)
Insurance Sales Agents (O*NET code 41-3021.00)	Little or none	$34,370
Sales Agents, Securities and Commodities (O*NET code 41-3031.01)	Much faster than average	$48,090

Job Title	Projected Growth	Average Earnings
Sales Agents, Financial Services (O*NET code 41-3031.02)	Much faster than average	$48,090

Typical College Courses

Business finance, business writing, calculus for business and social sciences, corporate finance, English composition, introduction to accounting, introduction to management information systems, introduction to marketing, introduction to psychology, investment analysis, legal environment of business, money and capital markets, operations management, principles of macroeconomics, principles of management and organization, principles of microeconomics, statistics for business and social sciences, strategic management.

Some Suggested High School Courses

Algebra, computer science, English, foreign language, geometry, science, trigonometry.

Essential Knowledge and Skills

Reading comprehension. **Values/Work Environment:** Good working conditions, working indoors, sitting.

Other Information Sources

Many career and education information sources use the standard cross-referencing systems noted below. You can use the codes to obtain substantial additional information on the major (via CIP code) and related occupations (via GOE code). The O*NET codes on the opposite page refer to another major career information system. See the Introduction for details on obtaining additional information.

Classification of Instructional Programs (CIP) code: 520801 Finance, General

Guide for Occupational Exploration (GOE) codes: 13.01 General Management Work and Management of Support Functions, 13.02 Management Support, 10.02 Sales Technology, 04.04 Public Safety, 12.03 Educational Services

---

Food Science

Career Snapshot

A glance at the label on a package of food will tell you that the science of making, packaging, and ensuring the quality of foods involves both biology and chemistry. Food science graduates work in research, product development, and quality control. A bachelor's degree is usually sufficient for an entry-level job in quality control. But for advancement and for research jobs, a graduate degree is a help.

Related Specialties and Careers

Food quality assurance, food research, management of food processing, product development.

Related Job Titles, Projected Growth, and Earnings		
Job Title	**Projected Growth**	**Average Earnings**
Industrial Production Managers (O*NET code 11-3051.00)	Declining	$56,320
Environmental Compliance Inspectors (O*NET code 13-1041.01)	Average	$36,820
Food Scientists and Technologists (O*NET code 19-1012.00)	Average	$42,340
Food Science Technicians (O*NET code 19-4011.02)	Little or none	$27,430
Chemical Technicians (O*NET code 19-4031.00)	Little or none	$31,450
Agricultural Sciences Teachers, Postsecondary (O*NET code 25-1041.00)	Faster than average	(No salary data available)
Biological Science Teachers, Postsecondary (O*NET code 25-1042.00)	Faster than average	(No salary data available)
Forestry and Conservation Science Teachers, Postsecondary (O*NET code 25-1043.00)	Faster than average	(No salary data available)
First-Line Supervisors/Managers of Production and Operating Workers (O*NET code 51-1011.00)	Little or none	$36,320

Typical College Courses

College algebra, English composition, food analysis, food bacteriology, food chemistry, food plant engineering, food processing, general biology, general chemistry, general physics, introduction to biochemistry, introduction to computer science, introduction to economics, introduction to food science and technology, microbiology, nutrition, oral communication, organic chemistry, statistics.

Some Suggested High School Courses

Algebra, biology, chemistry, computer science, English, geometry, home economics, public speaking, trigonometry.

Essential Knowledge and Skills

Reading comprehension. **Values/Work Environment:** Autonomy; working indoors; sitting; standing; using hands on objects, tools, or controls.

Other Information Sources

Many career and education information sources use the standard cross-referencing systems noted below. You can use the codes to obtain substantial additional information on the major (via CIP code) and related occupations (via GOE code). The O*NET codes on the opposite page refer to another major career information system. See the Introduction for details on obtaining additional information.

Classification of Instructional Programs (CIP) code: 020301 Food Sciences and Technology

Guide for Occupational Exploration (GOE) codes: 02.03 Life Sciences, 02.05 Laboratory Technology, 04.04 Public Safety, 08.01 Managerial Work in Industrial Production, 12.03 Educational Services

---

Forestry

Career Snapshot

Foresters manage wooded land. Most of them work for governments, concerned with conservation and fire prevention. Some work for logging companies and plan how to harvest timber economically, safely, and in keeping with environmental laws. Foresters also help plant and grow trees to regenerate forests. A bachelor's degree is usually a good preparation for this field, and the job outlook is good because of increasing interest in preserving the environment.

Related Specialties and Careers

Forest management, forest product production, forest restoration, urban forestry.

Related Job Titles, Projected Growth, and Earnings		
Job Title	**Projected Growth**	**Average Earnings**
Soil Conservationists (O*NET code 19-1031.01)	Average	$42,750
Foresters (O*NET code 19-1032.00)	Average	$42,750
Agricultural Sciences Teachers, Postsecondary (O*NET code 25-1041.00)	Faster than average	(No salary data available)
Biological Science Teachers, Postsecondary (O*NET code 25-1042.00)	Faster than average	(No salary data available)
Forestry and Conservation Science Teachers, Postsecondary (O*NET code 25-1043.00)	Faster than average	(No salary data available)

Typical College Courses

Calculus, computer applications in agriculture, dendrology, ecology, English composition, forest ecology, forest economics and valuation, forest inventory and growth, forest resources policy, forest surveying and mapping, forest watershed management, general biology, general chemistry, introduction to forestry, introduction to geology, introduction to soil science, introduction to wildlife conservation, oral communication, organic chemistry, remote sensing, silviculture, statistics, timber harvesting, tree pests and diseases, wood properties and utilization.

Some Suggested High School Courses

Algebra, biology, chemistry, computer science, English, geography, geometry, public speaking, trigonometry.

Essential Knowledge and Skills

Reading comprehension, information gathering, active learning, writing, mathematics. **Values/Work Environment:** Achievement; working indoors; sitting; standing; using hands on objects, tools, or controls.

Other Information Sources

Many career and education information sources use the standard cross-referencing systems noted below. You can use the codes to obtain substantial additional information on the major (via CIP code) and related occupations (via GOE code). The O*NET codes on the opposite page refer to another major career information system. See the Introduction for details on obtaining additional information.

Classification of Instructional Programs (CIP) code: 030501 Forestry, General

Guide for Occupational Exploration (GOE) codes: 02.03 Life Sciences, 12.03 Educational Services

---

 **French**

Career Snapshot

French is a native tongue on several continents and in parts of the United States, and it has a rich cultural heritage associated with the arts and literature. French majors may go into careers in international business, travel, or teaching.

Related Specialties and Careers

History and culture, language education, literature, translation.

Related Job Titles, Projected Growth, and Earnings		
Job Title	**Projected Growth**	**Average Earnings**
Foreign Language and Literature Teachers, Postsecondary (O*NET code 25-1124.00)	Faster than average	(No salary data available)
Interpreters and Translators (O*NET code 27-3091.00)	(No job growth data available)	(No salary data available)

Typical College Courses

Composition, conversation, European history and civilization, French history and civilization, French language, French literature, grammar, linguistics, phonetics.

Some Suggested High School Courses

English, French, history, literature, public speaking, social science.

Essential Knowledge and Skills

Reading comprehension, speaking, instructing, learning strategies, writing, critical thinking, information gathering, active listening, information organization, synthesis/reorganization. **Values/Work Environment:** Achievement, authority, ability utilization, autonomy, working indoors, sitting, standing.

Other Information Sources

Many career and education information sources use the standard cross-referencing systems noted below. You can use the codes to obtain substantial additional information on the major (via CIP code) and related occupations (via GOE code). The O*NET codes on the opposite page refer to another major career information system. See the Introduction for details on obtaining additional information.

Classification of Instructional Programs (CIP) code: 160901 French Language and Literature

Guide for Occupational Exploration (GOE) codes: 01.01 News, Broadcasting, and Public Relations; 12.03 Educational Services

Geography

Career Snapshot

Geography studies how people and their environments relate to one another. It analyzes the human habitat spatially and records information about it in various forms, with an increasing emphasis on databases. Geographers work for governments, public-interest organizations, and businesses. They help with site planning, environmental impact studies, market research, competitive intelligence, and military intelligence.

Related Specialties and Careers

Development, environmental science, geographic information systems, management and policy, urban planning.

Related Job Titles, Projected Growth, and Earnings		
Job Title	**Projected Growth**	**Average Earnings**
Surveyors (O*NET code 17-1022.00)	Little or none	$37,640
Geographers (O*NET code 19-3092.00)	Average	$38,990
Urban and Regional Planners (O*NET code 19-3051.00)	Average	$42,860

Typical College Courses

American history, economic geography, English composition, field geography, foreign language, geographic information systems (GIS), geography of a region, introduction to computer science, introduction to economics, introduction to geology, introduction to human geography, introduction to sociology, physical geography, quantitative methods in geography, remote sensing, research techniques in geography, statistics, thematic cartography, world history in the modern era.

Some Suggested High School Courses

Art, computer science, English, foreign language, geography, history, social science, trigonometry.

Essential Knowledge and Skills

Mathematics, writing, reading comprehension, active learning. **Values/Work Environment:** Autonomy; working outdoors; working indoors; sitting; standing; using hands on objects, tools, or controls.

Other Information Sources

Many career and education information sources use the standard cross-referencing systems noted below. You can use the codes to obtain substantial additional information on the major (via CIP code) and related occupations (via GOE code). The O*NET codes on the opposite page refer to another major career information system. See the Introduction for details on obtaining additional information.

Classification of Instructional Programs (CIP) code: 450701 Geography

Guide for Occupational Exploration (GOE) codes: 02.02 Physical Sciences, 02.04 Social Sciences, 02.08 Engineering Technology

---

 **Geology**

Career Snapshot

Geology is the study of the physical makeup, processes, and history of the earth. Geologists use knowledge of this field to locate water, mineral, and petroleum resources; to protect the environment; and to offer advice on construction and land-use projects. A bachelor's degree opens the door for many entry-level jobs, but a master's degree helps for advancement. Many research jobs in universities and the government require a Ph.D. Some field research requires going to remote places, but it is also possible to specialize in laboratory sciences.

Related Specialties and Careers

Engineering geology, geophysics, mineralogy, oceanography, paleontology, petroleum geology, stratigraphy, volcanology.

Related Job Titles, Projected Growth, and Earnings		
Job Title	**Projected Growth**	**Average Earnings**
Geologists (O*NET code 19-2042.01)	Average	$53,890
Hydrologists (O*NET code 19-2043.00)	Average	$53,890

Typical College Courses

Calculus, English composition, general chemistry, general physics, igneous and metamorphic petrology, introduction to computer science, introduction to geology, invertebrate paleontology, mineralogy, optical mineralogy, sedimentary petrology, stratigraphy, structural geology, summer field geology.

Some Suggested High School Courses

Algebra, calculus, chemistry, computer science, English, geometry, physics, pre-calculus, trigonometry.

Essential Knowledge and Skills

Mathematics, information gathering, science, writing, active learning, critical thinking, reading comprehension, problem identification, information organization. **Values/Work Environment:** Autonomy; ability utilization; moral values; responsibility; sitting; standing; working outdoors; working indoors; using hands on objects, tools, or controls.

Other Information Sources

Many career and education information sources use the standard cross-referencing systems noted below. You can use the codes to obtain substantial additional information on the major (via CIP code) and related occupations (via GOE code). The O*NET codes on the opposite page refer to another major career information system. See the Introduction for details on obtaining additional information.

Classification of Instructional Programs (CIP) code: 400601 Geology

Guide for Occupational Exploration (GOE) code: 02.02 Physical Sciences

Geophysics

Career Snapshot

Geophysics uses physical measurements and mathematical models to describe the structure, composition, and processes of the earth and planets. Geophysicists study seismic waves and variations in gravitation and terrestrial magnetism, thus learning where petroleum and minerals are deposited, where (and sometimes even when) earthquakes and volcanic eruptions are likely to strike, and how to solve environmental problems such as pollution. A bachelor's degree can lead to entry-level jobs, but a higher degree opens greater potential for advancement in research, as well as opportunities in college teaching.

Related Specialties and Careers

Atmospheric physics, physical oceanography, seismology, volcanology, remote sensing, geomagnetism, paleomagnetism, environmental geophysics.

Related Job Titles, Projected Growth, and Earnings		
Job Title	**Projected Growth**	**Average Earnings**
Geologists (O*NET code 19-2042.00)	Average	$53,890
Hydrologists (O*NET code 19-2043.00)	Average	$53,890

Typical College Courses

Calculus, English composition, exploration geophysics, general chemistry, general physics, igneous and metamorphic petrology, introduction to computer science, introduction to geology, mineralogy, physical oceanography, remote sensing, stratigraphy, structural geology, summer field geology.

Some Suggested High School Courses

Algebra, calculus, chemistry, computer science, English, geometry, physics, pre-calculus, trigonometry.

Essential Knowledge and Skills

Mathematics, information gathering, science, active learning, writing. **Values/Work Environment:** Autonomy; ability utilization; moral values; responsibility; sitting; standing; working indoors; working outdoors; using hands on objects, tools, or controls.

Other Information Sources

Many career and education information sources use the standard cross-referencing systems noted below. You can use the codes to obtain substantial additional information on the major (via CIP code) and related occupations (via GOE code). The O*NET codes on the opposite page refer to another major career information system. See the Introduction for details on obtaining additional information.

Classification of Instructional Programs (CIP) code: 400603 Geophysics and Seismology

Guide for Occupational Exploration (GOE) code: 02.02 Physical Sciences

German

Career Snapshot

United once again, Germany is a major economic and cultural force in Europe and the world. A degree in German can open many doors in international business, travel, and law. Many employers are looking for graduates with an understanding of a second language and culture. Those with a graduate degree in German may go into translation or college teaching.

Related Specialties and Careers

History and culture, language education, literature, translation.

Related Job Titles, Projected Growth, and Earnings		
Job Title	**Projected Growth**	**Average Earnings**
Foreign Language and Literature Teachers, Postsecondary (O*NET code 25-1124.00)	Faster than average	(No salary data available)
Interpreters and Translators (O*NET code 27-3091.00)	(No job growth data available)	(No salary data available)

Typical College Courses

Composition, conversation, European history and civilization, German history and civilization, German language, German literature, grammar, linguistics, phonetics.

Some Suggested High School Courses

English, German, history, literature, public speaking, social science.

Essential Knowledge and Skills

Reading comprehension, instructing, speaking, writing, learning strategies, information gathering, critical thinking, active listening, information organization, synthesis/reorganization. **Values/Work Environment:** Achievement, authority, ability utilization, autonomy, working indoors, sitting, standing.

Other Information Sources

Many career and education information sources use the standard cross-referencing systems noted below. You can use the codes to obtain substantial additional information on the major (via CIP code) and related occupations (via GOE code). The O*NET codes on the opposite page refer to another major career information system. See the Introduction for details on obtaining additional information.

Classification of Instructional Programs (CIP) code: 160501 German Language and Literature

Guide for Occupational Exploration (GOE) codes: 01.01 News, Broadcasting, and Public Relations; 12.03 Educational Services

Graphic Design, Commercial Art, and Illustration

Career Snapshot

Many consumer goods, such as books, magazines, and Web pages, consist primarily of graphic elements—illustrations and text. Other goods, such as cereal boxes, use graphic elements conspicuously. Graphic design teaches you how to represent ideas graphically and give maximum visual appeal to text and pictures. The program involves considerable studio time, and an important goal is creating a good portfolio of work. Ability to work with computers is becoming vital in this field. Graduates with an associate's or bachelor's degree work for publishers and design firms. Some freelance.

Related Specialties and Careers

Cartooning, illustration, letterform, typography, Web page design.

Related Job Titles, Projected Growth, and Earnings		
Job Title	**Projected Growth**	**Average Earnings**
Art Directors (O*NET code 27-1011.00)	Faster than average	$31,690
Painters and Illustrators (O*NET code 27-1013.01)	Faster than average	$31,690
Sketch Artists (O*NET code 27-1013.02)	Faster than average	$31,690
Cartoonists (O*NET code 27-1013.03)	Faster than average	$31,690
Commercial and Industrial Designers (O*NET code 27-1021.00)	Faster than average	$29,190
Graphic Designers (O*NET code 27-1024.00)	Faster than average	$29,190
Exhibit Designers (O*NET code 27-1027.02)	Faster than average	$29,190
Paste-Up Workers (O*NET code 51-5022.02)	Declining	$19,820
Precision Printing Workers (O*NET code 51-5023.01)	Declining	$29,386

Typical College Courses

Art history: prehistoric to Renaissance, art history: Renaissance to modern, art history: Renaissance to modern, basic drawing, college algebra, computer applications in graphic design, English composition, history of graphic design, introduction to graphic design, letterform, oral communication, presentation graphics, senior design project, three-dimensional design, two-dimensional design, typography, visual communication, visual thinking and problem solving.

Some Suggested High School Courses

Algebra, art, computer science, English, geometry, keyboarding, mechanical drawing, photography, pre-calculus, public speaking, trigonometry.

Essential Knowledge and Skills

Product inspection. **Values/Work Environment:** Moral values; working indoors; sitting; using hands on objects, tools, or controls.

Other Information Sources

Many career and education information sources use the standard cross-referencing systems noted below. You can use the codes to obtain substantial additional information on the major (via CIP code) and related occupations (via GOE code). The O*NET codes on the opposite page refer to another major career information system. See the Introduction for details on obtaining additional information.

Classification of Instructional Programs (CIP) code: 500402 Graphic Design, Commercial Art, and Illustration

Guide for Occupational Exploration (GOE) codes: 01.01 Visual Arts; 01.07 Graphic Arts; 08.03 Production Work; 01.01 Managerial Work in Arts, Entertainment, and Media

---

Health Information Systems Administration

Career Snapshot

Health information systems are needed for much more than billing patients or their HMOs. Many medical discoveries have been made when researchers have examined large collections of health information. Therefore, health information systems administrators must know about the health care system, about various kinds of diseases and vital statistics, about the latest database technologies, and about how researchers compile data to test hypotheses. Some people enter this field with a bachelor's degree, whereas others get a bachelor's degree in another field (perhaps related to health, information systems, or management) and complete a postgraduate certification program.

Related Specialties and Careers

Information technology, management.

Related Job Titles, Projected Growth, and Earnings		
Job Title	Projected Growth	Average Earnings
Medical and Health Services Managers (O*NET code 11-9111.00)	Faster than average	$48,870

Typical College Courses

Accounting, American health care systems, clinical classification systems, college algebra, English composition seminar (reporting on research), epidemiology, financial management of health care, fundamentals of medical science, health data and analysis, health data research, human resource management in health care facilities, introduction to business management, introduction to computer science, introduction to health records, introduction to medical terminology, introduction to psychology, legal aspects of health care, oral communication, statistics for business and social sciences.

Some Suggested High School Courses

Algebra, biology, chemistry, computer science, English, foreign language, geometry, office computer applications, pre-calculus, public speaking, social science, trigonometry.

Essential Knowledge and Skills

Management of financial resources; systems perception; systems evaluation.

Values/Work Environment: Good working conditions; working indoors; sitting.

Other Information Sources

Many career and education information sources use the standard cross-referencing systems noted below. You can use the codes to obtain substantial additional information on the major (via CIP code) and related occupations (via GOE code). The O*NET codes on the opposite page refer to another major career information system. See the Introduction for details on obtaining additional information.

Classification of Instructional Programs (CIP) code: 510706 Medical Records Administration

Guide for Occupational Exploration (GOE) code: 14.01 Managerial Work in Medical and Health Services

---

History

Career Snapshot

History studies past civilizations in order to understand the present, preserve our heritage, and appreciate the richness of human accomplishment. Almost every field—whether it be in the field of arts, science, or health—includes some study of its past. Therefore, many job opportunities in this field are in teaching. Other historians may work as archivists, genealogists, or curators. Some graduates use the critical-thinking skills they develop from history to go into administration or law.

Related Specialties and Careers

Applied history, genealogy, history education.

Related Job Titles, Projected Growth, and Earnings		
Job Title	**Projected Growth**	**Average Earnings**
Historians (O*NET code 19-3093.00)	Average	$38,990
Anthropology and Archeology Teachers, Postsecondary (O*NET code 25-1061.00)	Faster than average	(No salary data available)
Area, Ethnic, and Cultural Studies Teachers, Postsecondary (O*NET code 25-1062.00)	Faster than average	(No salary data available)
History Teachers, Postsecondary (O*NET code 25-1125.00)	Faster than average	(No salary data available)
Archivists (O*NET code 25-4011.00)	Average	$31,750
Curators (O*NET code 25-4012.00)	Average	$31,750
Museum Technicians and Conservators (O*NET code 25-4013.00)	Average	$31,750

Typical College Courses

American history, English composition, foreign language, introduction to international relations, introduction to philosophy, introduction to political science, seminar (reporting on research), theory and practice of history, world history in the modern era, world history to the early modern era.

Some Suggested High School Courses

Algebra, English, foreign language, history, social science, trigonometry.

Essential Knowledge and Skills

Reading comprehension, writing, speaking, information gathering, active learning, active listening, critical thinking. **Values/Work Environment:** Achievement, working indoors, sitting, standing.

Other Information Sources

Many career and education information sources use the standard cross-referencing systems noted below. You can use the codes to obtain substantial additional information on the major (via CIP code) and related occupations (via GOE code). The O*NET codes on the opposite page refer to another major career information system. See the Introduction for details on obtaining additional information.

Classification of Instructional Programs (CIP) code: 450801 History, General

Guide for Occupational Exploration (GOE) codes: 02.04 Social Sciences, 12.03 Educational Services

---

Home Economics Education

Career Snapshot

Home economics, sometimes called family and consumer sciences, is a combination of several concerns related to families and their economic needs and behaviors. Home economics educators teach these subjects, perhaps specializing in one or more, and they must also have mastered the techniques of education, including teaching strategies and classroom management. With a graduate degree, a home economics educator may work for the federal government as a cooperative extension agent.

Related Specialties and Careers

Child care and family life, clothing and textiles, family resource management, foods and nutrition.

Related Job Titles, Projected Growth, and Earnings		
Job Title	Projected Growth	Average Earnings
Vocational Education Teachers, Postsecondary (O*NET code 25-1194.00)	Average	$34,430
Middle School Teachers, Except Special and Vocational Education (O*NET code 25-2022.00)	Faster than average	$37,890
Vocational Education Teachers, Middle School (O*NET code 25-2023.00)	Faster than average	$34,430
Vocational Education Teachers, Secondary School (O*NET code 25-2032.00)	Faster than average	$34,430
Farm and Home Management Advisors (O*NET code 25-9021.00)	Declining	$37,200

Typical College Courses

Clothing and fashion, consumer economics, English composition, foods, history and philosophy of education, housing, human growth and development, introduction to interior design, introduction to nutrition, introduction to psychology, marriage and the family, oral communication, student teaching, textiles.

Some Suggested High School Courses

Algebra, English, foreign language, geometry, home economics, public speaking, science, trigonometry.

Essential Knowledge and Skills

Learning strategies, reading comprehension, speaking, instructing. **Values/Work Environment:** Authority, achievement, working indoors, standing, sitting.

Other Information Sources

Many career and education information sources use the standard cross-referencing systems noted below. You can use the codes to obtain substantial additional information on the major (via CIP code) and related occupations (via GOE code). The O*NET codes on the opposite page refer to another major career information system. See the Introduction for details on obtaining additional information.

Classification of Instructional Programs (CIP) code: 131308 Family and Consumer Sciences/Home Economics Teacher Education

Guide for Occupational Exploration (GOE) code: 12.03 Educational Services

---

Hospital/Health Facilities Administration

Career Snapshot

Hospital and health facilities administrators need to combine standard business management skills with an understanding of the American health care system and its current issues and trends. They may be generalists who manage an entire facility, or they may specialize in running a department or some specific service of the facility. Generalists are usually expected to have a master's degree, especially in large facilities; whereas specialists or those seeking employment in small facilities may enter with a bachelor's degree. Best employment prospects are in home health agencies, residential care facilities, and practitioners' offices and clinics.

Related Specialties and Careers

Health policy, hospital management, long-term care management.

Related Job Titles, Projected Growth, and Earnings		
Job Title	**Projected Growth**	**Average Earnings**
Medical and Health Services Managers (O*NET code 11-9111.00)	Faster than average	$48,870
Social and Community Service Managers (O*NET code 11-9151.00)	Average	$49,220
Health Specialties Teachers, Postsecondary (O*NET code 25-1071.00)	Faster than average	(No salary data available)

Typical College Courses

Accounting, American health care systems, college algebra, English composition, financial management of health care, health care and politics, human resource management in health care facilities, introduction to business management, introduction to economics, introduction to management information systems, introduction to medical terminology, introduction to psychology, legal aspects of health care, oral communication, statistics for business and social sciences, strategy and planning for health care.

Some Suggested High School Courses

Algebra, biology, chemistry, computer science, English, foreign language, geometry, home economics, office computer applications, pre-calculus, public speaking, social science, trigonometry.

Essential Knowledge and Skills

Reading comprehension, writing, speaking. **Values/Work Environment:** Authority, working indoors, sitting, standing.

Other Information Sources

Many career and education information sources use the standard cross-referencing systems noted below. You can use the codes to obtain substantial additional information on the major (via CIP code) and related occupations (via GOE code). The O*NET codes on the opposite page refer to another major career information system. See the Introduction for details on obtaining additional information.

Classification of Instructional Programs (CIP) code: 510702 Hospital/Health Facilities Administration

Guide for Occupational Exploration (GOE) codes: 12.01 Managerial Work in Education and Social Service, 12.03 Educational Services, 14.01 Managerial Work in Medical and Health Services

---

Hotel/Motel and Restaurant Management

Career Snapshot

Students of hotel/motel and restaurant management learn many skills required in any management program—economics, accounting, human resources, finance—plus the specialized skills needed for the hospitality industry. Some enter the field with an associate's degree, but opportunities are better with a bachelor's degree. Usually new hires enter an on-the-job training program where they learn all as-pects of the business. The outlook for employment is mostly good, especially in restaurants.

Related Specialties and Careers

Hotels/motels, resorts and theme parks, restaurants.

Related Job Titles, Projected Growth, and Earnings		
Job Title	Projected Growth	Average Earnings
Food Service Managers (O*NET code 11-9051.00)	Average	$26,700
Lodging Managers (O*NET code 11-9081.00)	Average	$26,700
Meeting and Convention Planners (O*NET code 13-1121.00)	Average	$37,060
First-Line Supervisors/Managers of Personal Service Workers (O*NET code 39-1021.00)	Average	$23,320
First-Line Supervisors/Managers of Retail Sales Workers (O*NET code 41-1011.00)	Average	$29,570
First-Line Supervisors/Managers of Non-Retail Sales Workers (O*NET code 41-1012.00)	Average	$29,570
First-Line Supervisors, Customer Service (O*NET code 43-1011.01)	Average	$31,090

Typical College Courses

Business finance, business writing, calculus for business and social sciences, English composition, field experience/internship, food and beverage production and management, food service and lodging operations, hospitality human resource management, hospitality technology applications, hotel financial management, introduction to accounting, introduction to management information systems, introduction to marketing, introduction to psychology, introduction to the hospitality industry, law and the hospitality industry, legal environment of business, marketing hospitality and leisure services, operations management, principles of macroeconomics, principles of management and organization, principles of microeconomics, statistics for business and social sciences, strategic management.

Some Suggested High School Courses

Algebra, computer science, English, foreign language, geometry, home economics, public speaking, science, trigonometry.

Essential Knowledge and Skills

Coordination. **Values/Work Environment:** Authority, working indoors, sitting, standing.

Other Information Sources

Many career and education information sources use the standard cross-referencing systems noted below. You can use the codes to obtain substantial additional information on the major (via CIP code) and related occupations (via GOE code). The O*NET codes on the opposite page refer to another major career information system. See the Introduction for details on obtaining additional information.

Classification of Instructional Programs (CIP) code: 520902 Hotel/Motel and Restaurant Management

Guide for Occupational Exploration (GOE) codes: 09.01 Managerial Work in Business Detail; 10.01 Managerial Work in Sales and Marketing; 11.01 Managerial Work in Recreation, Travel, and Other Personal Services

---

Human Resources Management

Career Snapshot

Human resource managers are responsible for attracting the right employees for an organization, training them, keeping them productively employed, and sometimes severing the relationship through outplacement or retirement. Generalists often enter the field with a bachelor's degree, although specialists may find a master's degree (or perhaps a law degree) advantageous. Generalists most often find entry-level work with small organizations. There is a trend toward outsourcing many specialized functions, such as outplacement, to specialized service firms.

Related Specialties and Careers

Compensation/benefits, job analysis, labor relations, training.

Related Job Titles, Projected Growth, and Earnings		
Job Title	**Projected Growth**	**Average Earnings**
Human Resources Managers (O*NET code 11-3040.00)	Average	$49,010
Compensation and Benefits Managers (O*NET code 11-3041.00)	Average	$49,010
Training and Development Managers (O*NET code 11-3042.00)	Average	$49,010
Equal Opportunity Representatives and Officers (O*NET code 13-1041.03)	Average	$36,820
Employment Interviewers, Private or Public Employment Service (O*NET code 13-1071.01)	Average	$36,482
Personnel Recruiters (O*NET code 13-1071.02)	Average	$36,482
Compensation, Benefits, and Job Analysis Specialists (O*NET code 13-1072.00)	Average	$37,710
Training and Development Specialists (O*NET code 13-1073.00)	Average	$37,710
Claims Takers, Unemployment Benefits (O*NET code 43-4061.01)	Faster than average	$31,110

Job Title	Projected Growth	Average Earnings
Human Resources Assistants, Except Payroll and Timekeeping (O*NET code 43-4161.00)	Little or none	$24,360

Typical College Courses

Business finance, business writing, calculus for business and social sciences, compensation and benefits administration, employment law, English composition, human resource management, industrial relations and labor management, introduction to accounting, introduction to management information systems, introduction to marketing, introduction to psychology, legal environment of business, operations management, organizational theory, principles of macroeconomics, principles of management and organization, principles of microeconomics, statistics for business and social sciences, strategic management, training and development.

Some Suggested High School Courses

Algebra, computer science, English, foreign language, geometry, public speaking, science, trigonometry.

Essential Knowledge and Skills

Reading comprehension. **Values/Work Environment:** Good working conditions, working indoors, sitting.

Other Information Sources

Many career and education information sources use the standard cross-referencing systems noted below. You can use the codes to obtain substantial additional information on the major (via CIP code) and related occupations (via GOE code). The O*NET codes on the opposite page refer to another major career information system. See the Introduction for details on obtaining additional information.

Classification of Instructional Programs (CIP) code: 521001 Human Resources Management

Guide for Occupational Exploration (GOE) codes: 04.04 Public Safety, 09.02 Administrative Detail, 09.07 Records Processing, 13.01 General Management Work and Management of Support Functions, 13.02 Management Support

---

Humanities

Career Snapshot

Humanities (sometimes called liberal arts) is an interdisciplinary major that covers a wide range of the arts and other non-scientific modes of thought, such as history, philosophy, religious studies, and language. Graduates of this major usually have strong skills for communicating and critical thinking, and they often advance further in the business world than those who hold more business-focused degrees. Some pursue careers in teaching, media, or the arts. Others get professional degrees in the law or medicine.

Related Specialties and Careers

Language, literature, the arts, history, religion, peace and justice studies, philosophy.

Related Job Titles, Projected Growth, and Earnings		
Job Title	**Projected Growth**	**Average Earnings**
Area, Ethnic, and Cultural Studies Teachers, Postsecondary (O*NET code 25-1062.00)	Faster than average	(No salary data available)
Art, Drama, and Music Teachers, Postsecondary (O*NET code 25-1121.00)	Faster than average	(No salary data available)
English Language and Literature Teachers, Postsecondary (O*NET code 25-1123.00)	Faster than average	(No salary data available)
Foreign Language and Literature Teachers, Postsecondary (O*NET code 25-1124.00)	Faster than average	(No salary data available)
History Teachers, Postsecondary (O*NET code 25-1125.00)	Faster than average	(No salary data available)
Philosophy and Religion Teachers, Postsecondary (O*NET code 25-1126.00)	Faster than average	(No salary data available)

Typical College Courses

Art and culture, European history and civilization, foreign language, literature, major thinkers and issues in philosophy, seminar (reporting on research), writing.

Some Suggested High School Courses

Algebra, English, foreign language, history, literature, public speaking, social science.

Essential Knowledge and Skills

Reading comprehension. **Values/Work Environment:** Achievement, ability utilization, autonomy, responsibility, working indoors, sitting, standing.

Other Information Sources

Many career and education information sources use the standard cross-referencing systems noted below. You can use the codes to obtain substantial additional information on the major (via CIP code) and related occupations (via GOE code). The O*NET codes on the opposite page refer to another major career information system. See the Introduction for details on obtaining additional information.

Classification of Instructional Programs (CIP) code: 240103 Humanities/Humanistic Studies

Guide for Occupational Exploration (GOE) code: 12.03 Educational Services

---

Industrial Design

Career Snapshot

Industrial designers develop every conceivable kind of manufactured product, from cars to computers to children's toys. They need to understand the technology that will make the product work, the human context in which the product will be used—such as the way it will be held in the hand—as well as the marketplace in which the product will compete. Therefore, this field requires students to learn a combination of technical, creative, and business skills. Demand for graduates is expected to be good.

Related Specialties and Careers

Computer modeling, product design.

Related Job Titles, Projected Growth, and Earnings		
Job Title	**Projected Growth**	**Average Earnings**
Commercial and Industrial Designers (O*NET code 27-1021.00)	Faster than average	$29,190

Typical College Courses

Art history: Renaissance to modern, basic drawing, college algebra, computer modeling, English composition, general physics, history of industrial design, human factors in design (ergonomics), industrial design materials and processes, introduction to economics, introduction to graphic design, introduction to marketing, oral communication, presentation graphics, professional practices for industrial design, senior design project, visual thinking and problem solving.

Some Suggested High School Courses

Algebra, art, computer science, English, geometry, mechanical drawing, photography, pre-calculus, public speaking, trigonometry.

Essential Knowledge and Skills

Reading comprehension, active learning. **Values/Work Environment:** Achievement; creativity; ability utilization; working indoors; sitting; standing; using hands on objects, tools, or controls.

Other Information Sources

Many career and education information sources use the standard cross-referencing systems noted below. You can use the codes to obtain substantial additional information on the major (via CIP code) and related occupations (via GOE code). The O*NET codes on the opposite page refer to another major career information system. See the Introduction for details on obtaining additional information.

Classification of Instructional Programs (CIP) code: 500404 Industrial Design

Guide for Occupational Exploration (GOE) code: 01.01 Visual Arts

Industrial and Labor Relations

Career Snapshot

Although labor unions are not as widespread as they once were, they still play an important role in American business. The "just in time" strategy that is popular in the manufacturing and transportation industries means that a strike lasting only a few hours can seriously disrupt business. Employers are eager to settle labor disputes before they start, and this creates job opportunities for labor-relations specialists working for either the employer or the union. Other job openings are found in government agencies that deal with labor. Many of these specialists hold bachelor's degrees, but a master's degree or law degree can be helpful for jobs involving contract negotiations and mediation.

Related Specialties and Careers

Arbitration, labor law, mediation, worker compensation, worker safety.

Related Job Titles, Projected Growth, and Earnings		
Job Title	**Projected Growth**	**Average Earnings**
Compensation and Benefits Managers (O*NET code 11-3041.00)	Average	$49,010
Human Resources Managers (O*NET code 11-3040.00)	Average	$49,010

Typical College Courses

Business finance, business writing, calculus for business and social sciences, employment law, English composition, human resource management, industrial relations and labor management, introduction to accounting, introduction to management information systems, introduction to marketing, introduction to psychology, legal environment of business, organizational behavior, principles of macroeconomics, principles of microeconomics, statistics for business and social sciences, systems of conflict resolution, training and development.

Some Suggested High School Courses

Algebra, computer science, English, foreign language, geometry, public speaking, social science, trigonometry.

Essential Knowledge and Skills

Management of personnel resources, problem identification. **Values/Work Environment:** Good working conditions, ability utilization, autonomy, authority, working indoors, sitting, standing.

Other Information Sources

Many career and education information sources use the standard cross-referencing systems noted below. You can use the codes to obtain substantial additional information on the major (via CIP code) and related occupations (via GOE code). The O*NET codes on the opposite page refer to another major career information system. See the Introduction for details on obtaining additional information.

Classification of Instructional Programs (CIP) code: 521002 Labor/Personnel Relations and Studies

Guide for Occupational Exploration (GOE) code: 13.01 General Management Work and Management of Support Functions

---

Industrial Engineering

Career Snapshot

Industrial engineers plan how an organization can most efficiently use staff, equipment, buildings, raw materials, information, and energy to output a product or service. They occupy the middle ground between management and the technology experts—for example, the mechanical or chemical engineers. Sometimes they make a career move into management positions. A bachelor's degree is good preparation for this field. The job outlook for industrial engineers is expected to be good, especially in non-manufacturing industries, as U.S. employers attempt to boost productivity to compete in a global workplace.

Related Specialties and Careers

Operations research, quality control.

Related Job Titles, Projected Growth, and Earnings		
Job Title	Projected Growth	Average Earnings
Engineering Teachers, Postsecondary (O*NET code 25-1032.00)	Faster than average	(No salary data available)
Industrial Engineers (O*NET code 17-2112.00)	Average	$52,610

Typical College Courses

Analysis of industrial activities, calculus, differential equations, dynamics, engineering economics, engineering systems design, English composition, facilities design, general chemistry, general physics, human factors and ergonomics, introduction to computer science, materials engineering, numerical analysis, operations research, quality control, senior design project, simulation, statics, technical writing, thermodynamics.

Some Suggested High School Courses

Algebra, calculus, chemistry, computer science, English, geometry, physics, pre-calculus, trigonometry.

Essential Knowledge and Skills

Mathematics, reading comprehension. **Values/Work Environment:** Ability utilization, autonomy, working indoors, sitting.

Other Information Sources

Many career and education information sources use the standard cross-referencing systems noted below. You can use the codes to obtain substantial additional information on the major (via CIP code) and related occupations (via GOE code). The O*NET codes on the opposite page refer to another major career information system. See the Introduction for details on obtaining additional information.

Classification of Instructional Programs (CIP) code: 141701 Industrial/Manufacturing Engineering

Guide for Occupational Exploration (GOE) code: 02.07 Engineering, 12.03 Educational Services

Industrial/Technology Education

Career Snapshot

As American industry progresses into a new century, the traditional "shop teacher" is evolving into a technology educator who teaches young people the high-tech skills they need to succeed in the new economy. In industrial/technology education, as in other teaching fields, a bachelor's degree is usually required for job entry, but a master's is often needed to build a career. In addition, it is helpful to get some genuine work experience in industry or agriculture. The job outlook is better for this field than for many other secondary-school specializations.

Related Specialties and Careers

A technology (such as welding), agriculture.

Related Job Titles, Projected Growth, and Earnings		
Job Title	**Projected Growth**	**Average Earnings**
Vocational Education Teachers, Middle School (O*NET code 25-2023.00)	Faster than average	$34,430
Vocational Education Teachers, Secondary School (O*NET code 25-2032.00)	Faster than average	$34,430

Typical College Courses

Classroom/laboratory management, English composition, evaluation in industrial education, history and philosophy of education, history and philosophy of industrial education, human growth and development, instructional materials in industrial education, introduction to psychology, methods of teaching industrial education, oral communication, safety and liability in the classroom, special needs in industrial education, student teaching.

Some Suggested High School Courses

Algebra, English, foreign language, geometry, industrial arts, mechanical drawing, public speaking, science, trigonometry.

Essential Knowledge and Skills

Learning strategies, speaking, reading comprehension, instructing, mathematics.
Values/Work Environment: Authority, achievement, responsibility, working indoors, standing, sitting.

Other Information Sources

Many career and education information sources use the standard cross-referencing systems noted below. You can use the codes to obtain substantial additional information on the major (via CIP code) and related occupations (via GOE code). The O*NET codes on the opposite page refer to another major career information system. See the Introduction for details on obtaining additional information.

Classification of Instructional Programs (CIP) code: 210101 Technology Education/Industrial Arts

Guide for Occupational Exploration (GOE) code: 12.03 Educational Services

Insurance

Career Snapshot

A bachelor's degree in insurance may lead to employment in an insurance company or agency. Graduates with outstanding mathematical ability may be hired for training as actuaries. Mergers and downsizing among agencies and brokerages may limit the number of job openings.

Related Specialties and Careers

Commercial risk management, life and health insurance, property and liability insurance.

Related Job Titles, Projected Growth, and Earnings		
Job Title	**Projected Growth**	**Average Earnings**
Claims Examiners, Property and Casualty Insurance (O*NET code 13-1031.01)	Average	$40,110
Insurance Adjusters, Examiners, and Investigators (O*NET code 13-1031.02)	Average	$38,290
Financial Analysts (O*NET code 13-2051.00)	Average	$40,534
Insurance Underwriters (O*NET code 13-2053.00)	Little or none	$38,710
Insurance Sales Agents (O*NET code 41-3021.00)	Little or none	$34,370

Typical College Courses

Business finance, business writing, calculus for business and social sciences, commercial risk management, employee benefit planning, English composition, insurance law, introduction to accounting, introduction to management information systems, introduction to marketing, introduction to psychology, legal environment of business, life and health insurance, operations management, principles of macroeconomics, principles of management and organization, principles of microeconomics, property and liability insurance, statistics for business and social sciences, strategic management.

Some Suggested High School Courses

Algebra, computer science, English, foreign language, geometry, science, trigonometry.

Essential Knowledge and Skills

Reading comprehension, information gathering. **Values/Work Environment:** Working indoors, sitting.

Other Information Sources

Many career and education information sources use the standard cross-referencing systems noted below. You can use the codes to obtain substantial additional information on the major (via CIP code) and related occupations (via GOE code). The O*NET codes on the opposite page refer to another major career information system. See the Introduction for details on obtaining additional information.

Classification of Instructional Programs (CIP) code: 520805 Insurance and Risk Management

Guide for Occupational Exploration (GOE) codes: 10.02 Sales Technology, 13.02 Management Support

---

Interior Design

Career Snapshot

Interior designers plan how to shape and decorate the interiors of all kinds of buildings, including homes and commercial structures. They may design new interiors or renovate existing places. They respond to their clients' needs and budgets by developing designs based on traditional forms, innovative uses of layout and materials, sound principles of engineering, and safety codes. A bachelor's degree in the field is not universally required, but it contributes to your qualifications for licensure (in some states) and membership in a professional association.

Related Specialties and Careers

Acoustics, bathrooms, computer-aided design, kitchens, public spaces, residential design, restoration.

Related Job Titles, Projected Growth, and Earnings		
Job Title	**Projected Growth**	**Average Earnings**
Exhibit Designers (O*NET code 27-1027.02)	Faster than average	$29,190
Interior Designers (O*NET code 27-1025.00)	Declining	$31,760
Set Designers (O*NET code 27-1027.01)	Faster than average	$29,190

Typical College Courses

Basic drawing, color and design, computer-aided design, construction codes and material rating, history of architecture, history of interiors, interior design studio, interior materials, introduction to interior design, lighting design, presentation graphics, senior design project.

Some Suggested High School Courses

Algebra, art, computer science, English, geometry, history, home economics, literature, physics, pre-calculus, trigonometry.

Essential Knowledge and Skills

Coordination, reading comprehension, active listening, visioning, management of financial resources, implementation planning. **Values/Work Environment:** Creativity; ability utilization; achievement; autonomy; working indoors; sitting; standing; using hands on objects, tools, or controls.

Other Information Sources

Many career and education information sources use the standard cross-referencing systems noted below. You can use the codes to obtain substantial additional information on the major (via CIP code) and related occupations (via GOE code). The O*NET codes on the opposite page refer to another major career information system. See the Introduction for details on obtaining additional information.

Classification of Instructional Programs (CIP) code: 500408 Interior Design

Guide for Occupational Exploration (GOE) code: 01.04 Visual Arts

International Relations

Career Snapshot

The study of international relations is a multidisciplinary effort that draws on political science, economics, sociology, and history, among other disciplines. It attempts to find meaning in the ways people, private groups, and governments relate to one another politically and economically. The traditional focus on sovereign states is opening up to include attention to other actors on the world stage, including non-governmental organizations, international organizations, multinational corporations, and groups representing a religion, ethnic group, or ideology. Now that American business is opening to the world more than ever before, this major is gaining in importance. Graduates often go on to law or business school, graduate school in the social sciences, the U.S. Foreign Service, or employment in businesses or organizations with an international focus.

Related Specialties and Careers

A regional specialization, development, diplomacy, global security, international political economy, U.S. foreign policy.

Related Job Titles, Projected Growth, and Earnings		
Job Title	Projected Growth	Average Earnings
Government Service Executives (O*NET code 11-1011.01)	Average	$55,030
Political Scientists (O*NET code 19-3094.00)	Average	$38,990
Area, Ethnic, and Cultural Studies Teachers, Postsecondary (O*NET code 25-1062.00)	Faster than average	(No salary data available)
Economics Teachers, Postsecondary (O*NET code 25-1063.00)	Faster than average	(No salary data available)
Political Science Teachers, Postsecondary (O*NET code 25-1065.00)	Faster than average	(No salary data available)

Typical College Courses

American foreign policy, comparative governments, English composition, foreign language, history of a non-western civilization, international economics, introduction to economics, introduction to international relations, introduction to political science, macroeconomic theory, microeconomic theory, seminar (reporting on research), world history in the modern era, world history to the early modern era, world regional geography.

Some Suggested High School Courses

Algebra, English, foreign language, history, social science, trigonometry.

Essential Knowledge and Skills

Reading comprehension, writing, active learning, information gathering, speaking, critical thinking, active listening, information organization, idea generation.

Values/Work Environment: Autonomy, achievement, ability utilization, working indoors, sitting, standing.

Other Information Sources

Many career and education information sources use the standard cross-referencing systems noted below. You can use the codes to obtain substantial additional information on the major (via CIP code) and related occupations (via GOE code). The O*NET codes on the opposite page refer to another major career information system. See the Introduction for details on obtaining additional information.

Classification of Instructional Programs (CIP) code: 450901 International Relations and Affairs

Guide for Occupational Exploration (GOE) codes: 12.03 Educational Services, 13.01 General Management Work and Management of Support Functions, 02.04 Social Sciences

---

 **Japanese**

Career Snapshot

Japan is a major trading partner of the United States, but comparatively few English speakers have mastered the Japanese language. This means that a major in Japanese can be a valuable entry route to careers in international business, travel, and law. A graduate degree in Japanese is good preparation for college teaching or translation.

Related Specialties and Careers

History and culture, language education, literature, translation.

Related Job Titles, Projected Growth, and Earnings		
Job Title	Projected Growth	Average Earnings
Foreign Language and Literature Teachers, Postsecondary (O*NET code 25-1124.00)	Faster than average	(No salary data available)
Interpreters and Translators (O*NET code 27-3091.00)	(No job growth data available)	(No salary data available)

Typical College Courses

Composition, conversation, East Asian literature, East Asian studies, grammar, Japanese language, Japanese literature, linguistics, phonetics.

Some Suggested High School Courses

English, foreign language, history, literature, public speaking, social science.

Essential Knowledge and Skills

Reading comprehension, instructing, speaking, learning strategies, writing, information gathering, critical thinking, active listening, synthesis/reorganization, information organization. **Values/Work Environment:** Achievement, ability utilization, authority, autonomy, working indoors, sitting, standing.

Other Information Sources

Many career and education information sources use the standard cross-referencing systems noted below. You can use the codes to obtain substantial additional information on the major (via CIP code) and related occupations (via GOE code). The O*NET codes on the opposite page refer to another major career information system. See the Introduction for details on obtaining additional information.

Classification of Instructional Programs (CIP) code: 160302 Japanese Language and Literature

Guide for Occupational Exploration (GOE) codes: 01.01 News, Broadcasting, and Public Relations; 12.03 Educational Services

Journalism and Mass Communications

Career Snapshot

Journalism is a good preparation not only for news reporting and writing, but also for advertising and (with specialized coursework) news media production. Competition for entry-level journalism jobs can be keen, especially for prestigious newspapers and media outlets. Expect to start in a smaller operation and move around to increasingly bigger employers as you build your career.

Related Specialties and Careers

Media management, news editing and editorializing, news reporting, photojournalism, radio and television news.

Related Job Titles, Projected Growth, and Earnings		
Job Title	**Projected Growth**	**Average Earnings**
Broadcast News Analysts (O*NET code 27-3021.00)	Little or none	$31,580
Reporters and Correspondents (O*NET code 27-3022.00)	Little or none	$26,040
Editors (O*NET code 27-3041.00)	Faster than average	$36,325
Creative Writers (O*NET code 27-3043.02)	Faster than average	$34,570

Typical College Courses

American government, communication ethics, copy editing, English composition, feature writing, foreign language, introduction to economics, introduction to mass communication, introduction to psychology, mass communication law, media management, news writing and reporting, oral communication, photojournalism, visual design for media, writing for mass media.

Some Suggested High School Courses

Algebra, art, English, foreign language, literature, public speaking, social science.

Essential Knowledge and Skills

Writing, reading comprehension. **Values/Work Environment:** Ability utilization, achievement, working indoors, sitting.

Other Information Sources

Many career and education information sources use the standard cross-referencing systems noted below. You can use the codes to obtain substantial additional information on the major (via CIP code) and related occupations (via GOE code). The O*NET codes on the opposite page refer to another major career information system. See the Introduction for details on obtaining additional information.

Classification of Instructional Programs (CIP) code: 090401 Journalism

Guide for Occupational Exploration (GOE) codes: 01.02 Writing and Editing; 01.03 News, Broadcasting, and Public Relations

Landscape Architecture

Career Snapshot

Landscape architects must have a good flair for design, ability to work with a variety of construction techniques and technologies, knowledge of the characteristics of many plants, plus business sense. A bachelor's degree is the usual entry route; some people enter the field with a master's degree after a bachelor's in another field. An internship is a very helpful credential. About 40 percent of landscape architects are self-employed.

Related Specialties and Careers

Arid lands, eco-tourism, historical and cultural landscapes, international studies, small-town and urban revitalization, urban design.

Related Job Titles, Projected Growth, and Earnings		
Job Title	Projected Growth	Average Earnings
Landscape Architects (O*NET code 17-1012.00)	Average	$37,930

Typical College Courses

Architectural computer graphics, architectural graphics, basic drawing, calculus, ecology, English composition, general biology, history of landscape architecture, introduction to horticulture, introduction to soil science, land planning, land surveying, landscape architectural design, landscape structures and materials, professional practice of landscape architecture, senior design project, site analysis.

Some Suggested High School Courses

Algebra, art, biology, calculus, computer science, English, geometry, physics, pre-calculus, trigonometry.

Essential Knowledge and Skills

Idea generation, solution appraisal, judgment and decision making, visioning, critical thinking, active listening, information gathering, active learning, idea evaluation, synthesis/reorganization. **Values/Work Environment:** Ability utilization; creativity; working indoors; working outdoors; sitting; using hands on objects, tools, or controls.

Other Information Sources

Many career and education information sources use the standard cross-referencing systems noted below. You can use the codes to obtain substantial additional information on the major (via CIP code) and related occupations (via GOE code). The O*NET codes on the opposite page refer to another major career information system. See the Introduction for details on obtaining additional information.

Classification of Instructional Programs (CIP) code: 040601 Landscape Architecture

Guide for Occupational Exploration (GOE) code: 02.07 Engineering

Law

Career Snapshot

Although most lawyers work in private practice, many work for government agencies, businesses, and non-profits. They enter the field by completing four years of college, three years of law school, and then passing the bar exam. The undergraduate major may be almost anything that contributes to skills in writing and critical thinking. Often it helps open doors to the kinds of careers that will be options after law school—for example, a bachelor's degree in a business field may help prepare for a career in tax law, labor relations law, or antitrust law.

Related Specialties and Careers

Environmental law, family law, intellectual property, international and comparative law, litigation.

Related Job Titles, Projected Growth, and Earnings

Job Title	Projected Growth	Average Earnings
Lawyers (O*NET code 23-1011.00)	Average	$78,170
Administrative Law Judges, Adjudicators, and Hearing Officers (O*NET code 23-1021.00)	Little or none	$33,870
Arbitrators, Mediators, and Conciliators (O*NET code 23-1022.00)	Little or none	$33,870
Judges, Magistrate Judges, and Magistrates (O*NET code 23-1023.00)	Little or none	$66,900

Typical College Courses

American history, civil procedure, constitutional law, contracts, criminal law, criminal procedure, English composition, evidence, foreign language, introduction to philosophy, introduction to political science, legal communication, legal research, legal writing, oral communication, professional responsibility, property, torts, trusts and estates.

Some Suggested High School Courses

Algebra, English, foreign language, geometry, history, public speaking, social science.

Essential Knowledge and Skills

Critical thinking, reading comprehension, active listening, judgment and decision making, information gathering, writing, speaking, active learning, synthesis/reorganization, information organization. **Values/Work Environment:** Autonomy, responsibility, security, good working conditions, working indoors, sitting.

Other Information Sources

Many career and education information sources use the standard cross-referencing systems noted below. You can use the codes to obtain substantial additional information on the major (via CIP code) and related occupations (via GOE code). The O*NET codes on the opposite page refer to another major career information system. See the Introduction for details on obtaining additional information.

Classification of Instructional Programs (CIP) code: 220101 Law (LL.B., J.D.)

Guide for Occupational Exploration (GOE) code: 04.02 Law

Law Enforcement

Career Snapshot

We live in a society that is governed by laws at the municipal, state, and federal levels. These laws are enforced by people who understand the laws themselves, the workings of the agencies that are empowered to enforce them, and the techniques for detecting violation of the laws, arresting violators, and processing them through the court system. Public concern about crime has created many job opportunities in this field, especially at the local level.

Related Specialties and Careers

Police administration, police work, security.

Related Job Titles, Projected Growth, and Earnings		
Job Title	**Projected Growth**	**Average Earnings**
Government Service Executives (O*NET code 11-1011.01)	Average	$55,030
Licensing Examiners and Inspectors (O*NET code 13-1041.02)	Average	$36,820
Government Property Inspectors and Investigators (O*NET code 13-1041.04)	Average	$36,820
Bailiffs (O*NET code 33-3011.00)	Average	$23,230
Correctional Officers and Jailers (O*NET code 33-3012.00)	Much faster than average	$28,540
Police Detectives (O*NET code 33-3021.01)	Faster than average	$48,029
Police Identification and Records Officers (O*NET code 33-3021.02)	Faster than average	$48,029
Criminal Investigators and Special Agents (O*NET code 33-3021.03)	Faster than average	$48,029
Child Support, Missing Persons, and Unemployment Insurance Fraud Investigators (O*NET code 33-3021.04)	Faster than average	$48,029

Job Title	Projected Growth	Average Earnings
Immigration and Customs Inspectors (O*NET code 33-3021.05)	Average	$36,820
Police Patrol Officers (O*NET code 33-3051.01)	Faster than average	$37,710
Sheriffs and Deputy Sheriffs (O*NET code 33-3051.03)	Faster than average	$28,270
Animal Control Workers (O*NET code 33-9011.00)	Average	$17,470

Typical College Courses

Criminal investigation, criminal law, criminal procedures, ethics, diversity and conflict, introduction to criminal justice, introduction to psychology, police organization and administration, police-community relations, seminar (reporting on research), technical writing.

Some Suggested High School Courses

Algebra, computer science, English, foreign language, history, public speaking, social science.

Essential Knowledge and Skills

Active listening. **Values/Work Environment:** Security, working indoors, standing, sitting, walking or running.

Other Information Sources

Many career and education information sources use the standard cross-referencing systems noted below. You can use the codes to obtain substantial additional information on the major (via CIP code) and related occupations (via GOE code). The O*NET codes on the opposite page refer to another major career information system. See the Introduction for details on obtaining additional information.

Classification of Instructional Programs (CIP) code: 430107 Law Enforcement/Police Science

Guide for Occupational Exploration (GOE) codes: 13.01 General Management Work and Management of Support Functions, 04.03 Law Enforcement, 04.04 Public Safety

Library Science

Career Snapshot

This major is sometimes called library and information science because increasingly the information that is needed by businesses, governments, and individuals is not available in books. Library science programs teach not only how to serve library users and manage library collections, but also how to retrieve and compile information from online databases. The master's degree is the entry-level credential in this field; a special librarian often needs an additional graduate or professional degree. The best employment opportunities will probably be in online information retrieval and in non-traditional settings.

Related Specialties and Careers

Archives, cataloguing, children's libraries, instructional libraries, map libraries, music libraries, online information retrieval, special-interest libraries.

Related Job Titles, Projected Growth, and Earnings		
Job Title	**Projected Growth**	**Average Earnings**
Librarians (O*NET code 25-4021.00)	Little or none	$38,470

Typical College Courses

Bibliographic control of library materials, English composition, foreign language, introduction to computer science, introduction to library and information science, library research and evaluation, management of libraries and information services, oral communication, reference services and resources.

Some Suggested High School Courses

Algebra, computer science, English, foreign language, keyboarding, office computer applications, public speaking, social science.

Essential Knowledge and Skills

Reading comprehension, information gathering. **Values/Work Environment:** Good working conditions, moral values, working indoors, sitting, standing.

Other Information Sources

Many career and education information sources use the standard cross-referencing systems noted below. You can use the codes to obtain substantial additional information on the major (via CIP code) and related occupations (via GOE code). The O*NET codes on the opposite page refer to another major career information system. See the Introduction for details on obtaining additional information.

Classification of Instructional Programs (CIP) code: 250101 Library Science/Librarianship

Guide for Occupational Exploration (GOE) code: 12.03 Educational Services

Management Information Systems

Career Snapshot

The management information systems major is considered a business major, which means that students get a firm grounding in economics, accounting, business law, finance, and marketing, as well as the technical skills needed to work with the latest business computer applications. Students may specialize in MIS at either the bachelor's or master's level, and may combine it with a degree in a related business field, such as accounting or finance, or in computer science. The job outlook is very good.

Related Specialties and Careers

Accounting, network programming, security and disaster recovery.

Related Job Titles, Projected Growth, and Earnings		
Job Title	Projected Growth	Average Earnings
Computer and Information Systems Managers (O*NET code 11-3021.00)	Much faster than average	$75,320
Computer Programmers (O*NET code 15-1021.00)	Faster than average	$49,570
Computer Support Specialists (O*NET code 15-1041.00)	Much faster than average	$37,120
Computer Systems Analysts (O*NET code 15-1051.00)	Much faster than average	$52,180
Database Administrators (O*NET code 15-1061.00)	Much faster than average	$47,980
Computer Security Specialists (O*NET code 15-1071.01)	Much faster than average	$38,822
Network Systems and Data Communications Analysts (O*NET code 15-1081.00)	Much faster than average	$51,344
Computer Science Teachers, Postsecondary (O*NET code 25-1021.00)	Faster than average	(No salary data available)
Computer Operators (O*NET code 43-9011.00)	Declining	$24,787

Typical College Courses

Business finance, business writing, calculus for business and social sciences, database management systems, decision support systems for management, English composition, introduction to accounting, introduction to management information systems, introduction to marketing, introduction to psychology, legal environment of business, networks and telecommunications, operations management, principles of macroeconomics, principles of management and organization, principles of microeconomics, statistics for business and social sciences, strategic management, systems analysis and design.

Some Suggested High School Courses

Algebra, computer science, English, foreign language, geometry, science, trigonometry.

Essential Knowledge and Skills

Reading comprehension. **Values/Work Environment:** Good working conditions; working indoors; sitting; using hands on objects, tools, or controls.

Other Information Sources

Many career and education information sources use the standard cross-referencing systems noted below. You can use the codes to obtain substantial additional information on the major (via CIP code) and related occupations (via GOE code). The O*NET codes on the opposite page refer to another major career information system. See the Introduction for details on obtaining additional information.

Classification of Instructional Programs (CIP) code: 521201 Management Information Systems and Business Data Processing

Guide for Occupational Exploration (GOE) codes: 02.06 Mathematics and Computers; 09.09 Clerical Machine Operation; 12.03 Educational Services; 02.01 Managerial Work in Science, Math, and Engineering

---

Marketing

Career Snapshot

Marketing is the study of how buyers and sellers of goods and services find one another, how businesses can tailor their offerings to meet demand, and how businesses can anticipate and influence demand. It uses the findings of economics, psychology, and sociology in a business context. A bachelor's degree is good preparation for a job in marketing research. Usually some experience in this field is required before a person can move into a marketing management position. Job outlook varies, with some industries looking more favorable than others.

Related Specialties and Careers

Marketing management, marketing research.

Related Job Titles, Projected Growth, and Earnings		
Job Title	Projected Growth	Average Earnings
Advertising and Promotions Managers (O*NET code 11-2011.00)	Faster than average	$57,300
Marketing Managers (O*NET code 11-2021.00)	Faster than average	$57,300
Sales Managers (O*NET code 11-2022.00)	Faster than average	$57,300

Typical College Courses

Business finance, business writing, buyer behavior, calculus for business and social sciences, decision support systems for management, English composition, introduction to accounting, introduction to management information systems, introduction to marketing, introduction to psychology, legal environment of business, marketing research, marketing strategy, operations management, principles of macroeconomics, principles of management and organization, principles of microeconomics, statistics for business and social sciences, strategic management.

Some Suggested High School Courses

Algebra, computer science, English, foreign language, geometry, home economics, science, trigonometry.

Essential Knowledge and Skills

Coordination, information gathering, solution appraisal, problem identification, judgment and decision making, speaking, visioning, idea evaluation, reading comprehension. **Values/Work Environment:** Good working conditions, working indoors, sitting, standing.

Other Information Sources

Many career and education information sources use the standard cross-referencing systems noted below. You can use the codes to obtain substantial additional information on the major (via CIP code) and related occupations (via GOE code). The O*NET codes on the opposite page refer to another major career information system. See the Introduction for details on obtaining additional information.

Classification of Instructional Programs (CIP) code: 521401 Business Marketing and Marketing Management

Guide for Occupational Exploration (GOE) code: 10.01 Managerial Work in Sales and Marketing

---

Materials Science

Career Snapshot

Materials scientists research the physical and chemical properties of ceramics, plastics, and other materials. They devise technologically elegant and economically valuable ways of creating and forming these materials. A bachelor's degree is a common entry route to this field, although those who want to do basic research or teach in college will need to get an advanced degree. The job outlook in this field is only fair, although workers will be needed to replace those who retire.

Related Specialties and Careers

Building materials, ceramics/glass, polymers, thin films.

Related Job Titles, Projected Growth, and Earnings		
Job Title	Projected Growth	Average Earnings
Materials Engineers (O*NET code 17-2131.00)	Little or none	$57,970
Materials Scientists (O*NET code 19-2032.00)	Little or none	$48,990
Engineering Teachers, Postsecondary (O*NET code 25-1032.00)	Faster than average	(No salary data available)

Typical College Courses

Calculus, differential equations, dynamics, English composition, senior design project, general chemistry, general physics, introduction to computer science, introduction to electric circuits, introduction to materials science, kinetics of chemical and physical reactions, materials characterization, mechanics of materials, microstructure and mechanical properties, numerical analysis, phase equilibrium, physical chemistry, statics, technical writing, thermodynamics.

Some Suggested High School Courses

Algebra, calculus, chemistry, computer science, English, geometry, physics, pre-calculus, trigonometry.

Essential Knowledge and Skills

Science, mathematics, active learning, reading comprehension, writing, critical thinking. **Values/Work Environment:** Ability utilization, autonomy, working indoors, sitting.

Other Information Sources

Many career and education information sources use the standard cross-referencing systems noted below. You can use the codes to obtain substantial additional information on the major (via CIP code) and related occupations (via GOE code). The O*NET codes on the opposite page refer to another major career information system. See the Introduction for details on obtaining additional information.

Classification of Instructional Programs (CIP) code: 143101 Materials Science

Guide for Occupational Exploration (GOE) codes: 12.03 Educational Services, 02.02 Physical Sciences, 02.07 Engineering

Mathematics

Career Snapshot

Mathematics is a science in its own right, in which researchers with graduate degrees continue to discover new laws. It is also a tool for understanding and organizing many aspects of our world. Many mathematics majors apply their knowledge by getting additional education or training, either in a master's program or on the job. For example, an insurance company might train them in actuarial science; a computer consulting company might train them in the latest computer language; they might get an economics, engineering, or accounting degree. Employment opportunities are very good for people who apply mathematical knowledge to other fields.

Related Specialties and Careers

Applied mathematics, mathematical statistics, mathematics education, theoretical mathematics.

Related Job Titles, Projected Growth, and Earnings		
Job Title	**Projected Growth**	**Average Earnings**
Mathematicians (O*NET code 15-2021.00)	Declining	$51,829
Statisticians (O*NET code 15-2041.00)	Little or none	$48,540
Mathematical Science Teachers, Postsecondary (O*NET code 25-1022.00)	Faster than average	(No salary data available)
Actuaries (O*NET code 15-2011.00)	Little or none	$65,560

Typical College Courses

Calculus, differential equations, introduction to abstract mathematics, introduction to computer science, linear algebra, programming in a language (for example, C++ or Java), statistics.

Some Suggested High School Courses

Algebra, calculus, computer science, geometry, physics, pre-calculus, trigonometry.

Essential Knowledge and Skills

Mathematics, active learning, information gathering, reading comprehension, critical thinking, learning strategies, idea generation, information organization, solution appraisal, writing. **Values/Work Environment:** Ability utilization, autonomy, good working conditions, working indoors, sitting.

Other Information Sources

Many career and education information sources use the standard cross-referencing systems noted below. You can use the codes to obtain substantial additional information on the major (via CIP code) and related occupations (via GOE code). The O*NET codes on the opposite page refer to another major career information system. See the Introduction for details on obtaining additional information.

Classification of Instructional Programs (CIP) code: 270101 Mathematics, General

Guide for Occupational Exploration (GOE) codes: 02.06 Mathematics and Computers, 12.03 Educational Services

---

Mechanical Engineering

Career Snapshot

Mechanical engineers design, test, and supervise the manufacture of various mechanical devices, including tools, motors, machines, and medical equipment. Their goal is to maximize both the technical efficiency and the economic benefits of the devices. Usually they enter their first job with a bachelor's degree. Sometimes they move from engineering to a managerial position. Despite an expected decline in manufacturing, job opportunities are expected to be good.

Related Specialties and Careers

Automotive design, heating and air conditioning, testing.

Related Job Titles, Projected Growth, and Earnings		
Job Title	**Projected Growth**	**Average Earnings**
Mechanical Engineers (O*NET code 17-2141.00)	Average	$53,290
Engineering Teachers, Postsecondary (O*NET code 25-1032.00)	Faster than average	(No salary data available)
Sales Engineers (O*NET code 41-9031.00)	Average	$54,600

Typical College Courses

Calculus, differential equations, dynamics, English composition, fluid mechanics, general chemistry, general physics, heat transfer, introduction to computer science, introduction to engineering, manufacturing processes, materials engineering, materials science, mechanical engineering design, numerical analysis, senior design project, statics, technical writing, thermodynamics.

Some Suggested High School Courses

Algebra, calculus, chemistry, computer science, English, geometry, physics, pre-calculus, trigonometry.

Essential Knowledge and Skills

Mathematics, active learning, reading comprehension, critical thinking, technology design, operations analysis, science, problem identification, solution appraisal.

Values/Work Environment: Ability utilization; working indoors; sitting; standing; using hands on objects, tools, or controls.

Other Information Sources

Many career and education information sources use the standard cross-referencing systems noted below. You can use the codes to obtain substantial additional information on the major (via CIP code) and related occupations (via GOE code). The O*NET codes on the opposite page refer to another major career information system. See the Introduction for details on obtaining additional information.

Classification of Instructional Programs (CIP) code: 141901 Mechanical Engineering

Guide for Occupational Exploration (GOE) codes: 02.07 Engineering, 12.03 Educational Services

Medical Technology

Career Snapshot

The detection, diagnosis, and prevention of disease depend heavily on various kinds of medical tests—of blood, urine, tissue samples, and so on. Medical technologists, also called clinical laboratory scientists, are trained to perform these tests after studying the principles of chemistry, microbiology, and other basic sciences, plus laboratory techniques that sometimes involve complex and sophisticated equipment. A bachelor's degree is the usual preparation. Job outlook is generally good, with best opportunities for those who have skills in multiple specializations.

Related Specialties and Careers

Blood banking, body fluid analysis, clinical chemistry, clinical microbiology, hematology, immunology.

Related Job Titles, Projected Growth, and Earnings		
Job Title	**Projected Growth**	**Average Earnings**
Health Specialties Teachers, Postsecondary (O*NET code 25-1071.00)	Faster than average	(No salary data available)
Medical and Clinical Laboratory Technologists (O*NET code 29-2011.00)	Average	$37,280

Typical College Courses

Body fluid analysis, clinical chemistry, clinical immunology and serology, clinical microbiology, college algebra, English composition, general biology, general chemistry, general microbiology, hematology and coagulation, human anatomy and physiology, immunohematology, introduction to biochemistry, introduction to computer science, medical technology education, medical technology management and supervision, organic chemistry, parasitology, statistics.

Some Suggested High School Courses

Algebra, biology, chemistry, computer science, English, geometry, physics, trigonometry.

Essential Knowledge and Skills

Reading comprehension, science, writing, information gathering, active learning, critical thinking, problem identification, speaking, active listening, learning strategies. **Values/Work Environment:** Ability utilization, working indoors, sitting, standing, common protective or safety attire.

Other Information Sources

Many career and education information sources use the standard cross-referencing systems noted below. You can use the codes to obtain substantial additional information on the major (via CIP code) and related occupations (via GOE code). The O*NET codes on the opposite page refer to another major career information system. See the Introduction for details on obtaining additional information.

Classification of Instructional Programs (CIP) code: 511005 Medical Technology

Guide for Occupational Exploration (GOE) codes: 12.03 Educational Services; 14.05 Medical Technology

---

Medicine

Career Snapshot

Medicine requires long years of education—four years of college, four years of medical school, and three to eight years of internship and residency, depending on the specialty. Entrance to medical school is highly competitive. Although "pre-med" is often referred to as a major, it is possible to meet the entry requirements for medical school while majoring in a non-scientific subject. This may be helpful to demonstrate that you are a well-rounded person and to prepare you for another career in case you are not admitted to medical school. Today, physicians are more likely than in the past to work as salaried employees of group practices or HMOs.

Related Specialties and Careers

Emergency medicine, family medicine, internal medicine, obstetrics/gynecology, pediatrics, psychiatry, radiology, surgery.

Related Job Titles, Projected Growth, and Earnings		
Job Title	**Projected Growth**	**Average Earnings**
Biological Science Teachers, Postsecondary (O*NET code 25-1042.00)	Faster than average	(No salary data available)
Health Specialties Teachers, Postsecondary (O*NET code 25-1071.00)	Faster than average	(No salary data available)
Family and General Practitioners (O*NET code 29-1062.00)	Faster than average	$124,821
Internists, General (O*NET code 29-1063.00)	Faster than average	$124,821
Obstetricians and Gynecologists (O*NET code 29-1064.00)	Faster than average	$124,821
Pediatricians, General (O*NET code 29-1065.00)	Faster than average	$124,821

Typical College Courses

Abnormal psychology, calculus, clinical experience in emergency medicine, clinical experience in family medicine, clinical experience in geriatrics, clinical experience in internal medicine, clinical experience in obstetrics/gynecology, clinical experience in pediatrics, clinical experience in psychiatry, clinical experience in surgery, clinical laboratory procedures, college algebra, English composition, ethics in health care, general biology, general chemistry, general microbiology, genetics, human anatomy and physiology, introduction to biochemistry, introduction to computer science, introduction to psychology, introduction to sociology, medical interviewing techniques, oral communication, organic chemistry, pathology, patient examination and evaluation, pharmacology.

Some Suggested High School Courses

Algebra, biology, chemistry, computer science, English, foreign language, geometry, physics, pre-calculus, public speaking, trigonometry.

Essential Knowledge and Skills

Reading comprehension, science, active learning, writing, critical thinking, problem identification, information gathering, speaking, active listening, mathematics.

Values/Work Environment: Achievement; ability utilization; social service; social status; responsibility; autonomy; working indoors; standing; sitting; using hands on objects, tools, or controls.

Other Information Sources

Many career and education information sources use the standard cross-referencing systems noted below. You can use the codes to obtain substantial additional information on the major (via CIP code) and related occupations (via GOE code). The O*NET codes on the opposite page refer to another major career information system. See the Introduction for details on obtaining additional information.

Classification of Instructional Programs (CIP) codes: 511201 Medicine (M.D.), 511901 Osteopathic Medicine (D.O.)

Guide for Occupational Exploration (GOE) codes: 12.03 Educational Services, 14.02 Medicine and Surgery

---

Metallurgical Engineering

Career Snapshot

Metallurgy is the science of refining and alloying metals, and shaping them to form structures and products. Metallurgical engineers apply principles of physics, chemistry, materials science, and economics to improve extractive and manufacturing processes. A bachelor's degree is often an entry route to this field, which may eventually lead to management. Job growth in this field is expected to be slow, but there will be some need to replace workers who retire.

Related Specialties and Careers

Chemical metallurgy, materials research, physical metallurgy, process engineering.

Related Job Titles, Projected Growth, and Earnings		
Job Title	**Projected Growth**	**Average Earnings**
Engineering Teachers, Postsecondary (O*NET code 25-1032.00)	Faster than average	(No salary data available)
Sales Engineers (O*NET code 41-9031.00)	Average	$54,600

Typical College Courses

Calculus, differential equations, English composition, general chemistry, general physics, hydroprocessing of materials, introduction to computer science, introduction to electric circuits, materials engineering, materials thermodynamics, mechanical metallurgy, metallurgical design, metallurgical transport phenomena, numerical analysis, organic chemistry, physics of metals, process modeling, optimization and control, senior design project, thermodynamics.

Some Suggested High School Courses

Algebra, calculus, chemistry, computer science, English, geometry, physics, pre-calculus, trigonometry.

Essential Knowledge and Skills

Mathematics, active learning, reading comprehension, critical thinking, science, instructing, learning strategies, writing, speaking, idea generation. **Values/Work Environment:** Achievement, ability utilization, authority, good working conditions, autonomy, responsibility, working indoors, sitting, standing.

Other Information Sources

Many career and education information sources use the standard cross-referencing systems noted below. You can use the codes to obtain substantial additional information on the major (via CIP code) and related occupations (via GOE code). The O*NET codes on the opposite page refer to another major career information system. See the Introduction for details on obtaining additional information.

Classification of Instructional Programs (CIP) code: 142001 Metallurgical Engineering

Guide for Occupational Exploration (GOE) codes: 02.07 Engineering, 12.03 Educational Services

Microbiology/Bacteriology

Career Snapshot

A bachelor's degree in microbiology or bacteriology may be an entry route to clinical laboratory work or to non-research work in industry or government. It also is good preparation for medical school. For a position in research or college teaching, a graduate degree is expected.

Related Specialties and Careers

Algae, bacteria, fungi (mycology), immunology, virology.

Related Job Titles, Projected Growth, and Earnings		
Job Title	**Projected Growth**	**Average Earnings**
Microbiologists (O*NET code 19-1022.00)	Faster than average	$46,140
Epidemiologists (O*NET code 19-1041.00)	Faster than average	$50,410
Medical Scientists, Except Epidemiologists (O*NET code 19-1042.00)	Faster than average	$50,410
Agricultural Sciences Teachers, Postsecondary (O*NET code 25-1041.00)	Faster than average	(No salary data available)
Biological Science Teachers, Postsecondary (O*NET code 25-1042.00)	Faster than average	(No salary data available)
Forestry and Conservation Science Teachers, Postsecondary (O*NET code 25-1043.00)	Faster than average	(No salary data available)

Typical College Courses

Bacterial genetics, bacterial physiology, calculus, English composition, general biology, general chemistry, general microbiology, general physics, genetics, immunology, introduction to biochemistry, introduction to computer science, organic chemistry.

Some Suggested High School Courses

Algebra, biology, calculus, chemistry, computer science, English, geometry, physics, pre-calculus, trigonometry.

Essential Knowledge and Skills

Reading comprehension, science, writing, active learning, instructing, critical thinking, information gathering, learning strategies, mathematics, problem identification. **Values/Work Environment:** Achievement; ability utilization; autonomy; social status; working indoors; sitting; standing; using hands on objects, tools, or controls.

Other Information Sources

Many career and education information sources use the standard cross-referencing systems noted below. You can use the codes to obtain substantial additional information on the major (via CIP code) and related occupations (via GOE code). The O*NET codes on the opposite page refer to another major career information system. See the Introduction for details on obtaining additional information.

Classification of Instructional Programs (CIP) code: 260501 Microbiology/Bacteriology

Guide for Occupational Exploration (GOE) codes: 02.03 Life Sciences, 12.03 Educational Services

---

Modern Foreign Language

Career Snapshot

The most popular foreign language majors—Chinese, French, German, Japanese, Russian, and Spanish—are described elsewhere in this book. But many colleges offer majors in other modern languages, such as Arabic, Hebrew, Hindi, Portuguese, Swahili, Swedish, or Turkish, to name just a few. As global trade continues to increase, a degree in a foreign language can lead to many job opportunities in international business, travel, and law. Many employers are looking for graduates with an understanding of a second language and culture. Translation or college teaching are options for those with a graduate degree in a foreign language.

Related Specialties and Careers

History and culture, language education, literature, regional studies, translation.

Related Job Titles, Projected Growth, and Earnings		
Job Title	Projected Growth	Average Earnings
Caption Writers (O*NET code 27-3043.03)	Declining	(No salary data available)
English Language and Literature Teachers, Postsecondary (O*NET code 25-1123.00)	Faster than average	(No salary data available)
Foreign Language and Literature Teachers, Postsecondary (O*NET code 25-1124.00)	Faster than average	(No salary data available)
Interpreters and Translators (O*NET code 27-3091.00)	(No job growth data available)	(No salary data available)
Forestry and Conservation Science Teachers, Postsecondary (ONET code 25-1043.00)	Faster than average	(No salary data available)

Typical College Courses

Composition, conversation, foreign language, foreign literature and culture, grammar, history of a world region, linguistics, phonetics.

Some Suggested High School Courses

English, foreign language, history, public speaking, social science.

Essential Knowledge and Skills

Reading comprehension, speaking, writing, instructing, learning strategies, information gathering, active listening, critical thinking, synthesis/reorganization, active learning, information organization. **Values/Work Environment:** Achievement, ability utilization, autonomy, authority, social service, good working conditions, working indoors, sitting, standing.

Other Information Sources

Many career and education information sources use the standard cross-referencing systems noted below. You can use the codes to obtain substantial additional information on the major (via CIP code) and related occupations (via GOE code). The O*NET codes on the opposite page refer to another major career information system. See the Introduction for details on obtaining additional information.

Classification of Instructional Programs (CIP) codes: 161101 Arabic Language and Literature; 160301 Chinese Language and Literature; 160399 East and Southeast Asian Languages and Literatures, Other; 160499 East European Languages and Literatures, Other; 160103 Foreign Language Interpretation and Translation; 160101 Foreign Languages and Literatures, General; 169999 Foreign Languages and Literatures, Other; 160901 French Language and Literature; 160501 German Language and Literature; 160599 Germanic Languages and Literatures, Other; 161102 Hebrew Language and Literature; 160902 Italian Language and Literature; 160302 Japanese Language and Literature; 160102 Linguistics; 161199 Middle Eastern Languages and Literatures, Other; 160904 Portuguese Language and Literature; 160999 Romance Languages and Literatures, Other; 160402 Russian Language and Literature; 160502 Scandinavian Languages and Literatures; 160403 Slavic Languages and Literatures (Other Than Russian); 160905 Spanish Language and Literature

Guide for Occupational Exploration (GOE) codes: 01.03 News, Broadcasting, and Public Relations; 12.03 Educational Services

 **Music**

Career Snapshot

Music majors study theory, composition, and performance. They learn how the success of a work of music depends on certain principles of what appeals to the ear, on the skill of the arranger, and on the interpretation of the performers. Relatively few graduates are able to support themselves as composers, arrangers, or performers, but many teach in schools or universities or give private instruction.

Related Specialties and Careers

Composition, music education, music theory, performance.

Related Job Titles, Projected Growth, and Earnings		
Job Title	**Projected Growth**	**Average Earnings**
Music Directors (O*NET code 27-2041.01)	Average	$22,440
Music Arrangers and Orchestrators (O*NET code 27-2041.02)	Average	$22,440
Composers (O*NET code 27-2041.03)	Average	$22,440
Singers (O*NET code 27-2042.01)	Average	$22,440
Musicians, Instrumental (O*NET code 27-2042.02)	Average	$32,120

Typical College Courses

Conducting, English composition, foreign language, harmony and counterpoint, introduction to music theory, music history and literature, performance technique with instrument/voice, piano proficiency, recital attendance, recital performance.

Some Suggested High School Courses

English, foreign language, music.

Essential Knowledge and Skills

Coordination. **Values/Work Environment:** Ability utilization, achievement, moral values, autonomy, creativity, working indoors, sitting, standing.

Other Information Sources

Many career and education information sources use the standard cross-referencing systems noted below. You can use the codes to obtain substantial additional information on the major (via CIP code) and related occupations (via GOE code). The O*NET codes on the opposite page refer to another major career information system. See the Introduction for details on obtaining additional information.

Classification of Instructional Programs (CIP) code: 360115 Music

Guide for Occupational Exploration (GOE) code: 01.01 Performing Arts

Nursing (R.N. Training)

Career Snapshot

The study of nursing includes a combination of classroom and clinical work. Students learn what science tells us about the origins and treatment of disease, how to care effectively for the physical and emotional needs of sick and injured people, and how to teach people to maintain health. Nurses work in a variety of health care settings, including patients' homes, schools and companies, and in desk jobs for HMOs. The employment outlook is good.

Related Specialties and Careers

Community health nursing, mental health nursing, nursing administration, pediatric nursing.

Related Job Titles, Projected Growth, and Earnings		
Job Title	**Projected Growth**	**Average Earnings**
Nursing Instructors and Teachers, Postsecondary (O*NET code 25-1072.00)	Faster than average	(No salary data available)
Registered Nurses (O*NET code 29-1111.00)	Faster than average	$40,690

Typical College Courses

Adult health nursing, clinical nursing experience, college algebra, community health nursing, English composition, ethics in health care, general biology, general chemistry, general microbiology, human anatomy and physiology, introduction to psychology, introduction to sociology, mental health nursing, nursing leadership and management, oral communication, patient examination and evaluation, pediatric nursing, pharmacology, reproductive health nursing.

Some Suggested High School Courses

Algebra, biology, chemistry, computer science, English, foreign language, geometry, public speaking, trigonometry.

Essential Knowledge and Skills

Reading comprehension, instructing, learning strategies, speaking. **Values/Work Environment:** Social service; achievement; ability utilization; working indoors; special uniform; standing; diseases/infections; common protective or safety attire; walking or running; using hands on objects, tools, or controls.

Other Information Sources

Many career and education information sources use the standard cross-referencing systems noted below. You can use the codes to obtain substantial additional information on the major (via CIP code) and related occupations (via GOE code). The O*NET codes on the opposite page refer to another major career information system. See the Introduction for details on obtaining additional information.

Classification of Instructional Programs (CIP) code: 511601 Nursing (R.N. Training, e.g., Diploma, A.S.N., B.S.N., MSN)

Guide for Occupational Exploration (GOE) codes: 14.02 Medicine and Surgery, 12.03 Educational Services

Occupational Health and Industrial Hygiene

Career Snapshot

Graduates with a bachelor's degree in occupational health and industrial hygiene are trained to protect workers from a variety of threats to their health and safety: chemical and biological contaminants, fire, noise, cramped bodily positions, dangerous machinery, and radiation. The major covers the nature of the risks from these and other hazards, the laws that exist to ban such hazards, how to recognize the presence and assess the risks of workplace hazards, and how to take steps to eliminate them.

Related Specialties and Careers

Hazardous materials, occupational health, safety.

Related Job Titles, Projected Growth, and Earnings		
Job Title	Projected Growth	Average Earnings
Health Specialties Teachers, Postsecondary (O*NET code 25-1071.00)	Faster than average	(No salary data available)
Environmental Compliance Inspectors (O*NET code 13-1041.01)	Average	$36,820

Typical College Courses

Biostatistics, calculus, chemistry of hazardous materials, English composition, environmental regulations, general biology, general chemistry, general physics, industrial fire prevention, introduction to computer science, introduction to environmental health, introduction to occupational health and safety, microbial hazards, occupational safety and health law, oral communication, organic chemistry, pollution science and treatment, safety organization and management, statistics, technical writing.

Some Suggested High School Courses

Algebra, chemistry, computer science, English, geometry, physics, pre-calculus, public speaking, trigonometry.

Essential Knowledge and Skills

Reading comprehension, writing; science, information gathering, instructing; active listening; critical thinking; active learning, idea evaluation, problem identification. **Values/Work Environment:** Achievement, ability utilization, authority, autonomy, responsibility, working indoors, standing, sitting.

Other Information Sources

Many career and education information sources use the standard cross-referencing systems noted below. You can use the codes to obtain substantial additional information on the major (via CIP code) and related occupations (via GOE code). The O*NET codes on the opposite page refer to another major career information system. See the Introduction for details on obtaining additional information.

Classification of Instructional Programs (CIP) code: 512206 Occupational Health and Industrial Hygiene

Guide for Occupational Exploration (GOE) codes: 04.04 Public Safety, 12.03 Educational Services

---

Occupational Therapy

Career Snapshot

Occupational therapists help people cope with disabilities and lead more productive and enjoyable lives. Some therapists enter the field with a bachelor's degree in occupational therapy; others get a master's after a bachelor's in another field. They learn about the nature of various kinds of disabilities—developmental, emotional, and so on—and how to help people overcome them or compensate for them in their daily lives. The long-range outlook for jobs is considered good, although it may be affected by cutbacks in Medicare coverage of therapies.

Related Specialties and Careers

Geriatric OT, pediatric OT, prosthetics.

Related Job Titles, Projected Growth, and Earnings		
Job Title	**Projected Growth**	**Average Earnings**
Health Specialties Teachers, Postsecondary (O*NET code 25-1071.00)	Faster than average	(No salary data available)
Occupational Therapists (O*NET code 29-1122.00)	Faster than average	$48,230

Typical College Courses

Abnormal psychology, administration of occupational therapy services, English composition, fundamentals of medical science, general biology, general chemistry, human anatomy and physiology, human growth and development, introduction to computer science, introduction to psychology, methods of facilitating therapeutic adaptation, neuroscience for therapy, occupational therapy fieldwork experience, occupational therapy for developmental problems, occupational therapy for physiological diagnoses, occupational therapy for psychosocial diagnoses, research methods in occupational therapy, seminar (reporting on research), statistics for business and social sciences.

Some Suggested High School Courses

Algebra, biology, chemistry, computer science, English, foreign language, geometry, physics, trigonometry.

Essential Knowledge and Skills

Reading comprehension, instructing, active listening, writing, speaking. **Values/ Work Environment:** Achievement, ability utilization, social service, working indoors, sitting, standing.

Other Information Sources

Many career and education information sources use the standard cross-referencing systems noted below. You can use the codes to obtain substantial additional information on the major (via CIP code) and related occupations (via GOE code). The O*NET codes on the opposite page refer to another major career information system. See the Introduction for details on obtaining additional information.

Classification of Instructional Programs (CIP) code: 512306 Occupational Therapy

Guide for Occupational Exploration (GOE) codes: 12.03 Educational Services, 14.06 Medical Therapy

---

Oceanography

Career Snapshot

Oceans cover more of the earth than does dry land, yet many of the physical and biological characteristics of the oceans are poorly understood. Oceanographers use techniques of physical sciences to study the properties of ocean waters and how these affect coastal areas, climate, and weather. Those who specialize in ocean life work to improve the fishing industry, to protect the environment, and to understand the relationship between oceanic and terrestrial life forms. It is possible to get started in this field with a bachelor's degree; for advancement and many research jobs, however, a master's degree or Ph.D. is helpful or required.

Related Specialties and Careers

Ocean biology, ocean chemistry, ocean geology, ocean meteorology.

Related Job Titles, Projected Growth, and Earnings		
Job Title	**Projected Growth**	**Average Earnings**
Geologists (O*NET code 19-2042.01)	Average	$53,890
Hydrologists (O*NET code 19-2043.00)	Average	$53,890

Typical College Courses

Agricultural power and machines, biological oceanography, calculus, chemical oceanography, differential equations, English composition, general chemistry, general physics, geological oceanography, introduction to computer science, physical oceanography, seminar (reporting on research).

Some Suggested High School Courses

Algebra, biology, calculus, chemistry, computer science, English, geometry, physics, pre-calculus, trigonometry.

Essential Knowledge and Skills

Mathematics, information gathering, science, writing, active learning, critical thinking, reading comprehension, problem identification, information organization. **Values/Work Environment:** Autonomy; ability utilization; moral values; responsibility; sitting; working indoors; working outdoors; standing; using hands on objects, tools, or controls.

Other Information Sources

Many career and education information sources use the standard cross-referencing systems noted below. You can use the codes to obtain substantial additional information on the major (via CIP code) and related occupations (via GOE code). The O*NET codes on the opposite page refer to another major career information system. See the Introduction for details on obtaining additional information.

Classification of Instructional Programs (CIP) code: 400702 Oceanography

Guide for Occupational Exploration (GOE) code: 02.02 Physical Sciences

Optometry

Career Snapshot

Optometrists measure patients' visual ability and prescribe visual aids such as glasses and contact lenses. They may evaluate patients' suitability for laser surgery and/or provide post-operative care, but they do not perform surgery. The usual educational preparation is at least three years of college, followed by a four-year program of optometry school. The job outlook is good because the aging population will need increased attention to vision. The best opportunities probably will be at retail vision centers and outpatient clinics.

Related Specialties and Careers

Contact lenses, low vision.

Related Job Titles, Projected Growth, and Earnings		
Job Title	Projected Growth	Average Earnings
Health Specialties Teachers, Postsecondary (O*NET code 25-1071.00)	Faster than average	(No salary data available)
Optometrists (O*NET code 29-1041.00)	Average	$68,480

Typical College Courses

Assessment of oculomotor system, calculus, clinical experience in optometry, contact lenses, English composition, ophthalmic optics, environmental and occupational vision, ethics in health care, general and ocular pharmacology, general biology, general chemistry, general microbiology, geometric, physical and visual optics, introduction to biochemistry, introduction to psychology, introduction to sociology, low vision and geriatric vision, microbiology for optometry, neuroanatomy, ocular anatomy and physiology, ocular disease, ocular health assessment, optical and motor aspects of vision, oral communication, organic chemistry, pathology, pediatric and developmental vision, professional practice management, strabismus and vision therapy, theory and methods of refraction, visual information processing and perception.

Some Suggested High School Courses

Algebra, biology, calculus, chemistry, computer science, English, foreign language, geometry, physics, pre-calculus, public speaking, trigonometry.

Essential Knowledge and Skills

Reading comprehension, science, writing, active listening, instructing, speaking.
Values/Work Environment: Achievement, responsibility, autonomy, social service, social status, good working conditions, working indoors, sitting, standing.

Other Information Sources

Many career and education information sources use the standard cross-referencing systems noted below. You can use the codes to obtain substantial additional information on the major (via CIP code) and related occupations (via GOE code). The O*NET codes on the opposite page refer to another major career information system. See the Introduction for details on obtaining additional information.

Classification of Instructional Programs (CIP) code: 511701 Optometry (O.D.)

Guide for Occupational Exploration (GOE) codes: 12.03 Educational Services, 14.04 Health Specialties

---

Orthotics/Prosthetics

Career Snapshot

Orthotics is the design and fitting of supportive or corrective braces for patients with musculoskeletal deformity or injury. Prosthetics is the fabrication and fitting of artificial limbs. People enter this field by getting a bachelor's degree in one or both specializations, or enrolling in a certification program after a bachelor's in another field (perhaps occupational therapy). The job outlook is expected to be good.

Related Specialties and Careers

Fabrication, fitting, orthotics, prosthetics.

Related Job Titles, Projected Growth, and Earnings		
Job Title	Projected Growth	Average Earnings
Health Specialties Teachers, Postsecondary (O*NET code 25-1071.00)	Faster than average	(No salary data available)
Orthotists and Prosthetists (O*NET code 29-2091.00)	Much faster than average	$27,260

Typical College Courses

Abnormal psychology, English composition, function of the locomotor system, fundamentals of medical science, general biology, general chemistry, general physics, human anatomy and physiology, human growth and development, immediate post-operative and early fitting, introduction to computer science, introduction to psychology, kinesiology, lower-extremity orthotics, lower-extremity prosthetics, neuroanatomy, psychological aspects of rehabilitation, spinal orthotics, statistics for business and social sciences, upper-extremity orthotics, upper-extremity prosthetics.

Some Suggested High School Courses

Algebra, biology, chemistry, computer science, English, foreign language, geometry, physics, trigonometry.

Essential Knowledge and Skills

Reading comprehension, speaking, active listening, writing, instructing, science.
Values/Work Environment: Achievement; social service; ability utilization; working indoors; standing; sitting; using hands on objects, tools, or controls.

Other Information Sources

Many career and education information sources use the standard cross-referencing systems noted below. You can use the codes to obtain substantial additional information on the major (via CIP code) and related occupations (via GOE code). The O*NET codes on the opposite page refer to another major career information system. See the Introduction for details on obtaining additional information.

Classification of Instructional Programs (CIP) code: 512307 Orthotics/Prosthetics

Guide for Occupational Exploration (GOE) codes: 12.03 Educational Services, 14.05 Medical Technology

Parks and Recreation Management

Career Snapshot

Interest in the outdoors and in fitness is growing. Americans want to make the most of their recreational time and the parks and other facilities that are set aside for recreational use. Those who major in parks and recreation management may want to emphasize either the managerial or the leadership and therapeutic aspects. With a bachelor's degree, they may find employment with government, commercial recreational and tourism organizations, camps, or theme parks.

Related Specialties and Careers

Exercise, interpretation, outdoor leadership, resource management, therapeutic recreation, tourism.

Related Job Titles, Projected Growth, and Earnings		
Job Title	Projected Growth	Average Earnings
Government Service Executives (O*NET code 11-1011.01)	Average	$55,030
Travel Guides (O*NET code 39-6022.00)	Average	$15,500
Recreation Workers (O*NET code 39-9032.00)	Average	$16,500

Typical College Courses

American government; conservation of natural resources; ecology; English composition; seminar (reporting on research); evaluation and research in parks and recreation; foundations of parks and recreation; introduction to business management; introduction to computer science; introduction to economics; introduction to psychology; introduction to sociology; methods of environmental interpretation; natural resource economics; oral communication; park planning and design; parks, recreation and diverse populations; recreation and tourism programs; statistics for business and social sciences; tourism management and planning.

Some Suggested High School Courses

Biology, chemistry, English, geometry, public speaking, social science.

Essential Knowledge and Skills

Coordination. **Values/Work Environment:** Autonomy, working indoors, sitting, standing, working outdoors, walking or running.

Other Information Sources

Many career and education information sources use the standard cross-referencing systems noted below. You can use the codes to obtain substantial additional information on the major (via CIP code) and related occupations (via GOE code). The O*NET codes on the opposite page refer to another major career information system. See the Introduction for details on obtaining additional information.

Classification of Instructional Programs (CIP) code: 310301 Parks, Recreation, and Leisure Facilities Management

Guide for Occupational Exploration (GOE) codes: 11.02 Recreational Services, 13.01 General Management Work and Management of Support Functions

---

Petroleum Engineering

Career Snapshot

Petroleum engineers devise technically effective and economically justifiable ways of locating, extracting, transporting, refining, and storing petroleum and natural gas. They apply basic principles of science to oil wells deep in the ground or high-towering refineries. Usually they begin with a bachelor's degree. Management is sometimes an option later in their careers. The job outlook in the United States depends on the price of oil. Although the price occasionally jumps, the overall trend seems to be downward because of the large reserves of petroleum in other countries.

Related Specialties and Careers

Distribution, drilling/extraction, exploration, refining.

Related Job Titles, Projected Growth, and Earnings		
Job Title	Projected Growth	Average Earnings
Mining and Geological Engineers, Including Mining Safety Engineers (O*NET code 17-2151.00)	Declining	$56,090
Petroleum Engineers (O*NET code 17-2171.00)	Declining	$74,260
Engineering Teachers, Postsecondary (O*NET code 25-1032.00)	Faster than average	(No salary data available)

Typical College Courses

Calculus, differential equations, drilling engineering, dynamics, engineering economics, English composition, fluid mechanics, formation evaluation, general chemistry, general physics, heat transfer, introduction to computer science, introduction to engineering, materials engineering, natural gas engineering, numerical analysis, petroleum development, petroleum geology, petroleum production methods, petroleum property management, physical geology, reservoir engineering, reservoir fluids, reservoir stimulation, sedimentary rocks and processes, senior design project, statics, technical writing, thermodynamics, well testing and analysis.

Some Suggested High School Courses

Algebra, calculus, chemistry, computer science, English, geometry, physics, pre-calculus, trigonometry.

Essential Knowledge and Skills

Mathematics, science, reading comprehension, active learning, critical thinking, writing, information gathering, operations analysis, solution appraisal, idea generation. **Values/Work Environment:** Ability utilization; autonomy; responsibility; working indoors; sitting; standing; using hands on objects, tools, or controls.

Other Information Sources

Many career and education information sources use the standard cross-referencing systems noted below. You can use the codes to obtain substantial additional information on the major (via CIP code) and related occupations (via GOE code). The O*NET codes on the opposite page refer to another major career information system. See the Introduction for details on obtaining additional information.

Classification of Instructional Programs (CIP) code: 142501 Petroleum Engineering

Guide for Occupational Exploration (GOE) codes: 02.07 Engineering, 12.03 Educational Services

---

Pharmacy

Career Snapshot

Pharmacists dispense medications as prescribed by physicians and other health practitioners and give advice to patients about how to use medications. Pharmacists must be knowledgeable about the chemical and physical properties of drugs, how they behave in the body, and how they may interact with other drugs and substances. Schools of pharmacy take about four years to complete and usually require at least one or two years of prior college work. Some pharmacists go on to additional graduate training to prepare for research, administration, or college teaching.

Related Specialties and Careers

Pharmaceutical chemistry, pharmacology, pharmacy administration.

Related Job Titles, Projected Growth, and Earnings		
Job Title	Projected Growth	Average Earnings
Health Specialties Teachers, Postsecondary (O*NET code 25-1071.00)	Faster than average	(No salary data available)
Pharmacists (O*NET code 29-1051.00)	Little or none	$66,220

Typical College Courses

Calculus, English composition, general biology, general chemistry, human anatomy and physiology, introduction to biochemistry, introduction to psychology, introduction to sociology, medicinal chemistry, microbiology and immunology, oral communication, organic chemistry, patient assessment and education, pharmaceutical calculations, pharmaceutics, pharmacokinetics, pharmacology, pharmacy law and ethics, therapeutics.

Some Suggested High School Courses

Algebra, biology, calculus, chemistry, computer science, English, foreign language, geometry, physics, public speaking, trigonometry.

Essential Knowledge and Skills

Reading comprehension, writing, science, instructing, active learning, critical thinking, active listening, problem identification. **Values/Work Environment:** Ability utilization; achievement; working indoors; standing; sitting; using hands on objects, tools, or controls.

Other Information Sources

Many career and education information sources use the standard cross-referencing systems noted below. You can use the codes to obtain substantial additional information on the major (via CIP code) and related occupations (via GOE code). The O*NET codes on the opposite page refer to another major career information system. See the Introduction for details on obtaining additional information.

Classification of Instructional Programs (CIP) code: 512001 Pharmacy (Pharm.D.)

Guide for Occupational Exploration (GOE) codes: 12.03 Educational Services, 14.02 Medicine and Surgery

Philosophy

Career Snapshot

Philosophy is concerned with the most basic questions about the human experience, such as what reality is, what the ultimate values are, and how we know what we know. Philosophy majors are trained to think independently and critically, and to write clearly and persuasively. They may go to work in a number of business careers where these skills are appreciated—perhaps most of all in the long run as these former philosophy majors advance to positions of leadership. Some find that a philosophy major combines well with further training in law, computer science, or religious studies. Those with a graduate degree in philosophy may teach in college.

Related Specialties and Careers

Aesthetics, ethics, history of philosophy, logic.

Related Job Titles, Projected Growth, and Earnings		
Job Title	Projected Growth	Average Earnings
Clergy (O*NET code 21-2011.00)	Average	$28,850
Creative Writers (O*NET code 27-3043.02)	Faster than average	$34,570

Typical College Courses

Classical philosophy, contemporary philosophy, English composition, esthetics, ethical/moral theory, foreign language, introduction to logic, major thinkers and issues in philosophy, modern philosophy.

Some Suggested High School Courses

Algebra, English, foreign language, geometry, history, social science.

Essential Knowledge and Skills

Service orientation, speaking, social perceptiveness, writing, reading comprehension, active listening. **Values/Work Environment:** Achievement, autonomy, ability utilization, working indoors, special uniform, standing, sitting.

Other Information Sources

Many career and education information sources use the standard cross-referencing systems noted below. You can use the codes to obtain substantial additional information on the major (via CIP code) and related occupations (via GOE code). The O*NET codes on the opposite page refer to another major career information system. See the Introduction for details on obtaining additional information.

Classification of Instructional Programs (CIP) code: 380101 Philosophy

Guide for Occupational Exploration (GOE) codes: 01.02 Writing and Editing, 12.02 Social Services

Physical Education

Career Snapshot

This major covers not only educational techniques, but also the workings of the human body. Thanks to a national concern for fitness and health, physical education graduates are finding employment not only as teachers, but also as instructors and athletic directors in health and sports clubs. Most jobs are still to be found in elementary and secondary schools, where a bachelor's degree is often sufficient for entry, but a master's may be required for advancement to a more secure and better-paid position. Some graduates may go on to get a master's in athletic training and work for a college or professional sports team.

Related Specialties and Careers

Coaching, health education, recreation, sports activities.

Related Job Titles, Projected Growth, and Earnings		
Job Title	Projected Growth	Average Earnings
Preschool Teachers, Except Special Education (O*NET code 25-2011.00)	Faster than average	$17,310
Kindergarten Teachers, Except Special Education (O*NET code 25-2012.00)	Average	$33,590
Elementary School Teachers, Except Special Education (O*NET code 25-2021.00)	Average	$36,110
Middle School Teachers, Except Special and Vocational Education (O*NET code 25-2022.00)	Faster than average	$37,890
Secondary School Teachers, Except Special and Vocational Education (O*NET code 25-2031.00)	Faster than average	$37,890

Typical College Courses

English composition, evaluation in physical education, first aid and CPR, history and philosophy of education, history and philosophy of physical education, human anatomy and physiology, human growth and development, introduction to psychology, introduction to special education, kinesiology, methods of teaching aerobics and weight training, methods of teaching dance, methods of teaching physical education, methods of teaching sports activities, oral communication, organization and administration of physical education, psychomotor development, special needs in physical education, student teaching, swimming and water safety.

Some Suggested High School Courses

Algebra, English, foreign language, geometry, public speaking, science, trigonometry.

Essential Knowledge and Skills

Learning strategies. **Values/Work Environment:** Authority, social service, achievement, responsibility, working indoors, standing, sitting, working outdoors.

Other Information Sources

Many career and education information sources use the standard cross-referencing systems noted below. You can use the codes to obtain substantial additional information on the major (via CIP code) and related occupations (via GOE code). The O*NET codes on the opposite page refer to another major career information system. See the Introduction for details on obtaining additional information.

Classification of Instructional Programs (CIP) code: 131314 Physical Education Teaching and Coaching

Guide for Occupational Exploration (GOE) code: 12.03 Educational Services

---

Physical Therapy

Career Snapshot

Physical therapists help people overcome pain and limited movement caused by disease or injury, and help them avoid further disabilities. They review patients' medical records and the prescriptions of physicians, evaluate patients' mobility, then guide patients through appropriate exercise routines and apply therapeutic agents such as heat and electrical stimulation. They need to be knowledgeable about many disabling conditions and therapeutic techniques. The master's program is becoming the standard requirement for entry into this field. Entry to master's programs is extremely competitive. The short-term job outlook has been hurt by cutbacks in Medicare coverage of therapy; however, the long-term outlook is expected to be good.

Related Specialties and Careers

Geriatric physical therapy, neurological physical therapy, orthopedics, physical therapy education, sports medicine.

Related Job Titles, Projected Growth, and Earnings		
Job Title	Projected Growth	Average Earnings
Health Specialties Teachers, Postsecondary (O*NET code 25-1071.00)	Faster than average	(No salary data available)
Physical Therapists (O*NET code 29-1123.00)	Faster than average	$56,600

Typical College Courses

Abnormal psychology, cardiopulmonary system, clinical applications of neurophysiology, clinical orthopedics, English composition, fundamentals of medical science, general biology, general chemistry, human anatomy and physiology, human growth and development, introduction to computer science, introduction to psychology, medical considerations in physical therapy, musculoskeletal system, neuroanatomy, neuroscience for therapy, physical and electrical agents in physical therapy, psychomotor development throughout the life span, psychosocial aspects of physical disability, research in physical therapy practice, statistics for business and social sciences, therapeutic exercise techniques.

Some Suggested High School Courses

Algebra, biology, chemistry, computer science, English, foreign language, geometry, physics, trigonometry.

Essential Knowledge and Skills

Reading comprehension, writing, instructing, active listening, science, critical thinking, problem identification, speaking, information gathering, active learning.

Values/Work Environment: Achievement, social service, ability utilization, working indoors, standing.

Other Information Sources

Many career and education information sources use the standard cross-referencing systems noted below. You can use the codes to obtain substantial additional information on the major (via CIP code) and related occupations (via GOE code). The O*NET codes on the opposite page refer to another major career information system. See the Introduction for details on obtaining additional information.

Classification of Instructional Programs (CIP) code: 512308 Physical Therapy

Guide for Occupational Exploration (GOE) codes: 12.03 Educational Services, 14.06 Medical Therapy

---

Physician Assisting

Career Snapshot

Physician assistants work under the supervision of physicians, but in some cases they provide care in settings where a physician may be present only a couple of days per week. They perform many of the diagnostic, therapeutic, and preventative functions that we are used to associating with physicians. The typical educational program results in a bachelor's degree. It often takes only two years to complete, but entrants usually must have at least two years of prior college and often must have work experience in the field of health care. Employment opportunities are expected to be good.

Related Specialties and Careers

Emergency medicine, family medicine, internal medicine, pediatrics.

Related Job Titles, Projected Growth, and Earnings		
Job Title	**Projected Growth**	**Average Earnings**
Health Specialties Teachers, Postsecondary (O*NET code 25-1071.00)	Faster than average	(No salary data available)
Physician Assistants (O*NET code 29-1071.00)	Much faster than average	$47,090

Typical College Courses

Clinical experience in emergency medicine, clinical experience in family medicine, clinical experience in geriatrics, clinical experience in internal medicine, clinical experience in obstetrics/gynecology, clinical experience in pediatrics, clinical experience in psychiatry, clinical experience in surgery, clinical laboratory procedures, college algebra, English composition, ethics in health care, general biology, general chemistry, general microbiology, human anatomy, human growth and development, human physiology, introduction to psychology, medical interviewing techniques, patient examination and evaluation, pharmacology.

Some Suggested High School Courses

Algebra, biology, chemistry, computer science, English, foreign language, geometry, pre-calculus, public speaking, trigonometry.

Essential Knowledge and Skills

Reading comprehension, science, writing, information gathering, problem identification, active listening, active learning, critical thinking, speaking. **Values/Work Environment:** Achievement, social service, ability utilization, working indoors, standing.

Other Information Sources

Many career and education information sources use the standard cross-referencing systems noted below. You can use the codes to obtain substantial additional information on the major (via CIP code) and related occupations (via GOE code). The O*NET codes on the opposite page refer to another major career information system. See the Introduction for details on obtaining additional information.

Classification of Instructional Programs (CIP) code: 510807 Physician Assistant

Guide for Occupational Exploration (GOE) codes: 12.03 Educational Services, 14.02 Medicine and Surgery

---

 **Physics**

Career Snapshot

Physics is the study of the basic laws of the physical world, including those that govern what matter and energy are and how they are created, move, and interact. This knowledge is the basis for our understanding of many fields, such as chemistry, biology, and engineering. Physics has direct applications in the technologies that we use every day for transportation, communication, and entertainment. Because most jobs are in basic research and development, a Ph.D. is most commonly required. Unfortunately, research is not expected to grow fast, if at all, so there will be keen competition for jobs.

Related Specialties and Careers

Acoustics, astronomy, elementary particles, nuclear physics, optics, plasma physics, solid-state physics, theoretical physics.

Related Job Titles, Projected Growth, and Earnings		
Job Title	**Projected Growth**	**Average Earnings**
Physicists (O*NET code 19-2012.00)	Little or none	$73,240
Physics Teachers, Postsecondary (O*NET code 25-1054.00)	Faster than average	(No salary data available)

Typical College Courses

Calculus, differential equations, electricity and magnetism, English composition, general chemistry, introduction to computer science, mechanics, modern experimental physics, modern physics, optics, quantum and atomic physics, thermal physics.

Some Suggested High School Courses

Algebra, calculus, chemistry, computer science, English, geometry, physics, pre-calculus, trigonometry.

Essential Knowledge and Skills

Mathematics, active learning, reading comprehension, writing, information gathering, science, critical thinking, solution appraisal, idea generation, information organization. **Values/Work Environment:** Ability utilization; autonomy; achievement; creativity; working indoors; sitting; using hands on objects, tools, or controls.

Other Information Sources

Many career and education information sources use the standard cross-referencing systems noted below. You can use the codes to obtain substantial additional information on the major (via CIP code) and related occupations (via GOE code). The O*NET codes on the opposite page refer to another major career information system. See the Introduction for details on obtaining additional information.

Classification of Instructional Programs (CIP) code: 400801 Physics, General

Guide for Occupational Exploration (GOE) codes: 02.02 Physical Sciences, 12.03 Educational Services

 **Podiatry**

Career Snapshot

Podiatrists are health care practitioners who specialize in the feet and lower extremities. The educational process is much like that for medical doctors—for almost all students, first a bachelor's degree, then four years of study and clinical practice in a school of podiatric medicine, followed by one to three years of a hospital residency program. The bachelor's degree can be in any subject as long as it includes certain coursework in science and math.

Related Specialties and Careers

Orthopedics, sports medicine, surgery.

Related Job Titles, Projected Growth, and Earnings		
Job Title	**Projected Growth**	**Average Earnings**
Health Specialties Teachers, Postsecondary (O*NET code 25-1071.00)	Faster than average	(No salary data available)
Podiatrists (O*NET code 29-1081.00)	Average	$79,530

Typical College Courses

Biomechanics, calculus, clinical experience in podiatric medicine, college algebra, dermatology, English composition, human physiology, general biology, general chemistry, general medicine, general microbiology, genetics, gross anatomy, histology, human anatomy and physiology, introduction to biochemistry, introduction to computer science, introduction to psychology, introduction to sociology, lower-extremity anatomy, microbiology and immunology, neuroanatomy, oral communication, organic chemistry, pathology, patient examination and evaluation, podiatric surgery, professional practice management, radiology, traumatology.

Some Suggested High School Courses

Algebra, biology, chemistry, computer science, English, foreign language, geometry, physics, pre-calculus, public speaking, trigonometry.

Essential Knowledge and Skills

Reading comprehension, active learning, active listening, idea evaluation, critical thinking, information gathering, writing, problem identification, speaking, idea generation. **Values/Work Environment:** Achievement, ability utilization, responsibility, autonomy, social service, social status, working indoors, standing, sitting.

Other Information Sources

Many career and education information sources use the standard cross-referencing systems noted below. You can use the codes to obtain substantial additional information on the major (via CIP code) and related occupations (via GOE code). The O*NET codes on the opposite page refer to another major career information system. See the Introduction for details on obtaining additional information.

Classification of Instructional Programs (CIP) code: 512101 Podiatry (D.P.M., D.P., Pod.D.)

Guide for Occupational Exploration (GOE) codes: 12.03 Educational Services, 14.04 Health Specialties

---

Political Science

Career Snapshot

Political science is the study of how political systems and public policy are created and evolve. It is concerned with many levels of political activity, from the campaigns of candidates for representation of a city precinct to the maneuvers of nations trying to resolve regional conflicts. Most political scientists work as researchers and teachers in universities, which means they generally have graduate degrees. Many graduates of political science programs use the bachelor's degree as an entry route to law school or public administration.

Related Specialties and Careers

Comparative politics, international relations, political theory, public administration, public opinion, public policy.

Related Job Titles, Projected Growth, and Earnings		
Job Title	Projected Growth	Average Earnings
Political Scientists (O*NET code 19-3094.00)	Average	$38,990
Area, Ethnic, and Cultural Studies Teachers, Postsecondary (O*NET code 25-1062.00)	Faster than average	(No salary data available)
Political Science Teachers, Postsecondary (O*NET code 25-1065.00)	Faster than average	(No salary data available)

Typical College Courses

American government, comparative governments, English composition, foreign language, introduction to economics, introduction to international relations, introduction to psychology, introduction to sociology, political science research methods, political theory, public policy analysis, seminar (reporting on research), state and local government, statistics, statistics for business and social sciences.

Some Suggested High School Courses

Algebra, English, foreign language, history, social science, trigonometry.

Essential Knowledge and Skills

Reading comprehension, writing, active learning, speaking, information gathering, active listening, critical thinking. **Values/Work Environment:** Autonomy, achievement, ability utilization, working indoors, sitting, standing.

Other Information Sources

Many career and education information sources use the standard cross-referencing systems noted below. You can use the codes to obtain substantial additional information on the major (via CIP code) and related occupations (via GOE code). The O*NET codes on the opposite page refer to another major career information system. See the Introduction for details on obtaining additional information.

Classification of Instructional Programs (CIP) code: 451001 Political Science and Government, General

Guide for Occupational Exploration (GOE) codes: 02.04 Social Sciences, 12.03 Educational Services

---

Psychology

Career Snapshot

Psychology is the study of human behavior. It may take place in a clinical, educational, industrial, or experimental setting. Those with a bachelor's degree usually must find employment in another field, such as marketing research. A bachelor's degree can also be a good first step toward graduate education in education, law, social work, or another field. To be licensed as a clinical or counseling psychologist, you usually need a Ph.D. About half of psychologists are self-employed. Because psychology is about behavior, many people don't realize that it uses scientific methods and that students are expected to become competent in statistics.

Related Specialties and Careers

Clinical/counseling psychology, educational psychology, industrial psychology, research clinical psychology.

Related Job Titles, Projected Growth, and Earnings		
Job Title	**Projected Growth**	**Average Earnings**
Educational Psychologists (O*NET code 19-3031.01)	Average	$48,050
Clinical Psychologists (O*NET code 19-3031.02)	Average	$48,050
Counseling Psychologists (O*NET code 19-3031.03)	Average	$48,050
Industrial-Organizational Psychologists (O*NET code 19-3032.00)	Average	$48,050
Psychology Teachers, Postsecondary (O*NET code 25-1066.00)	Faster than average	(No salary data available)

Typical College Courses

Abnormal psychology, biopsychology, cognitive psychology, developmental psychology, English composition, experimental psychology, introduction to psychology, psychological testing and measurements, psychology of learning, psychology of personality, quantitative analysis in psychology, research methods in speech pathology and audiology, sensation and perception, social psychology, statistics.

Some Suggested High School Courses

Algebra, biology, English, foreign language, social science, trigonometry.

Essential Knowledge and Skills

Reading comprehension, active listening, active learning, speaking, writing, information gathering, critical thinking, learning strategies, problem identification, instructing. **Values/Work Environment:** Achievement, autonomy, ability utilization, creativity, responsibility, good working conditions, working indoors, sitting, standing.

Other Information Sources

Many career and education information sources use the standard cross-referencing systems noted below. You can use the codes to obtain substantial additional information on the major (via CIP code) and related occupations (via GOE code). The O*NET codes on the opposite page refer to another major career information system. See the Introduction for details on obtaining additional information.

Classification of Instructional Programs (CIP) code: 420101 Psychology, General

Guide for Occupational Exploration (GOE) codes: 02.04 Social Sciences, 12.02 Social Services, 12.03 Educational Services

---

Public Administration

Career Snapshot

The public sector includes many kinds of agencies, working in the fields of health, law enforcement, environmental protection, transportation, and taxation, to name just a few. Because of this variety of fields, it is often useful to combine training in administrative skills (perhaps at the master's level) with specific training in another field, such as health, science, engineering, or accounting. Public administration programs usually include internships that give students actual experience working in a public agency.

Related Specialties and Careers

Economic development, finance and budgeting, personnel and labor relations, policy analysis, program management.

Related Job Titles, Projected Growth, and Earnings		
Job Title	Projected Growth	Average Earnings
Government Service Executives (O*NET code 11-1011.01)	Average	$55,030
Training and Development Managers (O*NET code 11-3042.00)	Average	$49,010
Postmasters and Mail Superintendents (O*NET code 11-9131.00)	Little or none	$44,730
Social and Community Service Managers (O*NET code 11-9151.00)	Average	$49,220
Equal Opportunity Representatives and Officers (O*NET code 13-1041.03)	Average	$36,820

Typical College Courses

Accounting, American government, college algebra, English composition, introduction to business management, introduction to economics, introduction to psychology, oral communication, organizational behavior, organizational theory, planning and change in public organizations, political science research methods, public finance and budgeting, public policy-making process, seminar (reporting on research), state and local government, statistics for business and social sciences, urban politics.

Some Suggested High School Courses

Algebra, computer science, English, foreign language, history, public speaking, social science, trigonometry.

Essential Knowledge and Skills

Reading comprehension. **Values/Work Environment:** Good working conditions, working indoors, sitting.

Other Information Sources

Many career and education information sources use the standard cross-referencing systems noted below. You can use the codes to obtain substantial additional information on the major (via CIP code) and related occupations (via GOE code). The O*NET codes on the opposite page refer to another major career information system. See the Introduction for details on obtaining additional information.

Classification of Instructional Programs (CIP) code: 440401 Public Administration

Guide for Occupational Exploration (GOE) codes: 13.01 General Management Work and Management of Support Functions, 04.04 Public Safety, 12.01 Managerial Work in Education and Social Service

---

Public Relations

Career Snapshot

Public relations specialists work for business, government, and non-profit organizations and encourage public support for the employer's policies and practices. Often several "publics" with differing interests and needs have to be targeted with different messages. The work requires understanding of psychology, the business and social environments, effective writing, and techniques used in various media for persuasive communications. A bachelor's degree is good preparation for an entry-level job in this competitive field. With experience, it may be possible to manage public relations campaigns.

Related Specialties and Careers

Creative process, management, new media.

Related Job Titles, Projected Growth, and Earnings		
Job Title	**Projected Growth**	**Average Earnings**
Agents and Business Managers of Artists, Performers, and Athletes (O*NET code 13-1011.00)	Average	$36,923
Public Relations Specialists (O*NET code 27-3031.00)	Faster than average	$34,550

Typical College Courses

Communication ethics, communications theory, English composition, introduction to communication research, introduction to economics, introduction to marketing, mass communication law, oral communication, organizational communications, principles of public relations, public relations media, public relations message strategy, public relations techniques and campaigns, public relations writing, visual design for media.

Some Suggested High School Courses

Algebra, art, English, foreign language, literature, public speaking, social science.

Essential Knowledge and Skills

Speaking. **Values/Work Environment:** Good working conditions, working indoors, sitting.

Other Information Sources

Many career and education information sources use the standard cross-referencing systems noted below. You can use the codes to obtain substantial additional information on the major (via CIP code) and related occupations (via GOE code). The O*NET codes on the opposite page refer to another major career information system. See the Introduction for details on obtaining additional information.

Classification of Instructional Programs (CIP) code: 090501 Public Relations and Organizational Communications

Guide for Occupational Exploration (GOE) codes: 01.01 Managerial Work in Arts, Entertainment, and Media; 01.03 News, Broadcasting, and Public Relations

Religion/Religious Studies

Career Snapshot

Interest in religion continues to grow in America, and many colleges were founded by churches, so the religious studies major continues to attract students, some of whom have no intention of becoming professional clergy. A graduate of a religious studies major has skills in language, literature, critical thinking, and writing that are valuable in many careers in the secular world. The amount of education required to be ordained in the clergy depends on the person's religious denomination. For some, there may be no formal requirement; most require several years of seminary training, often following four years of college. Clergy find work in churches, synagogues, and religious schools; as chaplains for hospitals, prisons, and the military; and as missionaries.

Related Specialties and Careers

Ecumenical studies, missionary work, pastoral counseling, pastoral studies, scriptural texts/language.

Related Job Titles, Projected Growth, and Earnings		
Job Title	Projected Growth	Average Earnings
Clergy (O*NET code 21-2011.00)	Average	$28,850

Typical College Courses

Contemporary theologies, English composition, ethical/moral theory, foreign language, Hebrew Bible, history of religion in the west, introduction to philosophy, introduction to religious studies, New Testament, non-western religions, philosophy of religion, religious ethics.

Some Suggested High School Courses

Algebra, English, foreign language, geometry, history, public speaking, social science.

Essential Knowledge and Skills

Speaking, social perceptiveness, service orientation, reading comprehension, writing, active listening. **Values/Work Environment:** Social status, achievement, autonomy, social service, security, working indoors, special uniform, standing, sitting.

Other Information Sources

Many career and education information sources use the standard cross-referencing systems noted below. You can use the codes to obtain substantial additional information on the major (via CIP code) and related occupations (via GOE code). The O*NET codes on the opposite page refer to another major career information system. See the Introduction for details on obtaining additional information.

Classification of Instructional Programs (CIP) code: 380201 Religion/Religious Studies

Guide for Occupational Exploration (GOE) code: 12.02 Social Services

 **Russian**

Career Snapshot

Despite the breakup of the Soviet Union, Russian is still an important world language that not many Americans know. As business and governmental ties with Russia continue to increase as it opens to free trade, a degree in Russian can lead to careers in international business, travel, and law. College teaching and translation are options for those with a graduate degree in Russian.

Related Specialties and Careers

History and culture, language education, literature, translation.

Related Job Titles, Projected Growth, and Earnings		
Job Title	Projected Growth	Average Earnings
Foreign Language and Literature Teachers, Postsecondary (O*NET code 25-1124.00)	Faster than average	(No salary data available)
Interpreters and Translators (O*NET code 27-3091.00)	(No job growth data available)	(No salary data available)

Typical College Courses

Composition, conversation, European history and civilization, grammar, linguistics, phonetics, Russian history and civilization, Russian language, Russian literature.

Some Suggested High School Courses

English, foreign language, history, literature, public speaking, social science.

Essential Knowledge and Skills

Reading comprehension, speaking, instructing, learning strategies, writing, critical thinking, information gathering, active listening, synthesis/reorganization, information organization. **Values/Work Environment:** Achievement, ability utilization, authority, autonomy, working indoors, sitting, standing.

Other Information Sources

Many career and education information sources use the standard cross-referencing systems noted below. You can use the codes to obtain substantial additional information on the major (via CIP code) and related occupations (via GOE code). The O*NET codes on the opposite page refer to another major career information system. See the Introduction for details on obtaining additional information.

Classification of Instructional Programs (CIP) code: 160402 Russian Language and Literature

Guide for Occupational Exploration (GOE) codes: 01.01 News, Broadcasting, and Public Relations; 12.03 Educational Services

Secondary Education

Career Snapshot

A bachelor's is the minimum for starting a secondary teaching career, and a master's may be required or encouraged for job security and a pay raise. A teacher-education program covers not only the subjects you will teach, but also basic principles of how young people learn and how to run a classroom. Demand for secondary school teachers is expected to be better than that for lower grades, but it will vary according to subject field and geographic area.

Related Specialties and Careers

Art education, bilingual education, language education, mathematics education, music education, remedial and developmental reading, science education, social studies education.

Related Job Titles, Projected Growth, and Earnings		
Job Title	**Projected Growth**	**Average Earnings**
Middle School Teachers, Except Special and Vocational Education (O*NET code 25-2022.00)	Faster than average	$37,890
Vocational Education Teachers, Middle School (O*NET code 25-2023.00)	Faster than average	$34,430
Secondary School Teachers, Except Special and Vocational Education (O*NET code 25-2031.00)	Faster than average	$37,890
Vocational Education Teachers, Secondary School (O*NET code 25-2032.00)	Faster than average	$34,430

Typical College Courses

Courses in the subject to be taught, educational alternatives for exceptional students, educational psychology, English composition, history and philosophy of education, human growth and development, introduction to psychology, oral communication, student teaching, teaching methods.

Some Suggested High School Courses

Algebra, English, foreign language, geometry, public speaking, science, trigonometry.

Essential Knowledge and Skills

Learning strategies, speaking, reading comprehension, instructing. **Values/Work Environment:** Authority, social service, achievement, responsibility, working indoors, standing, sitting.

Other Information Sources

Many career and education information sources use the standard cross-referencing systems noted below. You can use the codes to obtain substantial additional information on the major (via CIP code) and related occupations (via GOE code). The O*NET codes on the opposite page refer to another major career information system. See the Introduction for details on obtaining additional information.

Classification of Instructional Programs (CIP) code: 131205 Secondary Teacher Education

Guide for Occupational Exploration (GOE) code: 12.03 Educational Services

---

Social Work

Career Snapshot

Social workers improve people's lives by helping them cope with problems of bad health, substance abuse, disability, old age, family conflicts, mental illness, or poverty. A large number of them work for public agencies and health care institutions. A master's degree is becoming standard preparation for this field. Job opportunities are expected to be good, especially in rural areas.

Related Specialties and Careers

Advocacy, child welfare, domestic violence, health care, mental health, mental retardation, school social work, substance abuse.

Related Job Titles, Projected Growth, and Earnings		
Job Title	**Projected Growth**	**Average Earnings**
Social and Community Service Managers (O*NET code 11-9151.00)	Average	$49,220
Substance Abuse and Behavioral Disorder Counselors (O*NET code 21-1011.00)	Much faster than average	$25,942
Mental Health Counselors (O*NET code 21-1014.00)	Faster than average	$25,942
Child, Family, and School Social Workers (O*NET code 21-1021.00)	Much faster than average	$29,960
Medical and Public Health Social Workers (O*NET code 21-1022.00)	Much faster than average	$31,620
Mental Health and Substance Abuse Social Workers (O*NET code 21-1023.00)	Much faster than average	$31,620
Probation Officers and Correctional Treatment Specialists (O*NET code 21-1092.00)	Faster than average	$25,971

Typical College Courses

American government, cultural diversity, development of social welfare, English composition, field experience/internship, foreign language, human anatomy and physiology, human behavior and the social environment, human growth and development, introduction to philosophy, introduction to psychology, introduction to sociology, seminar (reporting on research), social welfare policy and issues, social work methods, social work research methods, statistics for business and social sciences.

Some Suggested High School Courses

Algebra, biology, English, foreign language, social science, trigonometry.

Essential Knowledge and Skills

Active listening, reading comprehension, social perceptiveness.

Values/Work Environment: Social service, working indoors, sitting.

Other Information Sources

Many career and education information sources use the standard cross-referencing systems noted below. You can use the codes to obtain substantial additional information on the major (via CIP code) and related occupations (via GOE code). The O*NET codes on the opposite page refer to another major career information system. See the Introduction for details on obtaining additional information.

Classification of Instructional Programs (CIP) code: 440701 Social Work

Guide for Occupational Exploration (GOE) codes: 12.01 Managerial Work in Education and Social Service, 12.02 Social Services

---

Sociology

Career Snapshot

Sociology studies how people behave within groups, such as families, religious denominations, social organizations, businesses, and political groups. Many graduates of bachelor's sociology programs go on to graduate school with the goal of research or teaching. Others branch out to a related field, perhaps with additional education, such as social work, the law, or marketing research.

Related Specialties and Careers

Anthropology, criminology, culture and social change, family and marriage, gerontology, human relations, social institutions/organizations, social problems.

Related Job Titles, Projected Growth, and Earnings		
Job Title	**Projected Growth**	**Average Earnings**
Sociologists (O*NET code 19-3041.00)	Average	$38,990
Anthropologists (O*NET code 19-3091.01)	Average	$38,990
Anthropology and Archeology Teachers, Postsecondary (O*NET code 25-1061.00)	Faster than average	(No salary data available)
Area, Ethnic, and Cultural Studies Teachers, Postsecondary (O*NET code 25-1062.00)	Faster than average	(No salary data available)
Sociology Teachers, Postsecondary (O*NET code 25-1067.00)	Faster than average	(No salary data available)

Typical College Courses

American government, contemporary social problems, English composition, foreign language, history of social thought, introduction to economics, introduction to psychology, introduction to social research, introduction to sociology, seminar (reporting on research), social inequality, statistics.

Some Suggested High School Courses

Algebra, English, foreign language, social science, trigonometry.

Essential Knowledge and Skills

Reading comprehension, active learning, writing, instructing, information gathering, speaking, critical thinking, active listening, learning strategies, idea generation.
Values/Work Environment: Achievement, ability utilization, autonomy, responsibility, working indoors, sitting, standing.

Other Information Sources

Many career and education information sources use the standard cross-referencing systems noted below. You can use the codes to obtain substantial additional information on the major (via CIP code) and related occupations (via GOE code). The O*NET codes on the opposite page refer to another major career information system. See the Introduction for details on obtaining additional information.

Classification of Instructional Programs (CIP) code: 451101 Sociology

Guide for Occupational Exploration (GOE) codes: 02.04 Social Sciences, 12.03 Educational Services

---

Soil Science

Career Snapshot

Soil is a lot more than just dirt. It is a complex ecosystem with chemical, physical, mineralogical, and biological properties that affect agricultural productivity and the larger environment. Soil scientists survey and map soils, advise farmers and landowners on how to use land in productive and ecologically sound methods, and consult with civil engineers about construction projects that involve soil. Many work for governments. Those with advanced degrees may go into college teaching or basic research.

Related Specialties and Careers

Land-use management, soil conservation, soil surveying, sustainable agriculture, waste/bioresource management.

Related Job Titles, Projected Growth, and Earnings		
Job Title	**Projected Growth**	**Average Earnings**
Soil Scientists (O*NET code 19-1013.02)	Average	$42,340
Soil Conservationists (O*NET code 19-1031.01)	Average	$42,750
Agricultural Sciences Teachers, Postsecondary (O*NET code 25-1041.00)	Faster than average	(No salary data available)
Biological Science Teachers, Postsecondary (O*NET code 25-1042.00)	Faster than average	(No salary data available)
Forestry and Conservation Science Teachers, Postsecondary (O*NET code 25-1043.00)	Faster than average	(No salary data available)

Typical College Courses

Calculus, computer applications in agriculture, ecology, ecology and renewable resource management, English composition, general biology, general chemistry, general physics, introduction to geology, introduction to ground water/hydrology, introduction to soil science, natural resource management and water quality, organic chemistry, soil analysis, soil chemistry, soil conservation engineering, soil fertility, soil mechanics, soil morphology, statistics.

Some Suggested High School Courses

Algebra, biology, chemistry, computer science, English, geometry, public speaking, trigonometry.

Essential Knowledge and Skills

Reading comprehension, science, active learning, critical thinking, writing, mathematics, information gathering, speaking, information organization, learning strategies. **Values/Work Environment:** Autonomy, working indoors, sitting, standing.

Other Information Sources

Many career and education information sources use the standard cross-referencing systems noted below. You can use the codes to obtain substantial additional information on the major (via CIP code) and related occupations (via GOE code). The O*NET codes on the opposite page refer to another major career information system. See the Introduction for details on obtaining additional information.

Classification of Instructional Programs (CIP) code: 020501 Soil Sciences

Guide for Occupational Exploration (GOE) codes: 02.03 Life Sciences, 12.03 Educational Services

---

 **Spanish**

Career Snapshot

Spanish has become the second language in the United States, as well as maintaining its importance as a world language, especially in the Western Hemisphere. A degree in Spanish can be useful preparation (perhaps with an additional degree) for many careers in business, travel, and public service, and not just with an international orientation.

Related Specialties and Careers

History and culture, language education, literature, translation.

Related Job Titles, Projected Growth, and Earnings		
Job Title	**Projected Growth**	**Average Earnings**
Foreign Language and Literature Teachers, Postsecondary (O*NET code 25-1124.00)	Faster than average	(No salary data available)
Interpreters and Translators (O*NET code 27-3091.00)	(No job growth data available)	(No salary data available)

Typical College Courses

Composition, conversation, European history and civilization, grammar, linguistics, phonetics, Spanish history and civilization, Spanish language, Spanish literature, Spanish-American literature.

Some Suggested High School Courses

English, history, literature, public speaking, social science, Spanish.

Essential Knowledge and Skills

Reading comprehension, instructing, speaking, writing, learning strategies, information gathering, critical thinking, active listening, synthesis/reorganization, information organization. **Values/Work Environment:** Achievement, authority, ability utilization, autonomy, working indoors, sitting, standing.

Other Information Sources

Many career and education information sources use the standard cross-referencing systems noted below. You can use the codes to obtain substantial additional information on the major (via CIP code) and related occupations (via GOE code). The O*NET codes on the opposite page refer to another major career information system. See the Introduction for details on obtaining additional information

Classification of Instructional Programs (CIP) code: 160905 Spanish Language and Literature.

Guide for Occupational Exploration (GOE) codes: 01.01 News, Broadcasting, and Public Relations; 12.03 Educational Services

Special Education

Career Snapshot

Special education covers a wide variety of learning and developmental disabilities and other conditions that require non-standard educational techniques. Many states require a master's degree for licensure, but some states are offering alternative entry routes. Job opportunity in this field is excellent, especially in rural areas and inner cities.

Related Specialties and Careers

Autism, multiple disabilities, specific learning disabilities, speech-language impairments, traumatic brain injury, visual impairments.

Related Job Titles, Projected Growth, and Earnings		
Job Title	Projected Growth	Average Earnings
Education Administrators, Preschool and Child Care Center/Program (O*NET code 11-9031.00)	Average	$60,400
Education Administrators, Elementary and Secondary School (O*NET code 11-9032.00)	Average	$60,400
Special Education Teachers, Preschool, Kindergarten, and Elementary School (O*NET code 25-2041.00)	Faster than average	$35,838
Special Education Teachers, Middle School (O*NET code 25-2042.00)	Faster than average	$35,838
Special Education Teachers, Secondary School (O*NET code 25-2043.00)	Faster than average	$35,838
Instructional Coordinators (O*NET code 25-9031.00)	Average	$38,870

Typical College Courses

Assessment in special education, behavior modification techniques in education, classroom/laboratory management, curriculum and methods for special education, education for moderate and severe disabilities, educational psychology, English composition, history and philosophy of education, human growth and development, introduction to psychology, introduction to special education, mathematics education, oral communication, psychology of the exceptional child, reading assessment and teaching, student teaching.

Some Suggested High School Courses

Algebra, English, foreign language, geometry, public speaking, science, trigonometry.

Essential Knowledge and Skills

Learning strategies, speaking, writing, reading comprehension, instructing, monitoring, social perceptiveness, active listening. **Values/Work Environment:** Achievement, ability utilization, working indoors, sitting, standing.

Other Information Sources

Many career and education information sources use the standard cross-referencing systems noted below. You can use the codes to obtain substantial additional information on the major (via CIP code) and related occupations (via GOE code). The O*NET codes on the opposite page refer to another major career information system. See the Introduction for details on obtaining additional information.

Classification of Instructional Programs (CIP) code: 131001 Special Education/Teaching, General

Guide for Occupational Exploration (GOE) codes: 12.01 Managerial Work in Education and Social Service, 12.03 Educational Services

---

Speech Pathology and Audiology

Career Snapshot

Speech pathologists and audiologists help people with a variety of communication disorders. About half work in schools, and most of the rest work for health care facilities. A master's degree is the standard entry route into this field, and it is possible to complete the requirements for entering the graduate program within a variety of undergraduate majors. Because of the aging of the population, demand for qualified practitioners is expected to increase.

Related Specialties and Careers

Audiology, speech-language pathology.

Related Job Titles, Projected Growth, and Earnings

Job Title	Projected Growth	Average Earnings
Health Specialties Teachers, Postsecondary (O*NET code 25-1071.00)	Faster than average	(No salary data available)
Audiologists (O*NET code 29-1121.00)	Much faster than average	$43,080
Speech-Language Pathologists (O*NET code 29-1127.00)	Much faster than average	$43,080

Typical College Courses

Anatomy of the speech and hearing mechanism, auditory anatomy and physiology, aural rehabilitation, diagnostic procedures in audiology, English composition, general biology, general physics, hearing problems, human growth and development, introduction to psychology, introduction to sociology, introduction to speech, language and hearing, linguistics, neuroscience, phonetics, psychoacoustics, psycholinguistics and speech perception, research methods in speech pathology and audiology, statistics, student teaching, stuttering and other fluency disorders, voice disorders.

Some Suggested High School Courses

Algebra, biology, chemistry, computer science, English, geometry, physics, precalculus, public speaking, social science, trigonometry.

Essential Knowledge and Skills

Reading comprehension, writing, instructing, speaking, information gathering, critical thinking, active learning, problem identification, learning strategies, idea generation. **Values/Work Environment:** Social service, achievement, ability utilization, authority, working indoors, sitting.

Other Information Sources

Many career and education information sources use the standard cross-referencing systems noted below. You can use the codes to obtain substantial additional information on the major (via CIP code) and related occupations (via GOE code). The O*NET codes on the opposite page refer to another major career information system. See the Introduction for details on obtaining additional information.

Classification of Instructional Programs (CIP) code: 510204 Speech Pathology and Audiology

Guide for Occupational Exploration (GOE) codes: 12.03 Educational Services, 14.06 Medical Therapy

---

 **Statistics**

Career Snapshot

Statistical analysis is a valuable tool that is used by every discipline that deals in quantitative information—social sciences, laboratory sciences, and business studies. Statisticians find meaningful patterns in data sets that are harvested from experiments, surveys, and other procedures such as bookkeeping. Graduates of statistics programs are in demand in many parts of the economy, from basic research to business management, from government to academia. Some get advanced degrees to specialize in research or college teaching, or get a degree in a second field such as psychology, computer science, or business.

Related Specialties and Careers

Computer applications, experimental design, mathematical statistics, probability, psychometrics.

Related Job Titles, Projected Growth, and Earnings		
Job Title	**Projected Growth**	**Average Earnings**
Statisticians (O*NET code 15-2041.00)	Little or none	$48,540
Mathematical Science Teachers, Postsecondary (O*NET code 25-1022.00)	Faster than average	(No salary data available)

Typical College Courses

Calculus, introduction to computer science, programming in a language (for example, C++ or Java), statistics, linear algebra, experimental design and analysis, mathematical statistics, seminar (reporting on research).

Some Suggested High School Courses

Algebra, calculus, computer science, geometry, physics, pre-calculus, trigonometry.

Essential Knowledge and Skills

Mathematics, reading comprehension, active learning, critical thinking, information gathering, idea generation, information organization, learning strategies, solution appraisal, writing. **Values/Work Environment:** Ability utilization, autonomy, achievement, good working conditions, responsibility, working indoors, sitting.

Other Information Sources

Many career and education information sources use the standard cross-referencing systems noted below. You can use the codes to obtain substantial additional information on the major (via CIP code) and related occupations (via GOE code). The O*NET codes on the opposite page refer to another major career information system. See the Introduction for details on obtaining additional information.

Classification of Instructional Programs (CIP) code: 270501 Mathematical Statistics

Guide for Occupational Exploration (GOE) codes: 02.06 Mathematics and Computers, 12.03 Educational Services

Transportation and Logistics Management

Career Snapshot

Transportation and logistics managers find the fastest and most cost-effective ways to keep materials flowing through our economy. Any business that produces goods or uses supplies—and that means practically every business—faces problems that these specialists are trained to solve. Some enter the field with a bachelor's in transportation and logistics management. Those interested in a technical specialization such as inventory control, packaging, or forecasting may major in (or get a master's degree in) management information systems, operations research, or industrial engineering.

Related Specialties and Careers

Inventory control, location analysis, management information systems, materials handling, order fulfillment, planning and forecasting, traffic and transportation management, warehouse operations.

Related Job Titles, Projected Growth, and Earnings		
Job Title	Projected Growth	Average Earnings
First-Line Supervisors, Administrative Support (O*NET code 43-1011.02)	Average	$31,090
First-Line Supervisors, Customer Service (O*NET code 43-1011.01)	Average	$31,090
First-Line Supervisors/Managers of Mechanics, Installers, and Repairers (O*NET code 49-1011.00)	Declining	(No salary data available)
First-Line Supervisors/Managers of Production and Operating Workers (O*NET code 51-1011.00)	Little or none	(No salary data available)
First-Line Supervisors/Managers of Transportation and Material-Moving Machine and Vehicle Operators (O*NET code 53-1031.00)	Average	(No salary data available)
Freight Inspectors (O*NET code 53-6051.06)	Average	(No salary data available)

Job Title	Projected Growth	Average Earnings
Production, Planning, and Expediting Clerks (O*NET code 43-5061.00)	Little or none	$29,270
Transportation Managers (O*NET code 11-3071.01)	Average	$52,810

Typical College Courses

Analysis and design of logistics systems, business finance, business writing, calculus for business and social sciences, English composition, human resource management, introduction to accounting, introduction to logistics, introduction to management information systems, introduction to marketing, introduction to psychology, inventory management, legal environment of business, principles of macroeconomics, principles of microeconomics, statistics for business and social sciences, transportation management.

Some Suggested High School Courses

Algebra, computer science, English, foreign language, geometry, pre-calculus, public speaking, trigonometry.

Essential Knowledge and Skills

Reading comprehension, coordination, writing, management of personnel resources, active listening. **Values/Work Environment:** Authority, activity, autonomy, responsibility, working indoors, sitting, standing.

Other Information Sources

Many career and education information sources use the standard cross-referencing systems noted below. You can use the codes to obtain substantial additional information on the major (via CIP code) and related occupations (via GOE code). The O*NET codes on the opposite page refer to another major career information system. See the Introduction for details on obtaining additional information.

Classification of Instructional Programs (CIP) code: 520203 Logistics and Materials Management

Guide for Occupational Exploration (GOE) codes: 05.01 Managerial Work in Mechanics, Installers, and Repairers; 07.01 Managerial Work in Transportation; 07.08 Support Work; 08.01 Managerial Work in Industrial Production; 09.01 Managerial Work in Business Detail; 09.04 Material Control

Urban Studies

Career Snapshot

Many different kinds of activities are concentrated in cities and towns—economic, social, political, architectural, and cultural—so urban studies is an interdisciplinary major. Degree holders go on to a variety of different careers, most often after getting a graduate or professional degree. Some work in urban planning or redevelopment, law, public administration, environmental planning, social work, or journalism.

Related Specialties and Careers

Community economic development, environmental design, ethnic studies, urban economics, urban planning, urban politics.

Related Job Titles, Projected Growth, and Earnings		
Job Title	**Projected Growth**	**Average Earnings**
Anthropology and Archeology Teachers, Postsecondary (O*NET code 25-1061.00)	Faster than average	(No salary data available)
Area, Ethnic, and Cultural Studies Teachers, Postsecondary (O*NET code 25-1062.00)	Faster than average	(No salary data available)
Economics Teachers, Postsecondary (O*NET code 25-1063.00)	Faster than average	(No salary data available)
History Teachers, Postsecondary (O*NET code 25-1125.00)	Faster than average	(No salary data available)
Political Science Teachers, Postsecondary (O*NET code 25-1065.00)	Faster than average	(No salary data available)
Psychology Teachers, Postsecondary (O*NET code 25-1066.00)	Faster than average	(No salary data available)
Sociologists (O*NET code 19-3041.00)	Average	(No salary data available)
Sociology Teachers, Postsecondary (O*NET code 25-1067.00)	Faster than average	(No salary data available)

Typical College Courses

English composition, history of cities, introduction to economics, introduction to sociology, introduction to urban planning, public policy analysis, seminar (reporting on research), statistics for business and social sciences, urban economics, urban politics.

Some Suggested High School Courses

Algebra, English, foreign language, history, social science, trigonometry.

Essential Knowledge and Skills

Reading comprehension, active learning, instructing. **Values/Work Environment:** Achievement, ability utilization, autonomy, responsibility, working indoors, sitting, standing.

Other Information Sources

Many career and education information sources use the standard cross-referencing systems noted below. You can use the codes to obtain substantial additional information on the major (via CIP code) and related occupations (via GOE code). The O*NET codes on the opposite page refer to another major career information system. See the Introduction for details on obtaining additional information.

Classification of Instructional Programs (CIP) code: 451201 Urban Affairs/Studies

Guide for Occupational Exploration (GOE) codes: 02.04 Social Sciences, 12.03 Educational Services

---

Veterinary Medicine

Career Snapshot

Veterinarians care for the health of animals—from dogs and cats to horses and cattle to exotic zoo animals—protect humans from diseases carried by animals, and conduct basic research on animal health. Most of them work in private practices. Some inspect animals or animal products for government agencies. Most students who enter the four-year veterinary school program have already completed a bachelor's degree that includes math and science coursework. Competition for entry to veterinary school is keen, but the job outlook is expected to be good.

Related Specialties and Careers

Companion animals, large animals (horses, cattle), public health, research.

Related Job Titles, Projected Growth, and Earnings		
Job Title	Projected Growth	Average Earnings
Health Specialties Teachers, Postsecondary (O*NET code 25-1071.00)	Faster than average	(No salary data available)
Veterinarians (O*NET code 29-1131.00)	Faster than average	$50,950

Typical College Courses

Animal nutrition and nutritional diseases, calculus, clinical veterinary experience, college algebra, English composition, general biology, general chemistry, general microbiology, genetics, human anatomy and physiology, introduction to biochemistry, introduction to computer science, introduction to psychology, introduction to sociology, neuroanatomy, oral communication, organic chemistry, pathology, pharmacology, public health, reproduction, veterinary gross anatomy, veterinary histology and cell biology, veterinary microbiology, veterinary ophthalmology, veterinary radiology, veterinary surgery, veterinary toxicology.

Some Suggested High School Courses

Algebra, biology, chemistry, computer science, English, foreign language, geometry, physics, pre-calculus, public speaking, trigonometry.

Essential Knowledge and Skills

Reading comprehension, science, information gathering, active learning, problem identification, writing, critical thinking, instructing, idea evaluation, speaking.

Values/Work Environment: Achievement, ability utilization, responsibility, autonomy, social status, working indoors, standing, sitting.

Other Information Sources

Many career and education information sources use the standard cross-referencing systems noted below. You can use the codes to obtain substantial additional information on the major (via CIP code) and related occupations (via GOE code). The O*NET codes on the opposite page refer to another major career information system. See the Introduction for details on obtaining additional information.

Classification of Instructional Programs (CIP) code: 512401 Veterinary Medicine (D.V.M.)

Guide for Occupational Exploration (GOE) codes: 03.02 Animal Care and Training; 12.03 Educational Services

Wildlife Management

Career Snapshot

The study of wildlife management combines a number of disciplines, including biology and public policy. Wildlife managers have to understand how wild creatures interact with their natural environment and how they react to the pressures put on them by human hunting and habitat destruction. Most wildlife managers work for governmental agencies.

Related Specialties and Careers

Fisheries management, public policy, terrestrial wildlife management.

Related Job Titles, Projected Growth, and Earnings		
Job Title	**Projected Growth**	**Average Earnings**
Government Service Executives (O*NET code 11-1011.01)	Average	$55,030
Agricultural Sciences Teachers, Postsecondary (O*NET code 25-1041.00)	Faster than average	(No salary data available)
Biological Science Teachers, Postsecondary (O*NET code 25-1042.00)	Faster than average	(No salary data available)
Forestry and Conservation Science Teachers, Postsecondary (O*NET code 25-1043.00)	Faster than average	(No salary data available)
Fish and Game Wardens (O*NET code 33-3031.00)	Average	$35,040

Typical College Courses

Animal physiology, animal population dynamics and management, calculus, ecology, English composition, general biology, general chemistry, general zoology, icthyology/herpetology, introduction to computer science, introduction to forestry, introduction to soil science, introduction to wildlife conservation, invertebrate zoology, mammalogy, natural resource biometrics, oral communication, organic chemistry, ornithology, regional wildlife management and policy, statistics, wildlife habitat management.

Some Suggested High School Courses

Algebra, biology, chemistry, computer science, English, geography, geometry, public speaking, trigonometry.

Essential Knowledge and Skills

Reading comprehension, critical thinking, writing, active learning, speaking, information gathering, active listening, learning strategies, problem identification, instructing. **Values/Work Environment:** Achievement, working indoors, sitting, standing.

Other Information Sources

Many career and education information sources use the standard cross-referencing systems noted below. You can use the codes to obtain substantial additional information on the major (via CIP code) and related occupations (via GOE code). The O*NET codes on the opposite page refer to another major career information system. See the Introduction for details on obtaining additional information.

Classification of Instructional Programs (CIP) code: 030601 Wildlife and Wildlands Management

Guide for Occupational Exploration (GOE) codes: 04.03 Law Enforcement, 12.03 Educational Services, 13.01 General Management Work and Management of Support Functions

---

Women's Studies

Career Snapshot

Women's studies is an interdisciplinary major that looks at the experience of women from the perspectives of history, literature, psychology, and sociology, among others. Graduates of this major may go into business fields where understanding of women's issues can be helpful—for example, advertising or human resources management. With further education, they may also find careers in fields where they can affect the lives of women, such as social work, law, public health, or public administration.

Related Specialties and Careers

Feminist theory, history of feminism, women's issues in art and culture, women's political issues.

Related Job Titles, Projected Growth, and Earnings		
Job Title	**Projected Growth**	**Average Earnings**
Anthropology and Archeology Teachers, Postsecondary (O*NET code 25-1061.00)	Faster than average	(No salary data available)
Area, Ethnic, and Cultural Studies Teachers, Postsecondary (O*NET code 25-1062.00)	Faster than average	(No salary data available)
Sociology Teachers, Postsecondary (O*NET code 25-1067.00)	Faster than average	(No salary data available)

Typical College Courses

American history, English composition, feminism from a global perspective, foreign language, historical and philosophical origins of feminism, introduction to women's studies, seminar (reporting on research), theories of feminism, women of color.

Some Suggested High School Courses

Algebra, English, foreign language, history, home economics, literature, public speaking, social science.

Essential Knowledge and Skills

Reading comprehension, instructing, speaking, active learning, active listening, writing, learning strategies, critical thinking, information gathering, idea generation. **Values/Work Environment:** Achievement, ability utilization, authority, responsibility, autonomy, working indoors, sitting, standing.

Other Information Sources

Many career and education information sources use the standard cross-referencing systems noted below. You can use the codes to obtain substantial additional information on the major (via CIP code) and related occupations (via GOE code). The O*NET codes on the opposite page refer to another major career information system. See the Introduction for details on obtaining additional information.

Classification of Instructional Programs (CIP) code: 050207 Women's Studies

Guide for Occupational Exploration (GOE) code: 12.03 Educational Services

Zoology

Career Snapshot

Zoologists study any form of animal life and therefore need a good background in biology and chemistry. A bachelor's degree in zoology can be a good first step toward a professional degree in medicine, veterinary science, or dentistry, or it may lead to entry-level work in some government and business fields. A graduate degree in zoology is good preparation for a career in research, college teaching, or agricultural extension service.

Related Specialties and Careers

Entomology, herpetology, ichthyology, mammalogy, ornithology.

Related Job Titles, Projected Growth, and Earnings		
Job Title	**Projected Growth**	**Average Earnings**
Biologists (O*NET code 19-1020.01)	Faster than average	$46,140
Biochemists (O*NET code 19-1021.01)	Faster than average	$46,140
Zoologists and Wildlife Biologists (O*NET code 19-1023.00)	Faster than average	$46,140
Epidemiologists (O*NET code 19-1041.00)	Faster than average	$50,410
Medical Scientists, Except Epidemiologists (O*NET code 19-1042.00)	Faster than average	$50,410
Agricultural Sciences Teachers, Postsecondary (O*NET code 25-1041.00)	Faster than average	(No salary data available)
Biological Science Teachers, Postsecondary (O*NET code 25-1042.00)	Faster than average	(No salary data available)
Forestry and Conservation Science Teachers, Postsecondary (O*NET code 25-1043.00)	Faster than average	(No salary data available)

Typical College Courses

Animal anatomy and physiology, calculus, cell biology, ecology, English composition, evolution, general biology, general chemistry, general physics, genetics, introduction to computer science, organic chemistry, statistics.

Some Suggested High School Courses

Algebra, biology, calculus, chemistry, computer science, English, geometry, physics, pre-calculus, trigonometry.

Essential Knowledge and Skills

Reading comprehension, science, writing, active learning, critical thinking, information gathering, mathematics, problem identification, information organization, idea generation. **Values/Work Environment:** Ability utilization; achievement; autonomy; working indoors; sitting; using hands on objects, tools, or controls.

Other Information Sources

Many career and education information sources use the standard cross-referencing systems noted below. You can use the codes to obtain substantial additional information on the major (via CIP code) and related occupations (via GOE code). The O*NET codes on the opposite page refer to another major career information system. See the Introduction for details on obtaining additional information.

Classification of Instructional Programs (CIP) code: 260701 Zoology, General

Guide for Occupational Exploration (GOE) codes: 12.03 Educational Services, 02.03 Life Sciences

Indexes

Careers Index

A

accountant, 80, 81, 224
acoustics specialist, 208, 272
actor, 148
actuary, 82, 83, 230
adjudicator, 218
administrative nurse, 246
administrative services manager, 122
advertising manager, 84, 85, 226
aerospace engineer, 86, 156
aesthetics specialist, 264
African-American expert, 88, 89
agricultural business manager, 91
agricultural economist, 90
agricultural educator, 94, 98, 112, 116, 118, 162, 168, 170, 204, 240, 310
agricultural engineer, 92, 93
agricultural financial specialist, 90
agricultural machinist, 92
agricultural marketing and sales representative, 90
agricultural structure technician, 92, 94, 98
agro-industrialist, 94
agronomist, 95
airframes and aerodynamics engineer, 86, 87
algae biologist, 240
American Studies expert, 97, 107
ancient civilizations specialist, 102
animal scientist, 98, 99
anthropologist, 100, 101, 102, 292
anthropology educator, 88, 96, 100, 102, 106, 140, 186
applied economist, 154
applied mathematician, 230
arbitrator, 200, 218
archeologist, 100, 102, 103, 134
archeology educator, 88, 96, 100, 102, 106, 140, 186

architect, 104–105
archivist, 186, 222
arid lands, specialist, 216
art conservator, 108
art director, 84, 108, 182
art educator, 108, 142, 148, 150, 158, 164, 196, 288
art historian, 108
arts, 88, 96, 109, 196
Asian expert, 107
astronomer, 110, 111, 152, 272
astrophysicist, 110
atmospheric physicist, 178
audiologist, 300
auditor, 80
autistic specialist, 298
automotive designer, 232

B

bacteriologist, 240
bailiff, 220
ballet dancer, 142
ballroom dancer, 142
behavioral and social inquiry specialist, 88
behavioral disorder counselor, 290
benefits/compensation specialist, 194
bilingual educator, 150, 158, 288
biochemist, 112, 113, 116
bioengineer, 115, 124
biological/forensic anthropologist, 100
biological science educator, 94, 98, 112, 116, 118, 162, 168, 170, 236, 240, 294, 310
biological technician, 94, 98
biologist, 117, 252, 314
biomechanic, 114
biomedical engineer, 114, 115
biophysicist, 112
blood bank technician, 234
body fluid analyst, 234
botanist, 116, 119
broadcaster, 156, 214
budget analyst, 80, 166

building materials specialist, 228
business administration manager, 123
business computer programmer, 138
business educator, 121

C

Canadian expert, 107
caption writer, 242
cartoonist, 108, 182
cataloger, 222
cell biologist, 116
ceramicist, 108
ceramics/glass technician, 228
chemical engineer, 124, 125
chemical metallurgist, 238
chemical technician, 168
chemist, 126, 127, 252
chemistry educator, 126
chief financial officer, 166
child care, 188
child welfare worker, 290
children's librarian, 222
Chinese language and literature educator, 129
chiropractor, 130–131
choreographer, 142
civil engineer, 132–133
claims examiner, property and casualty insurance, 206
claims taker, unemployment benefits, 194
classical civilization expert, 134, 135
clergy, 264, 284
climatologist, 152
clinical chemist, 234
clinical dietitian, 146
clinical microbiologist, 234
clinical psychologist, 278
clothing and textiles, 188
coach, 266
collector, 80
commercial designer, 182, 198, 199

commercial risk manager, 206
communications analyst, 156
community dietitian, 146
community economic developer, 306
community health nurse, 246
community service manager, 123, 190, 280, 290
companion animal trainer, 308
comparative politics expert, 276
compensation/benefits specialist, 194, 200
composer, music, 244
composite dancer, 142
computational bioengineer, 114
computer-aided designer, 208
computer applications and data manager, 90
computer engineer, 136, 137
computer modeler, 198
computer programmer, 156, 224
computer science educator, 138, 139, 224
conservator, 186, 240, 242
contact lens technician, 254
controlled drug delivery technician, 114
controllers, 166
controls engineer, 156
convention planner, 192
copy writer, 84
corporate financial analyst, 166
correctional officer/jailer, 220, 290
cosmologist, 110
cost accountant, 80
cost estimator, 123
counselor, 278, 284, 290, 292
creative processor, 84, 282
creative writer, 160, 164, 214, 264
criminologist, 140–141, 292
critic, film, 164
crop scientist, 95
cultural anthropologist, 100, 292
curator, 186
customer service, 304

D

dancer, 142–143
database programmer, 138, 224
dentist, 144–145
design and technology, theater, 148
development specialist, international, 210
developmental reading instructor, 288
diagnostic image technician, 130
dietitian, 146–147, 188
director, 148, 164
distribution manager, 122, 260
distributive educator, 120
domestic violence counselor, 290
drama educator, 108, 142, 148, 164, 196
driller/extractor, 260

E

earth sciences educator, 152, 153
East Asian expert, 107
Eastern European expert, 107
eco-tourism expert, 216
ecologist, 116
economic developer, 280, 306
economist, 90, 96, 106, 140, 154–155, 210
ecumenical specialist, 284
editor, 160, 164, 214
education administrator, 150
electrical engineer, 136, 156
elementary particles physicist, 272
elementary school educator, 150, 158, 159, 266, 298
emergency medical specialist, 236, 270
employment interviewer, 194
endodontist, 144
engineered biomaterial technician, 114
engineering educator, 86, 92, 114, 124, 132, 136, 156, 202, 228, 230, 238, 260
engineering geologist, 176
engineering manager, 132
English educator, 134, 160, 161, 196, 242

environmental compliance inspector, 168, 248
environmental designer, 306
environmental engineer, 92, 132, 162, 163
environmental geophysicist, 178
environmental lawyer, 218
epidemiologist, 112, 240, 314
equal opportunity representative and officer, 194, 280
ethics specialist, 264
ethnic studies specialist, 306
European expert, 107
exercise instructor, 258
exhibit designer, 182, 208
explorer, petroleum engineering, 260

F

fabricator, orthotics, 256
family and consumer sciences educator, 189
family lawyer, 218
family medical doctor, 236, 270
family resource manager, 188
farm business manager, 90, 98, 146, 188
feminist theorist, 312
field worker, 102
film critic, 164, 165
financial analyst, 80, 166, 206, 280
first-line supervisor, 98, 99, 168, 192
fish hatchery manager, 90, 310
folk dancer, 142
food and fiber processor, 92, 168
food quality assurance technician, 168
food researcher, 168
food services manager, 51, 58, 146, 192
foreign-language educator, 128, 134, 172, 180, 242, 286, 296
foreign policy expert, 210
forensic accountant, 80
forensic chemist, 112, 126
forensic science technician, 140

forester, 94, 98, 112, 116, 118, 162, 168, 170–171, 240, 242, 294, 310
fraud investigator, 220
freight inspector, 304
French teacher, 172–173

G

game warden, 310
gaming manager, 122
genealogist, 186
general practitioner, 236
geneticist, 116
geographer, 174
geological chemist, 126
geological engineer, 260
geologist, 176, 178, 252
geomagneticist, 178
geophysicist, 176
geotechnical engineer, 132
geriatric occupational therapist, 250
geriatric physical therapist, 268
German teacher, 180
gerontologist, 292
global security specialist, 210
government service executive, 122, 258, 280, 310
graphic designer, 182
Greek expert, 134
gynecologist, 236

H

hardware designer, computers, 136
hazardous materials technician, 248
health care worker, 290
health policymaker, 190
health services manager, 122, 184, 190
health specialties teacher, 144, 234, 236, 248, 250, 254, 256, 262, 266, 268, 270, 274, 300
hearing officer, 218
heating and air conditioning specialist, 232
hematologist, 234
historian, 88, 96, 106, 128, 172, 180, 186, 196, 212, 242, 286, 296
historical and cultural landscapes specialist, 216
home economics educator, 189
hospital manager, 190
hotel/motel manager, 192
human relations specialist, 292
human resources specialist, 194–195
hydrologist, 176, 178, 252

I

illustrator, 182
immunologist, 234, 240
industrial arts educator, 205
industrial designer, 182, 199
industrial engineer, 202
industrial psychologist, 278
information systems manager, 184, 224
instructional coordinator, 298
instructional librarian, 222
instrumental musician, 244
insurance agent, 82, 206
intellectual property lawyer, 218
interior designer, 208–209
international and comparative lawyer, 218
international business specialist, 122
international relations expert, 210–211, 276
Internet programmer, 138
internist, 236, 270
interpreter, 128, 172, 180, 212, 242, 258, 286, 296
inventory-control specialist, 304
investor, 82
irrigation technician, 92

J

Japanese teacher, 212
job analyst, 194
judge, 218

K

kindergarten educator, 266
kitchen designer, 208

L

labor lawyer, 200
labor-relations expert, 194, 280
laboratory technician, 234
land resources specialist, 162
land-use manager, 294
language and literature teacher, 88, 96, 106, 128, 160, 172, 180, 196, 212, 242, 286, 288, 296
Latin American expert, 107
Latin expert, 134
lawyer, 218–219
learning disabilities specialist, 298
librarian, 222–223
licensing examiner/inspector, 220
life and health insurance agent, 206
linguist, 134
literature/mythology teacher, 134, 160, 212, 242, 296
litigation lawyer, 218
location analyst, 304
logician, 264
long-term care manager, 190
low-vision specialist, 254

M

management information systems analyst, 304
manager, 84, 122, 184, 282, 304
map librarian, 222
marine scientist, 152
marketing analyst, 122, 154, 226
marriage counselor, 292
materials engineer, 228, 238
materials handler, 304
mathematician, 230
mathematics educator, 82, 158, 230, 288, 302
mechanical engineer, 232
media technologist, 12, 39, 44, 55, 56, 214, 282
mediator, 200, 218
medical image specialist, 114
medical manager, 122, 184, 190
medical records administrator, 185

medical scientist, 240
medical technologist, 234
meeting planner, 192
mental health counselor, 290
mental health nurse, 246
metallurgist, 238
meteorologist, 152, 252
microbiologist, 112, 116, 240
Middle Eastern expert, 107
middle school educator, 120, 188, 266, 288, 298
miner, 260
mineralogist, 176
missionary, 284
modern dance instructor, 142
molecular bioengineer, 114
museum librarian, 222
museum technician, 186
music educator, 108, 142, 148, 150, 158, 164, 196, 244, 288
musician, 244
mycologist, 240

N

natural history expert, 162
natural resources manager, 90, 162
network programmer, 224
neurological physical therapist, 268
news editor, 214
nuclear engineer, 124, 132
nuclear physicist, 272
nurse (R.N. training), 246
nursery and greenhouse manager, 90
nutritionist, 146–147, 188

O

obstetrician/gynecologist, 236
occupational health specialist, 248
occupational therapist, 250
oceanographer, 176, 178, 252
office manager, 120
online information retrieval specialist, 222
operations representative, 122
operations researcher, 202

optics physicist, 272
optometrist, 254
oral and maxillofacial surgeon, 144
oral pathologist, 144
order fulfillment specialist, 304
organizational psychologist, 278
orthodontist, 144
orthopedist, 130, 268, 274
orthotist, 256
outdoor leader, 258

P

Pacific area expert, 107
painter, 108, 182
paleomagneticist, 178
paleontologist, 176
paste-up worker, 182
pastoral counselor, 284
peace and justice expert, 196
pediatric nurse, 246, 270
pediatric occupational therapist, 250
pediatrician, 236, 270
penologist, 140
periodontist, 144
personal financial advisor, 166
personnel recruiter, 194, 280
petroleum geologist, 176, 260
pharmacist, 124, 262
pharmacological chemist, 112, 262
philosopher, 196, 264
photojournalist, 214
physical education, 266–267
physical metallurgist, 238
physical oceanographer, 178
physical therapist, 268
physician assistant, 270
physicist, 110, 152, 178, 272
phytopathologist, 118
planner/forecaster, 304
plant geneticist, 118
plant scientist, 94, 98
plasma physicist, 272
podiatrist, 274
police officer, 220
political science teacher, 96, 88, 106, 140, 210, 276

political scientist, 210, 276
polymers technician, 228
popular culture specialist, 96
postmaster and mail superintendent, 122, 280
power generation/transmission technician, 156
pre-elementary/early childhood/kindergarten educator, 151, 266, 298
precision printing worker, 182
prehistoric archeologist, 102
preschool teacher, 150–151
preservationist, 102
private-sector executive, 122, 166
probation officer, 290
process engineer, 238
producer, 148, 164
product designer, 198
product development, food, 168
production/planning/expediting clerk, 98
program director, 148
promotions manager, 84, 226
property and liability insurance agent, 206
property inspector, 220
propulsion engineer, 86
prosthetics and artificial organs technician, 114, 250, 256
psychiatrist, 236
psychologist, 278
psychology educator, 106, 140, 278
public administrator, 276, 280
public financial analyst, 166
public health dentist, 144
public opinion specialist, 276
public policymaker, 90, 276
public relations specialist, 282
public spaces designer, 208
public transportation inspector, 132
purchasing agent, 122, 123

Q

quality control representative, 124, 126, 202

R

radio and television news broadcaster, 214
radiologist, 236
ranch business manager, 90
reading instructor, 150, 158
recombinant DNA technician, 112
recreation worker, 258, 266
refiner, petroleum engineering, 260
registered nurse, 246
religion expert, 196, 284
remedial reading instructor, 288
remote sensing technician, 178
reporter, 214
research dietitian, 146
researcher, 112, 126, 306
residential designer, 208
resort/theme park manager, 192
resource manager, 258
restaurant manager, 192
restoration expert, 208
revenue agent, 80
Russian and Slavic expert, 107, 286

S

safety technician, 248
sales agent, securities and commodities, 166
sales engineer, 86, 92, 124, 156, 232, 238
sales manager, 84, 226
sales representative, agricultural, 98
Scandinavian expert, 107
science educator, 158, 162, 288
scientific programmer, 138
scientist, 240
screen printer, 108
screenwriter, 164
sculptor, 108
secondary school educator, 120, 266, 288, 298
securities analyst, 166

security and disaster recovery expert, computers, 138, 224
security guard, 220
seismologist, 178
self-enrichment educator, 148
set designer, 148, 208
singer, 244
sketch artist, 108, 182
small-town revitalization specialist, 216
social and community service manager, 123, 190, 280, 290
social studies educator, 288
sociologist, 100, 140, 292
sociology teacher, 88, 96, 102, 106, 140, 292
software/systems designer, computers, 136
soil and crop manager, 94
soil conservationist, 170, 294
solid-state physicist, 272
spacecraft technician, 86
Spanish educator, 296
special education worker, 298
special-interest librarian, 222
speech-language pathologist, 298, 300
sports activities director, 266
sports medicine manager, 130, 268, 274
statistician, 154, 230, 302
storage and distribution manager, 122
stratigrapher, 176
structural engineer, 132
studio artist, 108
substance abuse counselor, 290
supervisor, 304
surgeon, 236, 274
surveyor, 174, 294
systems analyst, 136, 224
systems programmer, 138

T

talent director, 148
tax examiner, 80
teacher, 150–151

technology educator, 205
testing engineer, 86, 232
theoretical mathematician, 230
theoretical physicist, 272
therapeutic recreation director, 258
traffic manager, 304
training and development manager, 194, 280
translator, 128, 172, 180, 212, 242, 286, 296
transportation engineering, 132
transportation manager, 122, 304, 305
travel guide, 258
treasurer, 166
turfgrass manager, 94
typographer, 182

U

urban forester, 170
urban planner, 174, 216, 306

V

veterinarian, 308
veterinary researcher, 98
virologist, 240
vision specialist, 254
vocational education educator, 120, 188, 204, 288
volcanologist, 176, 178

W

warehouse operator, 304
waste/bioresource management, 294
water resources engineer, 132, 152
Web page designer, 182
wildlife manager, 310
women's studies specialist, 312
worker compensation specialist, 200
writer, 160, 164, 214, 242, 264

Z

zoologist, 116, 314

College Majors Index

A

accounting, 20, 28, 29, 31, 32, 38, 43, 45, 46, 48, 50, 59, 61, 63, 74, 80, 81

actuarial science, 13, 18, 25, 27, 28, 31, 32, 38, 42, 43, 48, 57, 59, 63, 70, 82, 83, 84

advertising, 12, 17, 32, 38, 40, 45, 46, 50, 51, 53, 57, 60, 61, 71, 84

aeronautical/aerospace engineering, 14, 18, 25, 27, 31, 32, 34, 35, 38, 42, 43, 48, 56, 57, 63, 67, 86

African-American studies, 18, 25, 29, 32, 34, 35, 38, 45, 46, 50, 51, 53, 57, 60, 61, 67, 69, 70, 72, 88

agricultural business and economics, 13, 14, 25, 29, 32, 34, 35, 38, 40, 42, 43, 48, 63, 70, 90, 91

agricultural engineering, 14, 18, 25, 27, 31, 32, 34, 38, 40, 42, 43, 48, 57, 63, 67, 92, 93

agronomy and crop science, 13, 18, 32, 38, 40, 42, 43, 48, 57, 63, 69, 94, 95

American studies, 18, 25, 29, 32, 34, 35, 38, 45, 46, 50, 51, 53, 57, 60, 61, 68, 69, 70, 72, 96, 97

animal science, 13, 14, 17, 18, 32, 38, 41, 42, 43, 48, 57, 63, 70, 71, 98, 99

anthropology, 13, 18, 25, 27, 28, 32, 35, 38, 41, 42, 45, 46, 50, 51, 57, 60, 61, 68, 69, 71, 72, 100, 101

archeology, 13, 18, 25, 26, 27, 28, 29, 30, 32, 34, 35, 38, 41, 45, 46, 50, 51, 57, 60, 61, 68, 69, 71, 72, 102, 103

architectural engineering, 104

architecture, 14, 26, 32, 38, 40, 42, 43, 48, 57, 63, 68, 69, 71, 72, 73, 104, 105

area studies, 18, 25, 26, 27, 28, 29, 30, 32, 34, 35, 38, 45, 46, 50, 51, 53, 60, 61, 68, 69, 70, 71, 72, 73, 74, 106, 107

art, 12, 18, 28, 40, 45, 46, 50, 51, 53, 61, 68, 69, 71, 108, 109

astronomy, 13, 25, 27, 28, 31, 32, 33, 35, 38, 42, 43, 48, 56, 57, 63, 68, 71, 110, 111

B

biochemistry, 13, 18, 25, 28, 32, 33, 35, 38, 41, 42, 43, 48, 56, 57, 63, 68, 69, 71, 72, 112, 113

bioengineering, 27, 29, 31, 32, 33, 38, 41, 42, 43, 48, 56, 57, 63, 68, 69, 70, 114, 115

biology, 18, 25, 27, 28, 29, 30, 32, 33, 34, 35, 38, 41, 42, 43, 48, 56, 57, 63, 68, 69, 70, 71, 72, 73, 74, 116, 117

botany, 18, 25, 27, 29, 30, 31, 32, 38, 41, 42, 43, 48, 56, 57, 63, 68, 69, 70, 118, 119

business and economics, 18

business education, 19, 29, 30, 32, 34, 38, 45, 46, 48, 50, 52, 53, 55, 57, 58, 59, 61, 63, 69, 70, 72, 73, 120

business management, 13, 14, 15, 16, 17, 18, 20, 21, 32, 38, 43, 45, 46, 48, 50, 58, 59, 61, 63, 71, 122, 123

C

chemical engineering, 14, 19, 25, 27, 31, 32, 33, 35, 38, 42, 43, 48, 56, 57, 63, 68, 124, 125

chemistry, 13, 19, 25, 27, 28, 32, 33, 35, 38, 42, 43, 48, 56, 57, 63, 68, 69, 71, 126, 127

Chinese, 19, 29, 30, 32, 34, 35, 45, 51, 53, 58, 60, 68, 69, 70, 71, 128, 129

chiropractic, 19, 21, 26, 28, 31, 32, 33, 38, 41, 42, 43, 45, 46, 48, 50, 56, 57, 58, 62, 63, 68, 69, 71, 73, 130–131

civil engineering, 13, 14, 15, 19, 27, 28, 31, 32, 35, 38, 42, 43, 48, 56, 57, 63, 68, 132–133

classics, 19, 26, 27, 28, 29, 30, 32, 34, 35, 45, 46, 50, 51, 53, 58, 60, 62, 68, 70, 71, 134–135

commercial art and illustration, *see* graphic design, commercial art and illustration

computer engineering, 14, 19, 25, 27, 29, 31, 32, 33, 38, 42, 43, 48, 56, 57, 63, 68, 71, 72, 74, 136–137

computer science, 13, 19, 25, 27, 28, 32, 35, 38, 42, 43, 48, 56, 57, 63, 71, 138–139

criminology, 13, 15, 19, 25, 26, 27, 28, 29, 30, 31, 32, 34, 35, 38, 45, 46, 50, 60, 62, 63, 68, 71, 72, 140–141

D

dance, 12, 19, 29, 41, 44, 45, 46, 50, 54, 62, 68, 69, 71, 142–143

dentistry, 19, 21, 25, 27, 32, 33, 35, 38, 41, 42, 43, 45, 46, 48, 50, 56, 57, 58, 62, 63, 68, 69, 71, 72, 73, 144–145

design, 104

dietetics, 19, 21, 35, 38, 41, 42, 48, 51, 56, 60, 63, 73, 146–147

drama/theater arts, 12, 13, 19, 32, 44, 45, 46, 50, 53, 54, 58, 62, 68, 69, 71, 148–149

E

early childhood education, 18, 19, 30, 38, 45, 46, 48, 50, 54, 58, 59, 62, 70, 150–151

earth sciences, 25, 26, 27, 28, 29, 32, 34, 35, 36, 38, 42, 43, 48, 56, 57, 63, 68, 71, 152–153

economics, 13, 19, 20, 25, 28, 30, 32, 34, 36, 38, 45, 46, 50, 57, 60, 62, 63, 68, 69, 71, 154–155 electrical engineering, 14, 19, 25, 27, 31, 32, 36, 39, 42, 43, 48, 56, 57, 63, 68, 156–157

elementary education, 19, 30, 39, 45, 46, 48, 50, 54, 58, 59, 62, 63, 69, 70, 73, 158–159

English, 19, 28, 29, 30, 32, 34, 36, 46, 50, 51, 53, 58, 60, 62, 68, 69, 70, 71, 160–161

environmental science/studies, 13, 19, 20, 25, 27, 28, 32, 36, 39, 41, 42, 43, 47, 48, 58, 63, 68, 162–163

F

film/cinema studies, 12, 19, 27, 29, 30, 34, 36, 46, 50, 51, 53, 55, 62, 68, 69, 70, 71, 74, 164–165

finance, 13, 15, 16, 17, 19, 20, 32, 39, 43, 46, 48, 50, 59, 62, 63, 74, 166–167

food science, 13, 15, 16, 19, 32, 39, 41, 42, 43, 44, 48, 49, 51, 58, 63, 71, 168–169

forestry, 13, 16, 19, 25, 28, 31, 32, 36, 39, 41, 42, 44, 47, 49, 58, 63, 69, 170–171

French, 19, 29, 30, 32, 34, 35, 36, 46, 51, 53, 58, 60, 68, 69, 70, 71, 172–173

G

geography, 13, 14, 25, 31, 32, 36, 40, 44, 46, 47, 50, 51, 60, 62, 63, 71, 174–175

geology, 13, 25, 28, 31, 33, 36, 39, 42, 43, 44, 49, 56, 57, 63, 68, 71, 72, 176–177

geophysics, 25, 28, 31, 33, 36, 39, 42, 43, 44, 49, 56, 57, 63, 68, 71, 72, 178–179

German, 19, 29, 30, 32, 34, 35, 36, 50, 51, 53, 58, 60, 68, 69, 70, 71, 180–181

graphic design, commercial art and illustration, 12, 16, 32, 39, 40, 44, 49, 53, 54, 55, 57, 58, 63, 72

H

health facilities administration, 46

health information systems administration, 21, 35, 39, 41, 43, 44, 46, 49, 50, 55, 57, 58, 60, 62, 63, 74, 184–185

history, 13, 19, 25, 28, 32, 34, 36, 39, 46, 50, 51, 60, 62, 69, 104, 186–187

home economics education, 18, 19, 29, 30, 32, 34, 39, 46, 47, 49, 50, 51, 58, 59, 62, 63, 69, 70, 188–189

hospital/health facilities administration, 18, 19, 21, 32, 34, 36, 39, 41, 43, 44, 46, 47, 49, 50, 51, 55, 57, 58, 60, 62, 63, 70, 190–191

hotel/motel and restaurant management, 16, 17, 18, 26, 39, 44, 46, 47, 49, 50, 58, 59, 62, 70, 192–193

human resources management, 15, 16, 17, 19, 20, 32, 39, 44, 46, 47, 49, 50, 58, 59, 62, 63, 74, 194–195

humanities, 32, 39, 46, 47, 50, 51, 53, 58, 60, 62, 68, 69, 71, 73, 196–197

I

illustration, *see* graphic design, commercial art and illustration

industrial and labor relations, 30, 31, 39, 44, 46, 47, 49, 50, 58, 60, 62, 63, 68, 70, 74, 200–201

industrial design, 12, 25, 32, 39, 40, 44, 49, 54, 55, 57, 58, 63, 68, 69, 71, 198–199

industrial engineering, 14, 19, 25, 27, 31, 32, 33, 39, 42, 43, 44, 49, 56, 57, 63, 68, 71, 202–203

industrial/technology education, 19, 29, 30, 31, 32, 34, 39, 46, 47, 49, 50, 52, 54, 58, 59, 62, 63, 69, 70, 73, 204–205

insurance, 17, 20, 28, 32, 39, 44, 46, 47, 49, 50, 59, 62, 63, 206–207

interest areas, 22

interior design, 26, 32, 35, 39, 40, 44, 49, 51, 53, 56, 57, 63, 68, 69, 71, 208–209

international relations, 13, 19, 20, 25, 28, 32, 34, 36, 39, 46, 47, 50, 51, 60, 62, 63, 68, 69, 71, 210–211

J

Japanese, 19, 28, 29, 30, 32, 34, 36, 46, 51, 53, 58, 60, 68, 69, 70, 71, 212–213

journalism and mass communications, 12, 19, 32, 33, 36, 39, 40, 46, 47, 50, 53, 58, 60, 62, 68, 69, 214–215

L

landscape architecture, 14, 27, 28, 29, 34, 35, 39, 40, 41, 42, 44, 49, 56, 57, 63, 68, 71, 216–217

language, 29

law, 15, 26, 27, 28, 29, 33, 39, 46, 47, 49, 50, 51, 58, 60, 62, 71, 73, 74, 218–219

law enforcement, 15, 19, 20, 26, 39, 44, 46, 47, 50, 51, 58, 60, 62, 73, 220–221

library science, 19, 28, 33, 39, 44, 46, 47, 50, 53, 55, 58, 60, 62, 72, 74, 222–223

M

management information systems, 13, 14, 16, 17, 19, 33, 39, 44, 46, 47, 49, 50, 59, 62, 63, 74, 224–225

marketing, 17, 26, 28, 29, 31, 33, 34, 39, 44, 46, 47, 49, 50, 51, 59, 62, 63, 74, 226–227

mass communications, *see* journalism and mass communications

materials science, 13, 14, 19, 25, 31, 33, 36, 39, 42, 43, 44, 49, 56, 57, 63, 68, 71, 228–229

mathematics, 13, 19, 25, 27, 28, 31, 33, 36, 39, 42, 44, 49, 56, 57, 63, 68, 71, 74, 230–231 mechanical engineering, 14, 19, 25, 27, 31, 33, 35, 39, 42, 43, 44, 49, 56, 57, 64, 68, 232–233

medical technology, 19, 21, 25, 28, 30, 33, 36, 39, 41, 43, 44, 49, 56, 64, 68, 234–235

medicine, 19, 21, 25, 27, 31, 33, 36, 39, 41, 43, 44, 46, 47, 49, 50, 56, 57, 58, 62, 64, 68, 69, 71, 73, 236–237

metallurgical engineering, 19, 25, 27, 28, 31, 33, 39, 42, 43, 44, 49, 56, 57, 64, 68, 69, 70, 71, 73, 74, 238–239

microbiology/bacteriology, 13, 19, 25, 29, 31, 33, 36, 39, 41, 42, 43, 44, 49, 56, 57, 64, 68, 69, 71, 73, 240–241

modern foreign language, 12, 19, 25, 26, 27, 28, 29, 30, 33, 34, 35, 36, 46, 47, 50, 51, 58, 61, 62, 68, 69, 70, 71, 73, 74, 242–243

music, 12, 26, 46, 47, 50, 54, 62, 68, 69, 71, 72, 244–245

N

nursing (R.N. training), 19, 21, 29, 30, 33, 34, 39, 41, 43, 44, 46, 47, 49, 50, 58, 62, 64, 68, 69, 73, 246–247

O

occupational health and industrial hygiene, 19, 28, 29, 31, 33, 34, 36, 39, 43, 44, 49, 56, 57, 58, 64, 68, 69, 70, 71, 73, 248–249

occupational therapy, 19, 21, 26, 29, 33, 34, 36, 39, 41, 43, 44, 46, 47, 49, 50, 56, 62, 64, 68, 69, 73, 250–251

oceanography, 13, 25, 28, 31, 34, 36, 39, 41, 42, 43, 44, 49, 56, 57, 64, 68, 71, 72, 73, 252–253

optometry, 19, 21, 26, 29, 33, 34, 36, 39, 41, 42, 43, 44, 46, 47, 49, 50, 56, 57, 58, 62, 64, 69, 71, 73, 74, 254–255

orthotics/prosthetics, 19, 21, 26, 29, 33, 34, 36, 39, 41, 43, 44, 46, 47, 49, 50, 56, 62, 64, 68, 69, 73, 256–257

P

parks and recreation management, 12, 18, 20, 26, 27, 41, 43, 49, 58, 61, 71, 258–259

petroleum engineering, 14, 19, 25, 27, 28, 31, 33, 34, 39, 40, 42, 43, 44, 49, 56, 57, 64, 68, 71, 73, 260–261

pharmacy, 19, 21, 25, 29, 33, 34, 36, 39, 41, 42, 43, 44, 46, 47, 49, 50, 56, 58, 62, 64, 68, 69, 262–263

philosophy, 18, 33, 34, 36, 39, 47, 49, 50, 51, 61, 62, 69, 71, 73, 264–265

physical education, 12, 20, 30, 39, 47, 49, 50, 58, 59, 62, 64, 69, 70, 73, 266–267

physical therapy, 20, 21, 25, 26, 29, 33, 34, 36, 39, 41, 43, 44, 47, 49, 50, 56, 62, 64, 68, 69, 73, 268–269

physician assisting, 20, 21, 28, 31, 33, 34, 36, 40, 41, 43, 44, 47, 49, 50, 51, 57, 58, 62, 64, 68, 69, 73, 270–271

physics, 13, 20, 25, 28, 29, 31, 33, 36, 40, 42, 43, 44, 49, 56, 57, 64, 68, 69, 71, 272–273

podiatry, 20, 21, 26, 27, 28, 33, 40, 41, 43, 44, 47, 49, 51, 56, 57, 58, 62, 64, 68, 69, 71, 73, 274–275

political science, 13, 20, 26, 28, 33, 34, 36, 40, 47, 51, 61, 62, 64, 69, 71, 276–277

psychology, 13, 18, 20, 26, 29, 33, 35, 36, 40, 41, 47, 51, 61, 62, 64, 69, 71, 73, 74, 278–279

public administration, 14, 15, 16, 18, 20, 33, 40, 44, 51, 58, 61, 64, 74, 280–281

public relations, 12, 35, 40, 47, 51, 53, 58, 61, 62, 74, 282–283

R

religion/religious studies, 18, 33, 34, 35, 36, 40, 47, 49, 51, 58, 61, 62, 69, 71, 73, 284–285

Russian, 20, 29, 30, 33, 35, 36, 51, 53, 58, 61, 69, 70, 71, 286–287

S

secondary education, 20, 29, 30, 33, 35, 40, 47, 49, 51, 58, 59, 62, 64, 69, 70, 73, 288–289

social science, 41

social work, 15, 16, 18, 26, 33, 34, 40, 41, 47, 51, 61, 62, 290–291

sociology, 13, 20, 26, 28, 29, 33, 36, 40, 47, 51, 61, 62, 64, 69, 70, 71, 73, 292–293

soil science, 13, 20, 26, 27, 30, 33, 34, 36, 40, 43, 44, 49, 58, 64, 71, 294–295

Spanish, 20, 29, 30, 33, 35, 36, 51, 53, 58, 61, 62, 69, 70, 71, 296–297

special education, 18, 20, 29, 30, 33, 35, 36, 40, 47, 49, 51, 58, 59, 62, 64, 69, 70, 298–299

speech pathology and audiology, 20, 21, 28, 29, 33, 35, 36, 40, 41, 43, 44, 49, 56, 57, 58, 59, 61, 64, 69, 70, 300–301

statistics, 13, 20, 26, 27, 28, 29, 30, 31, 33, 34, 36, 40, 42, 44, 49, 56, 57, 64, 69, 70, 71, 73, 74

T

theory and criticism, 104

transportation and logistics management, 26, 27, 30, 33, 36, 40, 44, 47, 49, 51, 57, 59, 62, 64, 70, 71, 73, 304–305

U

urban studies, 26, 29, 33, 40, 47, 51, 61, 62, 63, 64, 69, 70, 71, 73, 104, 306–307

V

veterinary medicine, 14, 20, 26, 28, 31, 33, 34, 35, 40, 41, 43, 44, 47, 49, 51, 56, 57, 59, 64, 69, 70, 71, 73, 308–309

W

wildlife management, 15, 20, 26, 27, 29, 33, 35, 36, 40, 41, 43, 44, 47, 49, 59, 64, 70, 310–311

women's studies, 20, 26, 28, 29, 33, 35, 40, 47, 51, 53, 59, 61, 69, 70, 71, 73, 312–313

Z

zoology, 13, 20, 26, 27, 28, 33, 34, 36, 40, 42, 43, 44, 49, 56, 57, 64, 69, 70, 71, 314–315

High School Courses Index

algebra, 38, 39, 40, 81, 82, 84, 86, 88, 91, 92, 95, 96, 99, 101, 103, 104, 107, 110, 113, 114, 117, 118, 121, 123, 124, 126, 131, 133, 137, 138, 141, 144, 146, 151, 152, 154, 156, 158, 163, 167, 169, 171, 176, 178, 183, 184, 187, 189, 191, 193, 195, 197, 198, 200, 202, 204, 207, 208, 211, 214, 216, 219, 221, 222, 225, 226, 228, 230, 232, 234, 237, 238, 241, 246, 248, 250, 252, 254, 256, 261, 262, 264, 267, 269, 270, 272, 274, 276, 279, 281, 282, 284, 288, 291, 292, 295, 299, 300, 302, 305, 307, 308, 311, 312, 315

art, 40, 84, 104, 109, 174, 183, 198, 208, 214, 216, 282

biology, 40–41, 91, 92, 95, 99, 101, 103, 113, 117, 118, 131, 142, 144, 146, 163, 169, 171, 183, 184, 191, 216, 234, 237, 241, 246, 250, 252, 254, 256, 258, 262, 269, 270, 274, 279, 291, 295, 300, 308, 311, 315

calculus, 42, 82, 86, 92, 104, 110, 113, 114, 117, 118, 124, 126, 133, 137, 138, 152, 156, 176, 178, 202, 216, 228, 230, 232, 238, 241, 252, 254, 261, 262, 272, 302, 315

chemistry, 42–43, 86, 91, 92, 95, 99, 101, 110, 113, 114, 117, 118, 124, 126, 131, 133, 137, 138, 144, 146, 152, 156, 163, 167, 169, 171, 176, 178, 184, 191, 202, 228, 232, 234, 237, 238, 241, 246, 248, 250, 252, 254, 256, 258, 261, 262, 269, 270, 272, 274, 295, 300, 308, 315

computer science, 43, 44, 81, 82, 86, 91, 92, 95, 99, 104, 110, 113, 114, 117, 118, 123, 124, 126, 131, 133, 137, 138, 144, 152, 156, 163, 167, 169, 171, 174, 178, 183, 184, 191, 193, 195, 198, 200, 202, 207, 208, 216, 221, 222, 225, 226, 228, 230, 232, 234, 237, 238, 241, 246, 248, 250, 252, 254, 256, 261, 262, 269, 270, 272, 274, 281, 295, 300, 302, 305, 308, 311, 315

dance, 44, 142, 149

English, 45, 81, 82, 84, 86, 88, 91, 92, 95, 96, 99, 101, 103, 104, 107, 109, 110, 113, 114, 117, 118, 121, 124, 126, 128, 131, 133, 134, 137, 138, 141, 144, 146, 149, 151, 152, 154, 156, 158, 160, 163, 164, 167, 169, 171, 172, 174, 176, 178, 179, 180, 183, 184, 187, 189, 191, 193, 195, 197, 198, 200, 202, 204, 207, 208, 211, 212, 214, 216, 219, 221, 222, 225, 226, 228, 232, 234, 237, 238, 241, 242, 244, 246, 248, 250, 252, 254, 256, 258, 261, 262, 264, 267, 269, 270, 272, 274, 276, 279, 281, 282, 284, 286, 288, 291, 292, 295, 299, 300, 305, 307, 308, 311, 312, 315

foreign language, 45–46, 81, 84, 88, 96, 101, 103, 107, 109, 121, 123, 128, 131, 134, 141, 142, 144, 149, 151, 154, 158, 160, 164, 167, 174, 184, 187, 189, 191, 193, 195, 197, 200, 204, 207, 211, 212, 214, 219, 221, 222, 225, 226, 237, 242, 244, 246, 250, 254, 256, 262, 264, 267, 269, 270, 274, 276, 279, 281, 282, 284, 286, 288, 291, 292, 299, 305, 307, 308, 312

French, 46, 47, 172

geography, 47–48, 163, 171, 174, 311

geometry, 48–49, 81, 82, 86, 91, 92, 95, 99, 104, 110, 113, 114, 117, 118, 121, 123, 124, 126, 131, 133, 137, 138, 144, 146, 151, 152, 156, 158, 163, 167, 171, 176, 178, 183, 184, 189, 191, 193, 195, 198, 200, 202, 204, 207, 208, 216, 219, 225, 226, 228, 230, 232, 234, 237, 238, 241, 246, 248, 250, 252, 254, 256, 258, 261, 262, 264, 267, 269, 270, 272, 274, 284, 288, 295, 299, 300, 302, 305, 311, 315

German, 50–51, 180

history, 51, 88, 96, 101, 103, 107, 109, 128, 134, 160, 164, 172, 174, 180, 187, 197, 208, 211, 212, 219, 221, 242, 264, 276, 281, 284, 286, 296, 307, 312

home economics, 51–52, 84, 169, 189, 191, 193, 208, 226, 312

industrial arts, 52–53, 121, 204

keyboarding, 53, 121, 187, 222

language education, 296

literature, 53, 84, 88, 96, 107, 109, 128, 134, 149, 160, 164, 172, 180, 197, 208, 212, 214, 282, 286, 296, 312

mechanical drawing, 54, 183, 198, 204

music, 54, 142, 149, 151, 158, 244

office computer applications, 55, 121, 184, 191, 222

photography, 55, 164, 183, 198

physics, 56, 86, 104, 110, 113, 114, 117, 118, 124, 126, 131, 133, 137, 138, 144, 146, 152, 156, 176, 178, 202, 208, 216, 228, 230, 232, 234, 237, 238, 241, 248, 250, 252, 254, 256, 261, 262, 269, 272, 274, 300, 302, 308, 315

pre-calculus, 57, 82, 86, 92, 104, 110, 113, 114, 117, 118, 124, 126, 131, 133, 137, 138, 144, 152, 154, 156, 176, 178, 183, 184, 191, 198, 202, 208, 216, 228, 230, 232, 237, 238, 241, 248, 252, 254, 261, 270, 272, 274, 300, 302, 305, 308, 315

public speaking, 57–59, 84, 88, 95, 96, 99, 101, 103, 121, 123, 128, 131, 134, 144, 149, 151, 158, 167, 169, 171, 172, 180, 183, 184, 189, 191, 193, 195, 197, 198, 200, 204, 212, 214, 219, 221, 222, 237, 242, 246, 248, 254, 262, 267, 270, 274, 281, 282, 284, 286, 288, 295, 299, 300, 305, 311, 312

reading comprehension, 123

science, 59–60, 81, 82, 121, 123, 151, 158, 167, 189, 195, 204, 207, 225, 226, 267, 288, 299

social science, 60–61, 84, 88, 96, 101, 103, 107, 128, 134, 141, 146, 154, 160, 172, 174, 180, 184, 187, 191, 197, 200, 211, 212, 214, 219, 221, 222, 242, 258, 264, 276, 279, 281, 282, 284, 286, 291, 292, 300, 307, 312

Spanish, 61–63

translation, 296

trigonometry, 63–64, 81, 82, 86, 91, 92, 95, 99, 104, 110, 113, 114, 117, 118, 121, 123, 124, 126, 131, 133, 137, 138, 141, 144, 146, 151, 152, 154, 156,

158, 163, 167, 169, 171, 174, 176, 178, 183, 184, 187, 189, 191, 193, 195, 198, 200, 202, 204, 207, 208, 211, 216, 225, 226, 228, 230, 232, 234, 237, 238, 241, 246, 248, 250, 252, 254, 256, 261, 262, 267, 269, 270, 272, 274, 276, 279, 281, 288, 291, 292, 295, 299, 300, 302, 305, 307, 308, 311, 315

Interest Areas Index

arts, entertainment, and media, 12, 84, 104, 108, 142, 148, 164, 182, 208, 214, 244

business detail, 16, 80, 120, 122, 154, 166, 194, 200, 206, 210, 224

construction, mining, and drilling, 15

education and social services, 18, 19, 20, 88, 96, 100, 102, 106, 120, 122, 128, 134, 150, 158, 160, 172, 180, 186, 188, 196, 204, 210, 212, 222, 242, 264, 266, 276, 278, 280, 284, 286, 288, 290, 292, 296, 298, 300, 306, 312

general management and support, 20

industrial production, 16, 198, 200, 202, 204

law, law enforcement, and public safety, 14, 15, 140, 218, 220

mechanics, installers, and repairers, 15

medical and health services, 21, 130, 144, 146, 168, 184, 188, 190, 234, 236, 246, 248, 250, 254, 256, 262, 268, 274

plants and animals, 14, 90, 92, 94, 98, 170, 216, 258, 308, 310, 314

recreation, travel, and other personal services, 18, 192, 258

sales and marketing, 17, 84, 226

science, math, and engineering, 13, 14, 80, 82, 86, 92, 104,

110, 112, 114, 116, 118, 124, 126, 132, 136, 138, 152, 156, 162, 174, 176, 178, 202, 228, 230, 232, 238, 240, 252, 258, 260, 272, 294, 302

transportation, 16, 304

Work Groups Index

A

Accounting, 81

Actuarial Science, 83

Administrative Detail, 16, 26, 38, 45, 53, 55, 57, 60, 195

Advertising, 85

Aerospace, Aeronautical, and Astronautical Engineering, 87

African-American Studies, 89

Agricultural Business and Management, General, 91

Agricultural Engineering, 93

Agronomy and Crop Science, 95

Air Vehicle Operation, 38, 43, 47, 59, 67

American Studies/Civilization, 97, 107

Animal Care and Training, 14, 38, 40, 42, 309

Animal Sciences, General, 99

Anthropology, 101

Apparel, Shoes, Leather, and Fabric Care, 51, 52, 72

Arabic Language and Literature, 243

Archeology, 103

Architecture, 105

Art, 109

Asian Studies, 107

Astronomy, 111

B

Barber and Beauty Services, 40, 57, 73

Biochemistry, 113

Bioengineering and Biomedical Engineering, 115

Biology, General, 117

Botany, General, 119

Business Administration and Management, General, 123
Business Marketing and Marketing Management, 227
Business Teacher Education, 121

C

Canadian Studies, 107
Chemical Engineering, 125
Chemistry, 127
Chinese Language and Literature, 129, 243
Chiropractic, 131
Civil Engineering, General, 133
Classics and Classical Language and Literatures, 135
Cleaning and Building Services, 51
Clerical Machine Operation, 17, 38, 53, 55, 225
Communications, 53, 58
Computer Engineering, 137
Computer Science, 139
Construction, 43, 48, 54, 56, 59, 72
Craft Arts, 12, 40, 42, 45, 46, 50, 52, 54, 61, 72, 109
Criminology, 141
Customer Service, 17, 38, 55, 58

D

Dance, 143
Dentistry, 21, 32, 41, 42, 56, 57, 59, 60, 67, 69, 73, 145
Dietetics/Human Nutritional Services, 147
Drama/Theater Arts, General, 149

E

Earth and Planetary Sciences, 153
East and Southeast Asian Languages and Literatures, Other, 243
East European Languages and Literatures, 243
Economics, General, 155
Educational Services, *see* specific career; work group

Electrical and Electronic Systems, 43, 52, 54, 56, 57, 72, 157
Elementary Teacher Education, 159
Engineering, 14, 25, 26, 27, 28, 29, 31, 32, 33, 34, 35, 42, 43, 45, 54, 56, 68, 87, 93, 125, 133, 137, 157, 175, 203, 217, 233, 239, 261
English Language and Literature, 161
Environmental Science/Studies, 163
European Studies, 107

F

Family and Consumer Sciences/ Home Economics Teacher Education, 189
Film/Cinema Studies, 165
Finance, General, 167
Food and Beverage Services, 51, 58, 169
Foreign Language Interpretation and Translation, 243
Foreign Languages and Literatures, 243
Forestry, General, 171
French Language and Literature, 173, 243

G

General Management, 38, 43, 45, 58, 60
General Management Work and Management of Support Functions, 20, 26, 30, 31, 70, 123, 155, 163, 167, 195, 201, 211, 221, 259, 281, 311
General Sales, 38, 51, 55, 58, 60
Geography, 175
Geology, 177
Geophysics and Seismology, 179
German Language and Literature, 181, 243
Government Property Inspectors and Investigators, 220
Government Service Executives, 122, 154, 162, 210, 220

Graphic Arts, 12, 40, 44, 48, 54, 55, 72, 183
Graphic Design, Commercial Art, and Illustration, 182, 183

H

Hands-on Work: Loading, Moving, Hoisting, and Conveying, 38, 41, 48, 52, 54, 72
Health Protection and Promotion, 21, 39, 41, 51, 58, 147
Health Specialties, 21, 26, 32, 41, 42, 56, 57, 59, 60, 68, 69, 70, 72, 73, 130, 131, 144, 190, 255, 275
Hebrew Language and Literature, 243
Historians, 186
History, General, 187
History Teachers, Postsecondary, 88, 96, 102, 106, 140, 186, 196
Hospital/Health Facilities Administration, 191
Hotel/Motel and Restaurant Management, 193
Human Resources Assistants, Except Payroll and Timekeeping, 195
Human Resources Management, 194–195, 200
Humanities/Humanistic Studies, 197
Hydrologists, 176, 178

I

Industrial Design, 198, 199
Industrial/Manufacturing Engineering, 203
Insurance and Risk Management, 207
Insurance Sales Agents, 166, 206
Interior Design, 209
International Relations and Affairs, 211
Interpreters and Translators, 128, 172, 180, 212
Italian Language and Literature, 243

J

Japanese Language and Literature, 213, 243
Journalism, 215

L

Labor/Personnel Relations and Studies, 201
Laboratory Technology, 13, 41, 42, 44, 56, 57, 95, 99, 169
Landscape Architecture, 216–217
Latin American Studies, 107
Law, 15, 25, 26, 27, 28, 29, 32, 34, 35, 45, 46, 50, 51, 53, 58, 60, 62, 218–219
Law Enforcement/Police Science, 15, 26, 45, 46, 50, 55, 58, 60, 61, 141, 221, 311
Library Science/Librarianship, 223
Life Sciences, 13, 25, 28, 32, 33, 35, 41, 42, 43, 44, 56, 95, 99, 113, 163, 169, 171, 241, 295, 315
Linguistics, 243
Logistics and Materials Management, 305

M

Management Analysis, 123
Management Information Systems and Business Data Processing, 225
Management Support, 20, 28, 39, 42, 44, 52, 55, 57, 58, 81, 123, 155, 167, 195, 207
Managerial Work, 39, 41, 43, 44, 45, 46, 47, 48, 50, 52, 54, 55, 56, 57, 58, 59, 61, 62, 63
Managerial Work in Arts, Entertainment, and Media, 12, 30, 69, 70, 85, 105, 149, 165, 183, 283
Managerial Work in Business Detail, 16, 26, 30, 193, 305
Managerial Work in Construction, Mining, and Drilling, 15, 30, 70
Managerial Work in Education and Social Service, 18, 26, 28,

32, 34, 35, 123, 151, 191, 281, 291, 299
Managerial Work in Industrial Production, 16, 30, 70, 123, 169, 305
Managerial Work in Law, Law Enforcement, and Public Safety, 14, 31, 69, 70, 72, 73
Managerial Work in Mechanics, Installers, and Repairers, 15, 30, 70, 305
Managerial Work in Medical and Health Services, 21, 28, 32, 123, 185, 191
Managerial Work in Nursery, Groundskeeping, and Logging, 91, 99
Managerial Work in Plants and Animals, 14
Managerial Work in Recreation, Travel, and Other Personal Services, 18, 27, 31, 193
Managerial Work in Sales and Marketing, 17, 27, 85, 193, 227
Managerial Work in Science, Math, and Engineering, 13, 25, 27, 28, 29, 31, 32, 34, 35, 36, 133, 163, 225
Managerial Work in Transportation, 16, 305
Material Control, 17, 39, 55, 305
Materials Science, 229
Mathematical Detail, 17, 44, 53, 55, 57
Mathematical Statistics, 303
Mathematics and Computers, 13, 29, 31, 32, 42, 44, 56, 59, 83, 139, 155, 225, 231, 303
Mathematics, General, 231
Mechanical Engineering, 233
Mechanical Work, 39, 52, 54, 59, 72
Medical Records Administration, 185
Medical Technology, 21, 26, 41, 43, 56, 57, 60, 61, 235, 257
Medical Therapy, 21, 26, 40, 41, 43, 54, 56, 57, 60, 61, 73, 251,

269, 301
Medicine, 237
Medicine and Surgery, 21, 32, 41, 43, 56, 57, 60, 61, 68, 69, 73, 237, 247, 263, 271
Metal and Plastics Machine Technology, 39, 53, 54, 72
Metallurgical Engineering, 239
Microbiology/Bacteriology, 241
Middle Eastern Languages and Literatures, 243
Military, 46, 47, 50, 51, 55, 62
Mining and Drilling, 47, 48, 54, 60
Modeling and Personal Appearance, 52, 58
Music, 245

N

News, Broadcasting, and Public Relations, 12, 32, 36, 46, 48, 50, 51, 53, 58, 62, 129, 173, 181, 213, 215, 243, 283, 287, 297
Nursing (R.N. Training), 247

O

Occupational Health and Industrial Hygiene, 249
Occupational Therapy, 251
Oceanography, 253
Optometry, 255
Orthotics/Prosthetics, 257
Osteopathic Medicine, 237
Other Personal Services, 41, 43, 52, 61
Other Services Requiring Driving, 39, 58

P

Pacific Area Studies, 107
Parks, Recreation, and Leisure Facilities Management, 259
Patient Care and Assistance, 39, 41, 52, 61, 73
Performing Arts, 12, 27, 44, 45, 46, 47, 50, 51, 54, 59, 61, 62, 68, 69, 143, 149, 165, 245
Personal Soliciting, 59

Petroleum Engineering, 261

Pharmacy, 263

Philosophy, 265

Physical Education Teaching and Coaching, 267

Physical Sciences, 13, 25, 27, 28, 29, 31, 32, 33, 36, 42, 43, 44, 56, 68, 71, 111, 127, 153, 175, 177, 179, 229, 253, 273

Physical Therapy, 269

Physician Assistant, 271

Physics, General, 273

Podiatry, 275

Political Science and Government, General, 277

Portuguese Language and Literature, 243

Pre-Elementary/Early Childhood/Kindergarten Teacher Education, 151

Production Work, 16, 39, 53, 54, 55, 60, 72, 183

Psychology, General, 279

Public Administration, 281

Public Relations and Organizational Communications, 283

Public Safety, 15, 26, 39, 41, 43, 44, 45, 55, 61, 133, 167, 221, 249, 281

R

Rail Vehicle Operation, 39, 48

Records and Materials Processing, 17, 39, 53, 55, 59, 195

Recreational Services, 18, 27, 40, 48, 59, 259

Religion/Religious Studies, 285

Romance Languages and Literatures, Other, 243

Russian Language and Literature, 243, 287

S

Sales Technology, 17, 40, 52, 57, 59, 60, 61, 85, 99, 167, 207

Scandinavian Languages and Literatures, 243

Secondary Teacher Education, 289

Slavic Languages and Literatures (Other Than Russian), 243

Social Sciences, 13, 26, 27, 28, 29, 32, 36, 40, 45, 46, 47, 48, 50, 51, 61, 62, 71, 101, 103, 141, 155, 175, 187, 211, 265, 277, 279, 293, 307

Social Services, 18, 26, 33, 34, 40, 41, 45, 46, 47, 50, 59, 61, 62, 73, 91, 279, 285

Social Work, 291

Sociology, 293

Soil Sciences, 295

Spanish Language and Literature, 243, 297

Special Education/Teaching, General, 299

Speech Pathology and Audiology, 301

Sports: Coaching, Instructing, Officiating, and Performing, 12, 41, 59, 60, 61

Support Work, 53, 305

Systems Operation, 40, 43, 44, 56

T

Technology Education/Industrial Arts, 205

Transportation and Lodging Services, 52, 59

Truck Driving, 40, 48

U

Urban Affairs/Studies, 307

V

Vehicle Expediting and Coordinating, 40, 44, 48, 59

Veterinary Medicine, 309

Visual Arts, 12, 40, 46, 47, 50, 55, 62, 68, 69, 71, 109, 149, 183, 199, 209

W

Water Vehicle Operation, 40, 44, 48, 60

Wildlife and Wildlands Management, 311

Women's Studies, 313

Woodworking Technology, 40, 53, 54, 72

Writing and Editing, 12, 33, 36, 45, 46, 47, 50, 51, 53, 61, 62, 68, 69, 71, 85, 161, 165, 215, 265

Z

Zoology, General, 315